VISUAL QUICKSTART GUIDE

FILEMAKER PRO 5·5

FOR WINDOWS AND MACINTOSH

Nolan Hester

 Peachpit Press

Visual QuickStart Guide
FileMaker Pro 5.5 for Windows and Macintosh
Nolan Hester

Peachpit Press
1249 Eighth Street
Berkeley, CA 94710
(800) 283-9444
(510) 524-2178
(510) 524-2221

Find us on the World Wide Web at: www.peachpit.com

To report errors, please send a note to errata@peachpit.com

Peachpit Press is a division of Pearson Education

Copyright © 2002 by Nolan Hester

Editor: Nancy Davis
Production Coordinator: Lisa Brazieal
Production and Compositor: David Van Ness
Cover Design: The Visual Group, Mimi Heft
Indexer: Emily Glossbrenner

ISBN: 0-201-77320-1

0 9 8 7 6 5 4 3 2 1

Printed and bound in the United States of America

To Mary, my true home at the center of our little piece of terra infirma.

Special thanks to:
Nancy Davis whose sharp eye and sharper sensibility
keep me honest and on course; David Van Ness—the
man who never sleeps—for being the book's keel and
rudder; Emily Glossbrenner for the very best index a
reader could ever hope for (take a look, you'll see);
Mimi Heft for effortlessly solving problems that left
me scratching my head; Lisa Brazieal for the always
crucial behind-the-scenes production work; Becky
Morgan for helping us get over the hump to the
printer; Marjorie Baer for not saying I told you so
when I finally started to enjoy LA; and Nancy Aldrich-
Ruenzel for making this life of at-home work possible.
And home wouldn't be home without my study buddy,
Laika, who knows that walks keep all of us going.

TABLE OF CONTENTS

Chapter 6: **Using Spell Check and Dictionaries** **73**

Chapter 7: **Converting Files** **79**

PART III: **CREATING & DESIGNING DATABASES**

Chapter 8: **Planning Databases** **93**

Chapter 9: **Defining Fields** **99**

Chapter 10: Creating Layouts 129

Chapter 11: Working with Objects in Layouts 161

PART IV: PRINTING, NETWORKING, & THE WEB

PART V: APPENDICES

PART I

GETTING STARTED

1

USING FILEMAKER PRO 5.5

Welcome to the Visual QuickStart Guide for FileMaker Pro 5.5. If you've used earlier versions of FileMaker, you know how easy, flexible, and powerful the program is. If this is your first time using FileMaker, you're in for some pleasant surprises, including discovering how simple it is to create databases for the World Wide Web.

Why FileMaker?

Anyone who's used FileMaker much will readily sing its praises. It's the most popular Macintosh database program, which explains why many folks assume it's a Mac-only program. In truth, it's now also the second most popular stand-alone database program for Windows (Windows users now account for 60 percent of the program's users). Anyone who hasn't used FileMaker may wonder what the fuss is all about. Two words—clean, simple—explain FileMaker's appeal:

♦ **The interface:** FileMaker has been around since the mid-1980s, virtually forever in the constantly changing world of software. Unlike some programs, however, FileMaker's interface—the menus, buttons, windows, and steps required to get work done—has grown simpler, not more complex over time. This simplicity, and the resulting consistency that appears across the program, make it easy for you to focus on your work instead of puzzling over the program itself.

♦ **Cross-platform consistency:** FileMaker works so consistently on Windows and Macintoshes that your databases can move with you as you, and those using your databases, switch between platforms.

◆ **Simple yet powerful:** Folks who carp that FileMaker isn't as powerful as, say, Oracle, are missing the point. Heavy-duty database programs are super: super powerful, super hard to learn. FileMaker isn't. An example: FileMaker lets you build Web databases without learning CGI (Common Gateway Interface) scripting. If you are lucky enough to know CGI, FileMaker can use your scripts. More importantly, if you don't know a CGI from an SMB, FileMaker can help you solve your problems on your own. Even if your firm has its own Information Technology department, that staff is probably already overtaxed. With FileMaker, you won't need IT's help as often—and when you do, they'll also save time using FileMaker's powerful behind-the-scenes features.

WHY FILEMAKER?

What's New in FileMaker 5.5?

If you're a brand-new FileMaker user, all of FileMaker 5.5 is new. For FileMaker veterans, the biggest change is that FileMaker now fully supports the Macintosh OS X and Windows 2000 operating systems. It's also "Windows XP ready" though not yet certified as fully supported (see page 292). That means FileMaker can take advantage of the stability and protected memory of both new-generation operating systems. That change alone makes upgrading worthwhile, but FileMaker's improvements don't stop there:

New features and improvements

◆ **Record-level security:** File sharing security now can be set on a record-by-record basis, giving you more precise control over which users can read or change data. Previously, read-write privileges could not be assigned below the file level.

◆ **Query corporate-level data:** Continuing a trend first begun in FileMaker version 4.1, version 5.5 makes it even easier to integrate FileMaker and mainframe databases through built-in ODBC (Open Database Connectivity). FileMaker 5.5 can run calculation-based queries of corporate data sources, such as Oracle and Microsoft SQL Server. FileMaker can also run a simple query to import data from any ODBC-compliant database. Such features let you take advantage of FileMaker's easier-to-use interface yet still access enterprise-level data.

◆ **Update corporate-level data:** Updating ODBC databases now can be automated using a new "SQL Execute" script step. Once the script is written by a company's IT developers, FileMaker users can update a corporate database without having to create individual SQL queries.

◆ **Enhanced Instant Web Publishing:** Version 5.5 adds more options to its Instant Web Publishing feature, making Instant Web pages perform more like FileMaker's Custom Web Pages. For example, you can now hide FileMaker's status area, add your own navigation buttons, and trigger scripts through the Web browser. All of these changes make Instant Web pages behave more like regular Web pages.

◆ **Faster Web publishing performance:** FileMaker's Web Companion now is multi-threaded, making performance over an HTTP server twice as fast as it was in version 5.0.

◆ **Improved importing from Microsoft Excel:** Version 5.0 already allowed you to drag and drop an Excel spreadsheet into FileMaker. Version 5.5 now lets you import named cell ranges from Excel. Excel's named ranges make it easier to keep track of cells, and that advantage can be put to use in FileMaker.

◆ **Enhanced Table View:** You now can sort columns just by clicking the column header.

WHAT'S NEW IN FILEMAKER 5.5?

Using this Book

The key to this book, like all of Peachpit's Visual QuickStart Guides, is that word *visual*. As much as possible, I've used illustrations with succinct captions to explain FileMaker's major functions and options. Ideally, you should be able to quickly locate what you need by scanning the page tabs, illustrations, and captions. Once you find a relevant topic, the text provides details and tips.

If you're new to FileMaker, you'll find it easy to work your way through the book chapter by chapter. By the final pages, you'll know FileMaker better than most of the folks who use it daily.

But if you've got an immediate FileMaker problem or question that you need answered right now, the book makes it easy for you to dive right in and get help quickly. For those of you who find even a QuickStart Guide too slow, consider jumping straight to pages 20–30, where FileMaker's menus and context-sensitive screens are explained with an extra serving of illustrations and screen shots.

One program, one book for Windows and Macintosh

FileMaker was one of the first programs that performed similarly whether you were using a Windows or Macintosh computer. In fact, the two versions are so similar now that anyone comfortable with FileMaker in general will find it relatively easy to pick up and move to FileMaker on the other platform—a real boon for anyone working in today's typical office with a mix of PCs and Macs. Still, there are some differences between FileMaker's Windows and Mac versions.

◆ Minor differences—different looking menus, dialog boxes, window icons—are not highlighted in the text. I've alternated illustrations from both platforms when such differences aren't important to how FileMaker functions. But in many of the book's illustrations, you can't necessarily tell which platform is being used.

◆ Small but important differences between the versions are handled like so: "Under the Help menu, select FileMaker Help (Windows) or Show Balloons (Mac)."

◆ Major distinctions are highlighted with two icons:

  Ⓦ This icon marks special instructions or features for the Windows version of FileMaker.

  Ⓜ This icon marks special instructions or features for the Macintosh version of FileMaker.

◆ **Tips:** Signified by a ✔ in the margin, tips highlight shortcuts for performing common tasks or ways you can use your new FileMaker skills to solve common problems.

(continued)

Using this Book

◆ **Italic words:** When *italicized* words appear in the book's text, you'll find the very same words on the FileMaker screen itself when you reach that step in the program. The italicized term might appear as a button or tab label, the name of a text window or an option button in a dialog box, or as one of several choices in a drop-down menu. Whatever the context, the italics are meant to help you quickly find the item in what can sometimes be a crowded screen. If the step includes an accompanying illustration, use it to help you find the item being discussed. For example: Select *Open an existing file...* and click *OK*.

◆ **Code font:** When a word or words appears in `code font`, it's used to indicate the literal text you need to type into FileMaker. For example: In the text window, type `http://localhost` and press Enter. Web addresses are also in code font.

◆ **Menu commands and keyboard shortcuts:** Menu-based commands are shown as: File > Define Fields. Keyboard-based shortcuts (when available) are shown in parentheses after the first step in which they can be used. For example: (Ctrl L) means that you should press the Ctrl and L keys at the same time to switch to the Layout mode.

◆ **Fades in figures:** Sometimes a FileMaker dialog box or menu is so deep that it can be hard to fit on the page with all the other figures and still leave it large enough to read. In those cases, I fade out the middle or end of the figure to save some space (**Figure 1.1**). Nothing critical to understanding the step is ever left out. And it sure beats running teeny, tiny figures.

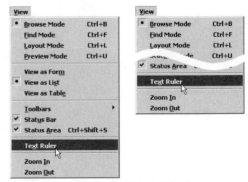

Figure 1.1 Sometimes the original dialog boxes or deep menus (left) will be faded out in the middle to save space on the page (right).

Updates and feedback

For FileMaker updates and patches, make a point of checking FileMaker's Web site from time to time: www.filemaker.com

This book also has a companion Web site where you'll find examples from the book, and tips and tricks based on real-world tasks. So drop by www.peachpit.com/vqs/filemaker when you can. You're also welcome to write me directly at filemaker@waywest.net with your own tips or—heaven forbid—any mistakes you may have spotted.

DATABASE BASICS

If you're new to databases, this chapter covers some basic concepts that will help you start off on the right foot in tapping the power of databases. If you're already familiar with databases, you may want to skip ahead to *FileMaker Basics* on page 19.

While you might not think of them as such, databases are everywhere: address books, cookbooks, television program listings, to-do lists scribbled on envelopes—examples abound. None of those examples involves a computer, but they illustrate a fundamental concept: databases *organize* information.

It slices! It dices!

An address book organizes information alphabetically. A cookbook organizes information by ingredient or by course. Television listings organize information by time and channel. To-do lists organize information by task and time. Each lets you find what you need precisely because of how the information is organized. A computer database is not so different except for one major advantage: it can quickly organize the *same* information in *multiple* ways.

In some ways, a database is like that late-night TV perennial, the Veg-o-Matic: It slices! It dices! It's ten kitchen tools in one! A database can slice the same basic information any number of ways: as address book entries, as mailing labels, as billing invoices—whatever's needed.

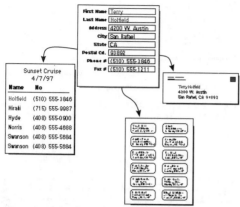

Figure 2.1 A database's real power comes from being able to display a single record's data in multiple ways.

Content vs. form

Understanding content vs. form is the key to tapping the real power of any database. Do not confuse what a database contains (the content) with how it looks (the form). As important as data may be, it's not what gives a database its power. Instead, the power is in the program's ability to organize—and instantly reorganize—the display of that data (**Figure 2.1**).

Many people use spreadsheet programs to organize and analyze data. At times a spreadsheet is the best tool for such work, but a database often offers far more flexibility. Spreadsheet information, for example, is confined to rows and columns. Database programs like FileMaker can break free of that grid to display data as tables, lists, address labels, or in almost any form you need. Since FileMaker lets you drag data from Microsoft Excel and drop it right into a layout, making the switch couldn't be easier.

Tapping the power behind any database boils down to understanding and effectively using just a few items: fields, records, and layouts. Let's take a look at the role of each in a database program like FileMaker.

Anatomy of a Database

Databases often contain huge amounts of information, yet tiny pieces of that data can be fetched almost instantly. What's the secret? It's because everything within even the largest database is organized piece by piece into categories, or *fields* (**Figure 2.2**). Each field—the smallest unit within a database—contains information describing its contents. With that field information, the database can go to work. And by understanding the power of fields, so can you.

The field—the smallest unit

Fields let a database keep track of what information goes where. Each field contains data but also carries a description, called a *field name*. The field name helps the database sort, sift, and manipulate without necessarily needing to deal directly with the data itself. It can be a bit confusing, but remember: fields, field names, and the data inside the fields are three different things (**Figure 2.3**).

The more specific the fields you create within a database, the more powerful the database. Hang on to this idea as you learn more about FileMaker. For now here's an obvious example of why it's so important to make fields as specific as possible.

Though surely you wouldn't do this, imagine you've built an employee database with just one name field. With only a single name field, an alphabetical sort yields an immediate problem: Dennis Smith appears before Jennifer Norriz because D precedes J (**Figure 2.4**). Obviously that's not what you want. Creating two name fields lets you sort the last and first names alphabetically and independently (**Figure 2.5**). Obvious yes, but it's an idea that's easily forgotten in the heat of designing a new database. See Part III, starting on page 91, for more on defining and using fields with precision.

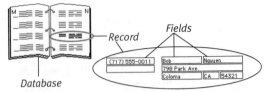

Figure 2.2 Every database organizes its information into individual records, which then contain fields for each bit of data.

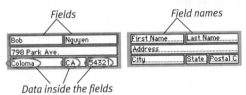

Figure 2.3 Each field contains data but also carries a description, called a field name, which makes it possible to quickly manipulate even a large database.

Name	Home Phone
Dennis Smith	205-555-9876
Jennifer Norriz	702-555-4688
Jeremy Smith	503-555-4655
John Winford	414-555-9987
Julie Davidson	415-555-0900
Michael St. Lorant	415-555-0143
Pamela Day	712-555-5245
Sonia Long	508-555-6899

Figure 2.4 Smith before Norriz: Having only *one* name field highlights the problem of not breaking fields into the smallest pieces possible. Figure 2.5 shows a better approach.

First Name	Last Name	Home Phone
Julie	Davidson	415-555-0900
Pamela	Day	712-555-5245
Sonia	Long	508-555-6899
Jennifer	Norriz	702-555-4688
Dennis	Smith	205-555-9876
Jeremy	Smith	503-555-4655
Michael	St. Lorant	415-555-0143
John	Winford	414-555-9987

Figure 2.5 By breaking data into smaller pieces, such as adding *two* name fields, you gain more control over your information. This concept is crucial to building powerful, yet precise, databases.

The record— grouping related fields

Put a bunch of fields together and you have what FileMaker calls a *record*. A single record contains related information about a single topic, person, or activity. In an address book, for example, the equivalent of a record would be the entry for one person. That entry or record would contain several related items: the person's name, address, and telephone number. As you already know, those three items are equivalent to fields in a database.

The database— a group of related records

Combine a bunch of records on a single topic, for example customers, and you have a *database*. A database also can contain records on several related topics, such as customers, their addresses, invoices, and past orders. The ability to connect or relate *different* databases is what's meant by a *relational* database, like FileMaker.

One of the advantages of a relational database is that you can make such connections between databases without duplicating the information in each database. When you're dealing with thousands of records, that can save a lot of disk space—and lots of time.

ANATOMY OF A DATABASE

The layout— one record, many forms

A *layout*, sometimes called a *view*, is simply a way to control how the information in a database is displayed. When you first begin building FileMaker databases, you may find yourself occasionally confusing records with layouts. Again, the difference boils down to content vs. form: One record (content) can have many different layouts (forms) (**Figure 2.6**).

At its most basic, a record is *all* of the information for a single entry, while a layout shows a view of only the portion you need at the moment. Layouts also offer a way to hide everything you don't need at the moment. Let's go back to our paper address book example.

For each person in your book, you've probably listed their name, address, and phone number. If you're sending someone a birthday card, obviously you don't need to see their phone number. Similarly, if you want to call someone, you don't need their address. The paper address book shows you both. With databases, layouts enable you to show only what's relevant to the task at hand. So if you need mailing labels, you can take those address records and create layouts that only show the address. This notion of showing only what you need becomes especially important when you're working with a huge database containing dozens, or hundreds, of records and fields.

No matter whether you're using FileMaker or some other database program, these terms and concepts remain much the same. Now you're ready to delve into the particulars of FileMaker itself.

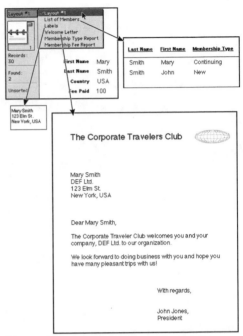

Figure 2.6 Using FileMaker's layout pop-up, the content of a single record can be displayed in many different forms, or layouts.

FileMaker Basics

If you hate to read computer books, this chapter's for you. By taking a brief look at the menus assembled here and the explanations of how they and various commands work, you'll get a quick overview of FileMaker that will allow you to dive right in—if that's your style.

For readers who prefer a go-slow approach, this chapter's brief explanations also include page references to where in the book you'll find all the details you could want.

No matter which approach you prefer, this chapter provides a visual map for learning all of FileMaker's major functions.

FileMaker's Screen and Modes

When using FileMaker, you will always be working in one of four views or what it calls modes: Browse, Find, Layout, or Preview. Reached using the View menu, each mode is used for a different set of tasks. For that reason, FileMaker's screen, menus, and their related options change from mode to mode.

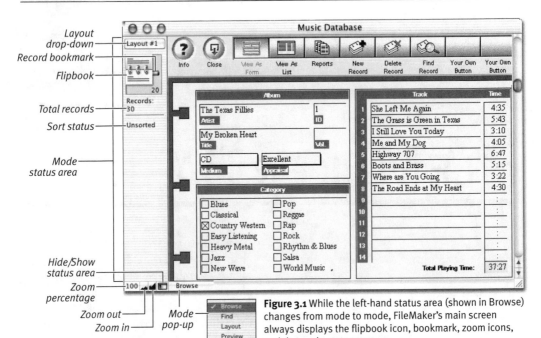

Layout drop-down

Record bookmark

Flipbook

Total records

Sort status

Mode status area

Hide/Show status area

Zoom percentage

Zoom out

Zoom in

Mode pop-up

Figure 3.1 While the left-hand status area (shown in Browse) changes from mode to mode, FileMaker's main screen always displays the flipbook icon, bookmark, zoom icons, and the mode status pop-up.

The FileMaker screen

Certain features of the FileMaker screen (**Figure 3.1**) remain constant: the flipbook icon at the upper left, the status area along the left side (unless you elect to hide it), the Zoom-in and Zoom-out icons, and the pop-up bar at the bottom of the screen, which lets you quickly choose your mode. As you switch from one view or mode to another, however, the left-hand status area displays a different set of tools and icons (**Figure 3.2**). The main record area also will change from mode to mode. For example, in Layout mode, the names of fields appear instead of the data itself.

Here's a quick rundown of the main elements of the FileMaker screen:

◆ **Layout pop-down:** Clicking your cursor on the box reveals all the layouts for the current record. For more on using Layout mode, see *Creating and Designing Databases* on page 91.

◆ **Record bookmark:** Using your cursor to click on and drag the bookmark allows you to quickly jump forward or backward through a database's records. For more on using the bookmark, see *Viewing Records* on page 41.

◆ **Flipbook:** This icon represents all the records in the current database. Clicking on the upper or lower pages of the flipbook moves you forward or backward one record at a time. For more on using the flipbook, see *Viewing Records* on page 41.

◆ **Current record, Total records:** The current record number tells you where you are among all the database's records, which is represented by the Total records number. By clicking on the Current record number, you can type in the number of a particular record you're seeking. For more information, see *Viewing Records* on page 41.

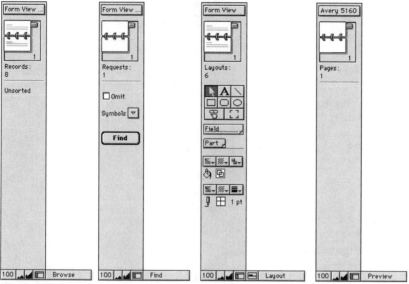

Figure 3.2 Tools and icons tailored to each mode appear in the left-hand status area as you switch among the (left to right): Browse, Find, Layout, and Preview modes.

◆ **Sort status:** This simply tells you whether the records you're working with have been sorted or remain unsorted. For more on sorting records, see *Finding and Sorting Records* on page 49.

◆ **Mode status area:** Running along the left-hand side of your screen, the status area displays the icons and tools for whichever mode you're in (**Figure 3.2**). For more on each mode's tools and icons, see pages 22–23.

◆ **Hide/Show status area:** Clicking on this icon allows you to hide or show the entire left-hand status area. This can be handy when you want to give the record itself as much screen space as possible.

◆ **Zoom percentage, Zoom in, Zoom out:** Clicking the Zoom-in or Zoom-out icon allows you to magnify or shrink your view of the current record. Clicking on the Zoom percentage box lets you toggle between the current magnification view

and the 100 percent view. This makes it easy, for example, to jump between an extreme close-up view (400 percent) and a regular view (100 percent) in a single click instead of the multiple clicks required by the Zoom-in and Zoom-out icons.

◆ **Mode pop-up:** This pop-up box at the bottom left of the screen displays FileMaker's current mode (**Figure 3.3**). By clicking on it, you can quickly move to another mode—just as you can by clicking on View in the menu bar. For more on modes, see the next section.

Figure 3.3 Click your cursor on the status mode pop-up and you can quickly switch to another mode.

Browse mode

Browse mode is the view where you'll spend most of your time if you're working with existing databases (**Figure 3.4**). Whenever you open a FileMaker database, it first appears in Browse mode. In Browse, you can view, sort, add, omit, and delete records. For more on using Browse mode, see *Viewing Records* on page 41 and *Finding and Sorting Records* on page 49.

Find mode

Find mode offers a powerful set of tools for locating individual records, or groups of records, within a database (**Figure 3.5**). In Find, you can search for records that match or don't match particular criteria based on text or mathematical values. For more on using Find mode, see *Finding and Sorting Records* on page 49.

Figure 3.4 The status area for Browse mode appears to the left of the current record—though you can hide it if you want more screen space for the record.

Figure 3.5 The Find mode status area offers tools for locating individual records, or groups of records, within a database.

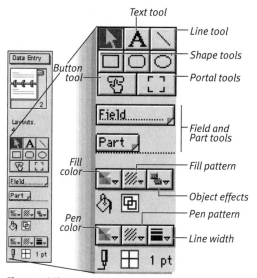

Figure 3.6 The most elaborate of the four modes, the Layout mode's status area contains tools to control the appearance of the records and record views you design.

Figure 3.7 The Preview mode lets you control the appearance of printed FileMaker records.

Layout mode

Layout mode is where you design the appearance of the fields and records that display your data (**Figure 3.6**). In Layout, you can control every detail of fonts, field borders, button design—as well as the overall look of forms and entry screens. For more on using Layout mode, see *Creating and Designing Databases*, on page 91.

Preview mode

Preview mode lets you control how your files look when printed (**Figure 3.7**). In Preview, you can set margins, get rid of unwanted gaps between fields, hide fields if you desire, and control how everything prints out, from reports to labels to envelopes. For more on using Preview mode, see *Printing*, on page 237.

FileMaker's Menus

This section provides a quick run-through of FileMaker's contextual menus, which change to reflect which mode you're in (**Figure 3.8**). Many of the menu commands and options are no different than those in any application: Open File, for example, is a fairly universal action. Some of the commands specific to FileMaker are highlighted on the following pages. Follow the page references for details on the various menu commands and options.

| File Edit View Insert Format **Records Scripts Window Help** |

| File Edit View Insert Format **Requests Scripts Window Help** |

| File Edit View Insert Format Layouts Arrange Scripts Window Help |

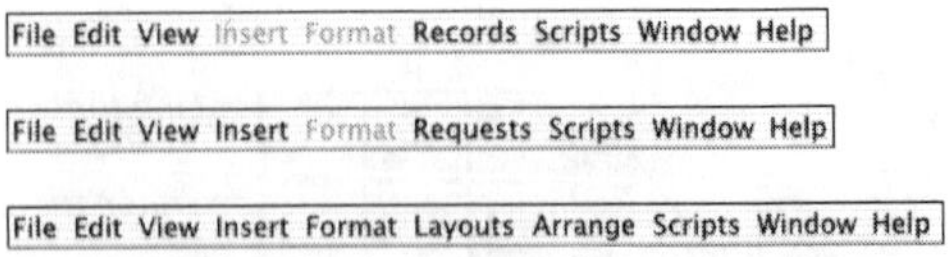

Figure 3.8 FileMaker's contextual menu bar changes depending on which mode you're in.

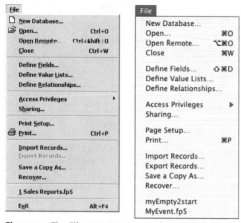

Figure 3.9 The File menu's commands are available in all four modes.

The File menu

As the name implies, all the commands within the File menu control actions related directly to file management (**Figure 3.9**). The File menu appears in all four FileMaker modes, with all its functions available.

◆ **New Database, Open, Open Remote, Close:** With the exception of Open Remote, these commands operate much as they do in most programs. The Open Remote command lets you open a FileMaker database shared over a network. For more information, see *Networking* on page 243.

◆ **Define Fields, Define Value Lists, Define Relationships:** Use the second group of commands to create fields, set options for entering data in them, and establish relationships among the fields. For more information, see *Defining Fields* on page 99 and *Creating Relational Databases* on page 221.

◆ **Access Privileges, Sharing:** Both commands control network-related functions. For more on determining which files can be seen on a network, who can see them, and which files can be shared, see *Networking* on page 243.

◆ **Print Setup/Page Setup, Print:** These commands operate much as they do in all programs. For more information, see *Printing* on page 237.

◆ **Import/Export Records, Save a Copy As, Recover:** These commands help you convert other database files to the current FileMaker format. For more on importing and exporting, see *Converting Files* on page 79.

◆ **Exit/Quit:** Use this command to quit FileMaker. If you are running Mac OS X, the Quit command resides under the separate FileMaker Pro menu (**Figure 3.42**).

FILEMAKER'S MENUS

25

The Edit menu

Most of this menu's commands operate just as they do in other programs—except for a few explained below (**Figure 3.10**). The Edit menu appears in all four FileMaker modes, though not all its functions are available in every mode. (Dimmed items indicate functions not available within that mode.)

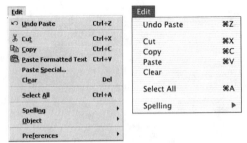

Figure 3.10 The Edit menu appears in all four modes, though not all functions are available in every mode.

W **Paste Special:** This command can be a tremendous time saver. Essentially, it lets you paste the contents of the clipboard into any FileMaker document.

W **Object:** This command takes advantage of a standard Windows feature, OLE (Object Linking and Embedding), which allows you to cut and paste data from other applications. The great advantage of OLE is that the data is updated automatically within the FileMaker record whenever it's changed in the original application. For more information, see *Creating Layouts* on page 129.

◆ **Spelling** offers the usual options. For more information, see *Using Spell Check and Dictionaries* on page 73.

◆ **Preferences:** Setting FileMaker's preferences early on will save you time and frustration. The preference dialog boxes control a variety of items, including how FileMaker works with your modem, network, memory, and Web plug-ins. If you are running Mac OS X, the preferences command resides under the separate FileMaker Pro menu. For more information, see *Setting FileMaker's Preferences* on page 301.

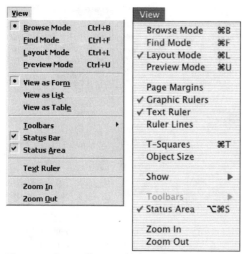

Figure 3.11 Depending on which mode you're in (Browse on the left, Layout on the right), the View menu's commands and functions change.

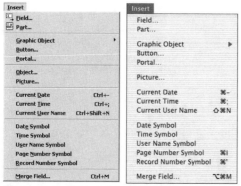

Figure 3.12 Available only in Find and Layout modes, the Insert menu lets you quickly paste in a field, a part, a picture, date, or user name.

The View menu

FileMaker operates in one of four modes: Browse, Find, Layout, or Preview. Each mode is used for a different set of tasks and, so, the options offered under the View menu change depending on which mode you're in (**Figure 3.11**). In each of the four contextual mode menus, however, the top section remains the same, allowing you to quickly switch to another mode.

The rest of the menu changes based on which mode you're in. For example, the Layout mode (right, **Figure 3.11**) includes Show and an extensive submenu, which replaces FileMaker 4's stand-alone Show menu.

The Insert menu

The Insert menu, available only in Find and Layout modes, offers a fast way to paste a field, part, object, button, portal, or picture into a layout (**Figure 3.12**). It also enables you to paste in the date, time, a user name, an indexed item, or selected content of the previous record. In FileMaker 4, most of these same functions were found under the Edit menu's *Paste Special* item. For more information on inserts, see *Finding and Sorting Records* on page 49 and *Using Variable Fields* on page 148. For more on indexing, see *Storage options* on page 110.

The Format menu

The Format menu appears in all modes except Preview, but offers the most functions in Layout mode (**Figure 3.13**). The availability of the functions also varies depending on what you've selected within the current record. In general, the functions within the Format menu start at the character level and move toward the field level. For more information, see *Formatting and Graphics in Layouts*, on page 175.

◆ **Font** through **Text Color:** The top six functions control attributes *at the character level* within a selected field.

◆ **Text** through **Portal:** The second group of functions controls attributes at the field level, that is, what *type* of content the field contains: text, numbers, a date, a time, a graphic, button, or portal (record view).

◆ **Field Format, Field Borders, Sliding/Printing:** The third and fourth groups of Format menu functions control the style and behavior of the field *container*, that is, whether it's a standard field or one that offers a pop-up list or repeats itself.

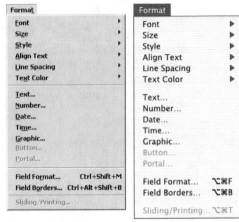

Figure 3.13 The Format menu appears in all modes except Preview, but offers the most functions in Layout mode.

Figure 3.14 Available only in Find and Preview modes, the Records menu lets you create, duplicate, and delete records.

Figure 3.15 Available only in the Find mode, the Requests menu replaces FileMaker 4 functions found under the now-defunct Select menu.

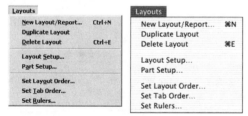

Figure 3.16 The Layouts menu, available only in Layout mode, lets you create, duplicate, and delete layouts.

The Records menu

The Records menu (**Figure 3.14**), available only in Find and Preview modes, lets you create, duplicate, and delete records. It also contains commands for changing previous find requests for records and working with sorts of the records. In practice, you'll find yourself using the Records menu in tandem with the Requests menu, explained below. In FileMaker 4, most of these functions were found under the Mode menu when you were in Browse mode or in the now-defunct Select menu. For more information, see *Finding and Sorting Records*, on page 49.

The Requests menu

The Requests menu (**Figure 3.15**), available only in Find mode, contains commands used for finding records. In FileMaker 4, these functions were found under the Select menu. For more information, see *Finding and Sorting Records*, on page 49.

The Layouts menu

The Layouts menu (**Figure 3.16**), which naturally enough appears only in Layout mode, lets you create, duplicate, and delete layouts. It also lets you control which layouts will be visible in which modes. In FileMaker 4, most of these functions were found under the Mode menu when you were in Layout mode. For more information, see *Creating Layouts* on page 129.

The Arrange menu

The Arrange menu (**Figure 3.17**), which appears only in Layout mode, lets you control the layering and grouping of objects as you design a layout. For more information, see *Creating Layouts*, on page 129.

The Scripts menu

Don't let this menu's unassuming appearance fool you (**Figure 3.18**). Choosing ScriptMaker will launch a powerful FileMaker feature that enables you to automate many of the program's operations. Existing scripts for the current file appear in the menu's second section. For more information, see *Using Templates and Scripts*, on page 199.

The Window menu

This works much like the Window menu in most programs: The bottom half of the menu lists all currently open FileMaker databases, enabling you to arrange what's visible on your desktop (**Figure 3.19**).

The Help menu

FileMaker's Help menu has some of the best built-in help of any program (**Figure 3.20**). For the quickest route to the answers you need, choose Help > Contents and Index. When the Topics dialog box appears, click the *Contents* tab for big-picture topics or the *Index* tab to find more specific items.

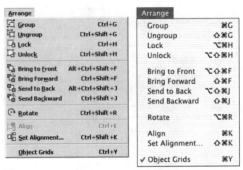

Figure 3.17 Use the Arrange menu, which appears only in Layout mode, to control the layering and grouping of objects as you design a layout.

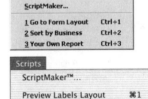

Figure 3.18 Use the Scripts menu to launch ScriptMaker, which enables you to automate many of FileMaker's operations.

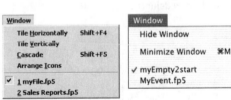

Figure 3.19 Use the Window menu to arrange multiple FileMaker databases on your desktop.

Figure 3.20 FileMaker's Help menu offers some of the best built-in help of any program, but the multiple options can seem confusing initially.

FileMaker's Toolbars

By default, only the Standard toolbar appears when you launch FileMaker, though its appearance changes depending on which mode you're working in (**Figures 3.21–3.22**). FileMaker also includes a Text Formatting toolbar (**Figure 3.23**), which can be very handy when you're creating layouts and naming fields. The Arrange and Tools toolbars are available only in Layout mode (**Figures 3.24–3.25**).

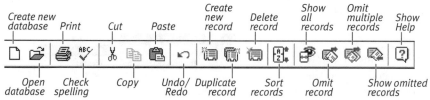

Figure 3.21 FileMaker's Standard toolbar looks pretty much the same in Browse, Find, and Preview modes, though different icons are dimmed.

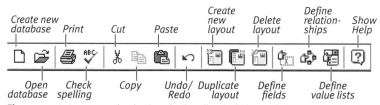

Figure 3.22 In Layout mode, the Standard toolbar includes tools for creating layouts and defining their parts and relationships.

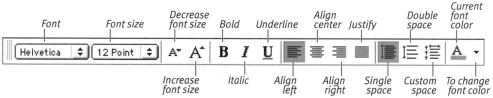

Figure 3.23 Available in all four modes, the Text Formatting toolbar provides quick access to FileMaker's major text-related tools.

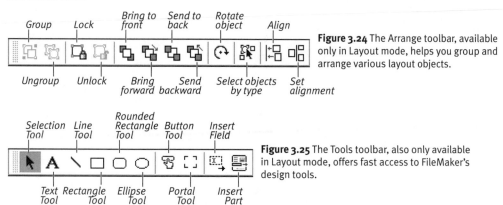

Figure 3.24 The Arrange toolbar, available only in Layout mode, helps you group and arrange various layout objects.

Figure 3.25 The Tools toolbar, also only available in Layout mode, offers fast access to FileMaker's design tools.

To turn on/off toolbars:

1. Choose View > Toolbars and select a tool-bar from the submenu to turn on or off (**Figure 3.26**). Checked toolbars are already on; unchecked ones are off.

2. Release your cursor on the selected tool-bar and by default, it will appear in the area below FileMaker's menu bar.

✔ Tip

■ The mode you're working in dictates which toolbars will be available: the Arrange and Tools toolbars cannot be turned on unless you're in Layout mode.

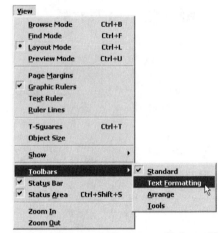

Figure 3.26 To turn toolbars on or off, choose View > Toolbars and make a selection from the submenu.

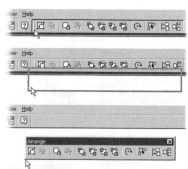

Figure 3.27 To move toolbars to your desktop, click on any toolbar's left edge (top), drag to the desktop (middle), and release your cursor (bottom).

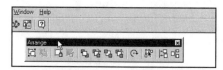

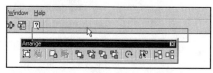

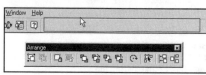

Figure 3.28 To dock a toolbar below FileMaker's menu bar, click the toolbar's title (top), drag it toward the menu bar (middle), and release the cursor (bottom).

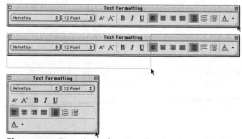

Figure 3.29 To resize a *freestanding* toolbar, click its outer edge (Windows) or lower-right corner (Mac) and drag the cursor to shrink or enlarge the toolbar.

Rearranging the toolbars

FileMaker makes it easy to rearrange the toolbars to suit your work setup. Sometimes it's easiest to have your activated toolbars "docked," that is, running horizontally across the top of FileMaker's main window. For some tasks, however, you may prefer to have a toolbar sitting out on the desktop itself. You also can resize toolbars when they're on your desktop.

To move toolbars to the desktop:

1. To move a docked toolbar (those running across FileMaker's main window), click your cursor on the vertical bar marking the toolbar's left-hand edge (top, **Figure 3.27**).

2. Continue pressing the cursor and drag the toolbar to a new spot on the desktop (middle, **Figure 3.27**).

3. Release the cursor and the toolbar will appear with its own title (bottom, **Figure 3.27**).

To dock toolbars in the main window:

1. To move a freestanding toolbar into a docked position below FileMaker's menu bar, click on the toolbar's title (top, **Figure 3.28**).

2. Continue pressing the cursor and drag the toolbar to the area just below the menu bar (middle, **Figure 3.28**).

3. Release the cursor and the toolbar will snap into place (bottom, **Figure 3.28**).

To resize freestanding toolbars:

◆ To resize a freestanding toolbar, click an outer edge (Windows) or its lower-right corner (Mac) and drag the cursor to shrink or enlarge the toolbar (**Figure 3.29**).

Opening, Closing, and Saving Files

Opening and closing files in FileMaker works like most programs. Unlike many programs, however, FileMaker automatically saves data as you enter it. If by habit, you type Ctrl S or ⌘ S, the Sort dialog box will appear. Just click *Done* and you'll be back to where you were with no harm done.

While FileMaker's save feature works automatically, you can control how often and under what circumstances saves take place. For more information, see *Setting FileMaker's Preferences*, on page 301.

To open a file:

1. If you haven't started the FileMaker program, do so now by either choosing Programs\FileMaker Pro from the Start menu (**Figure 3.30**) or double-clicking the FileMaker Pro icon in the FileMaker Pro 5.5 folder (Mac).

2. A dialog box will appear asking whether you want to create a new file using a template, create a new empty file, or open an existing file (**Figure 3.31**). Make your choice and click *OK*.

3. Depending on your choice in step 2, a dialog box will appear asking you to create and name a copy of the selected template (**Figure 3.32**), open an existing file, or create and name a new file. For more information on templates see *Using Templates and Scripts*, on page 199.

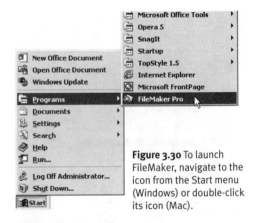

Figure 3.30 To launch FileMaker, navigate to the icon from the Start menu (Windows) or double-click its icon (Mac).

Figure 3.31 When FileMaker's opening dialog box appears, you may open a new template-based file, a new empty file, or an existing file.

Figure 3.32 If you use one of FileMaker's templates, a dialog box will ask you to create and name a copy of the selected template.

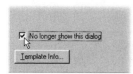

Figure 3.33 To skip FileMaker's opening dialog box, check the *No longer show this dialog* box.

Figure 3.34 You also can open an existing file using the File menu.

Figure 3.35 To create a new file, choose File > New Database.

✔ Tips

■ If you'd rather not see the dialog box that asks whether you want to open a template, a new file, or an existing file every time you launch FileMaker, check the *No longer show this dialog* box (**Figure 3.33**). In the future, when FileMaker starts up, you can then go directly to the File menu.

■ If you've turned off the opening dialog box (see the *Tip* above), you still can open an existing file by choosing File > Open (**Figure 3.34**). Or use your keyboard: Ctrl O (Windows) or ⌘O (Mac).

To create a new file:

◆ Choose File > New Database (**Figure 3.35**).

Closing a file

Because FileMaker automatically saves your data, closing a file is simple. You can close a file several different ways.

To close a file:

◆ Choose File > Close (**Figure 3.36**). The keyboard equivalents are: Ctrl W (Windows) or ⌘ W (Mac).

or

Ⓦ Click the close button in the record's upper-right corner (**Figure 3.37**) or double-click the FileMaker icon in the upper-left corner of the menu bar (**Figure 3.38**).

Ⓜ Click the close box in the left corner of the record's title bar (in OS X, it's a red circle marked with an X) (**Figure 3.39**).

Figure 3.36 To close a file, choose File > Close.

Figure 3.37 To close a Windows FileMaker file, click the close button in the upper right of the document.

Figure 3.38 You also can close a Windows FileMaker file by double-clicking the FileMaker icon at the far left of the menu bar.

Figure 3.39 To close a Macintosh FileMaker file, click the close icon in the upper left of the document.

CLOSING FILES

Figure 3.40 To make a backup copy of a record, choose *Save a Copy As* under the File menu.

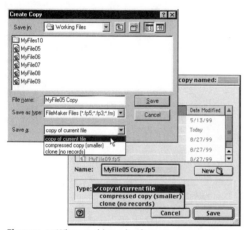

Figure 3.41 When making a backup copy, you can save it as a regular record, a compressed version, or a layout-only clone. Select one and click *Save*.

Saving files

Though FileMaker saves your work as you go, you may want to make a copy of a database right before making a lot of changes to the original.

To save a copy of a database file:

1. Choose File > Save a Copy As (**Figure 3.40**).

2. When the dialog box appears, you can either accept the default name or type in a new name. Choose where you want to store the copy by navigating through the folder icons at the top of the dialog box. At the bottom of the dialog box (**Figure 3.41**), you also have the option to save the copy as a regular database file, a space-saving compressed file, or a clone. The clone option lets you save a database's layout, scripts, and field definitions but without any data.

3. Once you've picked your file name, destination, and file type, click *Save*.

To quit FileMaker:

◆ Choose File > Exit (Windows) or File > Quit (pre-OS X Mac) or FileMaker Pro > Quit FileMaker Pro (OS X Mac) (**Figure 3.42**). The keyboard equivalents are: Alt F4 or Ctrl Q (Windows) or ⌘ Q (Mac, all operating systems).

✔ Tip

■ If you don't quit FileMaker properly (for example, your machine crashes), the next time you open a FileMaker record the program will pause to run a consistency check. This takes only a moment, and then FileMaker is usually ready to go.

Figure 3.42 To quit FileMaker, choose File > Exit (left, Windows) or File > Quit (right, in OS X Mac).

PART II

WORKING WITH RECORDS & FILES

VIEWING RECORDS

As eager as you might be to start creating your own database, the truth is you'll spend most of your time using FileMaker to view and modify *existing* records. Whether it's zipping through a big corporate health benefits database or working with your personal cookie recipes, knowing how to get around FileMaker records efficiently will save you lots of work over the long haul.

Opening a File

If you're working alone and this is your first time using FileMaker, you may not have any records to view. Never fear. To spare you the bother of having to create some records just for viewing, we'll be using some of the existing records that came with your copy of FileMaker. If you already have a FileMaker database to work with, feel free to use it.

By the way, when you first open a FileMaker file it automatically appears in Browse mode, which enables you to look at a record without worrying about the layout or how it'll print. For more on each of FileMaker's four modes, see page 22.

To open a FileMaker database file:

1. If you haven't started the FileMaker program, do so now by either choosing Programs\FileMaker Pro from the Start menu (Windows) (**Figure 3.30**) or double-clicking the FileMaker Pro icon in the FileMaker Pro 5.5 folder (Mac) (**Figure 4.1**).

2. A dialog box will appear asking whether you want to create a *new* file using a template, create a new *empty* file, or open an *existing* file. Select *Open an existing file...* and click *OK* (**Figure 4.2**). See *Using Templates and Scripts* on page 199 to learn how templates can save you time in creating your own databases.

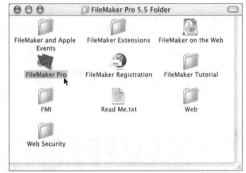

Figure 4.1 To launch the FileMaker Pro application, double-click its icon in the FileMaker Pro 5.5 folder.

Figure 4.2 When FileMaker's opening dialog box appears, choose *Open an existing file...* and click *OK*.

Figure 4.3 You also can open an existing file via FileMaker's File Menu.

Figure 4.4 FileMaker's existing *Sample02.fp5* file.

3. If you've turned off the opening dialog box (see *Tip* on page 35), you still can open an existing file by choosing File > Open (**Figure 4.3**). Or use your keyboard: Ctrl O (Windows) or ⌘ O (Mac).

4. At this point, you can open a FileMaker file you may already have, in which case navigate your way through the dialog boxes to find it. If you don't have your own file, see the next step to open the example file featured in this chapter.

5. Navigate your way down to the file *Sample02.fp5*, nested inside these folders: FileMaker\FileMaker Pro 5.5\FileMaker Tutorial\Sample Files\. Open the file by double-clicking it, clicking the Open button, or using the keyboard commands: Ctrl O (Windows) or ⌘ O (Mac). Now that you have the *Sample02.fp5* file onscreen (**Figure 4.4**), we'll use it to explain how to view records, move from one record to another, and get around within individual records.

Viewing Multiple or Single Records

FileMaker lets you view records three different ways: as single records using the View as Form choice or as multiple records using the View as List or View as Table choices. Viewing one record at a time helps you see more detail within a particular record. Inspecting multiple records at the same time makes it easier to compare one to another.

To view multiple records:

◆ Our example, *Sample02.fp5,* opens showing just one record (**Figure 4.4**). To view several records at once, choose View > View as List or View > View as Table (**Figure 4.5**). Depending on your choice, the file will display as many individual records as your screen can accommodate (**Figure 4.6**) or display a table of records (**Figure 4.7**).

To view a single record:

◆ To view one record at a time, choose View > View as Form (**Figure 4.8**). The file will shift back to a view with only one record showing.

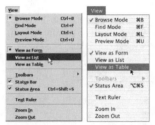

Figure 4.5 To see more than one record at once, choose View > View as List (left) or View > View as Table (right).

Figure 4.6 The View as List choice will display multiple records in the current layout, enabling you to compare one record to another.

Figure 4.7 The View as Table choice uses a simple table layout to display as many records as your screen can accommodate.

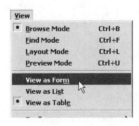

Figure 4.8 Choosing View > View as Form switches the file back to a single-record view.

Figure 4.9 Click on the flipbook pages to move forward or backward one record at a time.

Figure 4.10 A blank page means you've reached the end of the record sequence.

Figure 4.11 Jump ahead in the records by grabbing the book-mark bar and dragging it down-ward. Dragging it upward will let you move backward through the records.

Moving from Record to Record

FileMaker offers you three ways to quickly jump from record to record within any file. And, as with most things in FileMaker, you have several options within each view.

Navigating records in forms

◆ Click on the flipbook's pages to move for-ward or backward—one record at a time. Click the lower page to move forward in the sequence (**Figure 4.9**); click the upper page to move back. A blank upper or lower page indicates there are no more records in that direction (**Figure 4.10**).

◆ To quickly skip ahead or back within the records, click and drag the flipbook's bookmark bar. Dragging it down will skip you ahead in the sequence (**Figure 4.11**); dragging it up moves you back.

Navigating records in lists and tables

◆ You can use the flipbook pages and book-mark bar in List or Table view as well (**Figures 4.12–4.13**).

◆ The List and Table views also allow you to skip from record to record simply by clicking anywhere within the records visible on your screen (**Figure 4.14**). This is especially handy when you need to change data in one field within each record. Clicking directly on that field will highlight it, enabling you to begin entering your new data.

✔ Tip

■ When you're working in List or Table view, a thin black bar just left of the records highlights the current record (**Figure 4.13**).

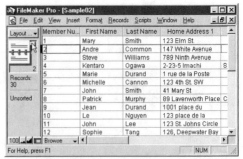

Figure 4.12 Dragging the bookmark works in the List and Table views as well. Just grab, drag, and ...

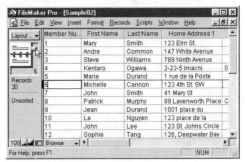

Figure 4.13 ... jump ahead in your records. Note how the black highlight in the thin bar left of the records now marks the Michelle Cannon entry.

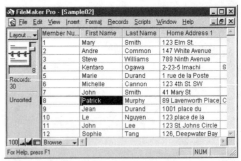

Figure 4.14 When in List or Table view, you can click directly on any field and it will become highlighted. Once highlighted, you can change a portion or all of the data within the field.

Figure 4.15 You can directly enter a record number by clicking the number just below the flipbook or by pressing the [Esc] key. Type in a new record number, press [Enter] (Windows) or [Return] (Mac), and you're there.

Navigating directly by record number

◆ If you know the number of a particular record, you can go right to it by clicking on the current record number, typing in the desired number, and pressing [Enter] (Windows) or [Return] (Mac) (**Figure 4.15**). Pressing [Esc] will automatically highlight the current record number, allowing you to work mouse-free. This method works in Form, List, or Table view.

Moving within a Record

Getting around within a single FileMaker record couldn't be easier, but as usual, there are several ways to do it.

Using your cursor to directly select a field works best when you need to change only a couple of items within a particular record. Using the ⌈Tab⌉ key generally works best when you're filling in new *blank* records or when you want to keep your hands on the keyboard. Both methods work in either Form or List View.

To move by direct selection:

◆ Click on any field you want to modify (left, **Figure 4.16**). Once the field becomes highlighted, type in your data (right, **Figure 4.16**). To reach another spot in the record, click your cursor on the desired field.

To move with the Tab key:

◆ After a record opens, press the ⌈Tab⌉ key to reach the first field. Continue pressing the ⌈Tab⌉ key until you reach the desired field. To move backward among the fields, press ⌈Shift⌉⌈Tab⌉.

✔ Tips

■ You can't tab to fields that contain calculations or summaries. But the contents of those fields are based on values set in other fields, so it's not really a problem. Just keep it in mind.

■ FileMaker lets you set the tab order for all the fields in a record. Reordering the tabs is particularly handy if you need to reach only a few scattered fields within each record. For more on setting the tab order, see page 160.

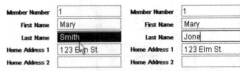

Figure 4.16 To enter data or modify a field, just click on it and type in your data once the field is highlighted.

FINDING AND SORTING RECORDS

5

Finding and sorting records are like two halves of the same process. Together, they give you the power to spotlight particular records in a particular order. That ability allows you to complete such mundane work as correcting entry errors as well as big-picture tasks like analyzing trends.

With Find you can hunt down a record that needs changing without having to go through the records one by one. While records normally are displayed in the order they were created, the Sort command lets you arrange the view to what best suits your needs.

Virtually every Find or Sort you do can be set up as a script using FileMaker's ScriptMaker. Creating a script for a complicated Find allows you to save it for future use. For more information, see *Using Templates and Scripts* on page 199.

Finding related field information in relational databases is covered in *Creating Relational Databases* on page 221.

Finding Records

Understanding a few key terms—the Find request and the found set, along with *And* vs. *Or* searches—will make it easier to use FileMaker's Find features (**Figure 5.1**).

The Find Request: What FileMaker calls a *Find request* simply represents all the criteria entered for a particular search. Whether they're plain or fancy, all the field criteria associated with a single search represent one Find request.

The Found Set: FileMaker calls the records returned in any search the *found set*, which represents only the records activated by the current Find request. The rest of the file's records still exist but are not displayed and make up what FileMaker calls the *omitted set*. For more information, see *Omitting Records* on page 62 and *Deleting Records* on page 65.

Working with a found set allows you to focus on tailoring it for sorting, printing, exporting, etc. You can return to working with the full set of records within a file at any time. To do so, choose the *Show All Records* command under the Requests or Records menus. Or use your keyboard: [Ctrl][J] (Windows) or [⌘][J] (Mac). In effect, this turns the entire file into the found set.

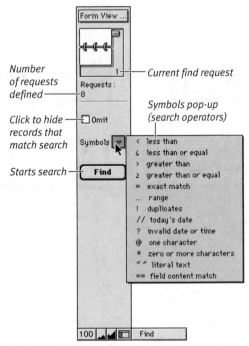

Figure 5.1 Switching to Find mode calls up search-related tools and buttons in FileMaker's left-hand status area.

***And* vs. *Or* Searches:** Find's features allow you to create wonderfully specific search requests but they all involve variations of two kinds of searches: the *And* search vs. the *Or* search.

Any time you create a Find request that looks for data in two or more *different* fields in a record, you're performing what's called a logical *And* search. FileMaker also calls this a *simple search*. If, for example, you create a Find request that asks for any records within a file where the city is San Francisco and the state is California, you're asking FileMaker to find records that contain San Francisco *and* California. Such *And* searches tend to narrow your search since you're not just looking for records containing California but a smaller group within that group that also contains San Francisco.

Any time you create a Find request that looks for *different* values within the *same* field, you're performing what's called a logical *Or* search. FileMaker also calls this a *multiple search*. If, for example, you create a Find request for all records containing California *or* Arizona, that will require FileMaker to search the database's state field for two different values. Such *Or* queries tend to widen your search.

Doing a Simple Search

The database used for examples in this section contains house sales information for a neighborhood collected from the county assessor: the address, the most recent sales price, when the house was last sold, the square footage, etc. It's intended to show how Find allows you to search the same information in a variety of ways.

To do a simple search for one item:

1. You can't search for information in a particular field unless you have a layout with that field in it. Switch to the layout of your database that contains the field or fields you want to search.

2. Once the correct layout appears, choose View > Find Mode (**Figure 5.2**). Or use your keyboard: Ctrl F (Windows) or ⌘ F (Mac). A blank version of the selected layout will appear.

3. In our example we want to find all the houses on Pomona Avenue, so type Pomona into the Street Name field (**Figure 5.3**). Click the *Find* button in the mode status area along the left-hand side of the screen (**Figure 5.1**), or simply press Enter (Windows) or Return (Mac). (You can also choose Requests > Perform Find but using the keyboard is much easier.) Nine records appear that contain "Pomona" in the Street Name field (**Figure 5.4**). Notice that the left-hand mode status area shows the number of found records (9), along with the total record count (49).

✔ Tip

■ If you want to follow along with the real estate database examples, you can download the database at: www.peachpit.com/vqs/filemaker.

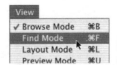

Figure 5.2 To start a search, choose View > Find Mode.

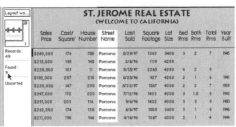

Figure 5.3 Type into any field the data you're seeking.

Figure 5.4 Once you click Find, FileMaker displays any records matching your search.

Figure 5.5 Entering data into multiple fields allows you to narrow your search, in this case to two-bedroom houses costing $200,000 or less.

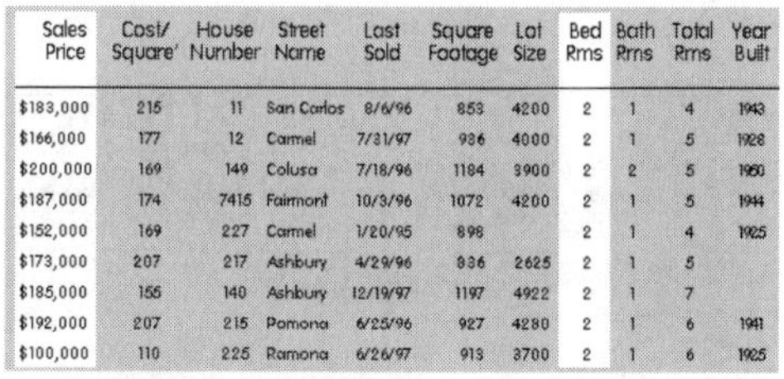

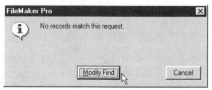

Figure 5.6 The search results show only records that match criteria in *both* fields.

FileMaker Pro	×
No records match this request.	
Modify Find	Cancel

Figure 5.7 If no records match your request, click *Modify Find*.

To do a simple search for several items simultaneously:

1. Select the database and layout you want to search. To start, choose View > Find Mode or use your keyboard: Ctrl F (Windows) or ⌘F (Mac).

2. When a blank version of the layout appears, type your various criteria into the appropriate fields. In this example, we're searching for any two-bedroom houses costing $200,000 or less (**Figure 5.5**).

3. Click the *Find* button in the mode status area, or press Enter (Windows) or Return (Mac). The results show only records matching both request items (**Figure 5.6**).

✔ Tips

■ If nothing in the database matches your search criteria, FileMaker will tell you and give you the chance to revise your search by clicking *Modify Find* (**Figure 5.7**).

■ As long as each item you're requesting appears in a *different* field, you can make such requests as specific as you like: all two-bedroom, two-bath homes built since 1975 costing less than $200,000, for example. Many times this simple *And* search will be all you need. To search for different values within the *same* field, you'll need to make a multiple search request (see page 54).

■ Once you've found a set of records, you can copy their data into another application, such as a spreadsheet, though FileMaker's field formatting will not be copied. Just use the copy command: Ctrl C (Windows) or ⌘C (Mac).

Doing Multiple Criteria Searches

What distinguishes a multiple criteria search from a simple search is that you're looking for several values within the *same* field. To go back to our real estate example, you may want to find homes on Pomona Avenue *and* San Carlos Avenue. Both items would appear in the Street Name field, so you'll need to make a multiple criteria search.

To do a multiple criteria search:

1. Choose View > Find Mode or use your keyboard: Ctrl F (Windows) or ⌘F (Mac). Type what you're seeking into the relevant field. Do *not* hit Enter or Return just yet.

2. To add your second search item, choose Requests > Add New Request (**Figure 5.8**). Or use your keyboard: Ctrl N (Windows) or ⌘N (Mac). A duplicate set of blank fields will appear (**Figure 5.9**).

3. Type what you're seeking into the duplicate of the field you used in the first request. Within the left-hand mode status area, the number of requests you've made within this set of records is displayed. If you want, you can continue to add multiple criteria by repeating this step.

4. When you're ready, click the *Find* button in the mode status area or press Enter (Windows) or Return (Mac). The search will display all records that match any of your criteria requests (**Figure 5.10**).

Figure 5.8 To add another request to your search, choose Requests > Add New Request.

Figure 5.9 In a multiple criteria search, a second set of fields will appear—allowing you to look for several values within the *same* field.

Sales Price	Cost/ Square'	House Number	Street Name	Last Sold	Square Footage	Lot Size	Bed Rms	Bath Rms	Total Rms	Year Built
$240,000	189	115	San Carlos	11/12/97	1271	3900	2	1	7	1941
$183,000	215	11	San Carlos	8/6/96	853	4200	2	1	4	1943
$241,000	258	5	San Carlos	2/14/97	934	5000	2	2	4	1956
$250,000	139	200	San Carlos	0/30/96	1804	5000	2	2	9	1943
$201,000	204	216	San Carlos	1/20/97	983	4200	2	1	5	1940
$228,000	155	232	San Carlos	2/28/97	1474	4625	3	1	7	1943
$240,000	176	755	Pomona	5/29/97	1363	5400	3	2	7	1945
$218,000	195	145	Pomona	3/6/96	1119	4200				
$228,500	101	11	Pomona	8/15/97	2265	4280	4	2	9	
$192,000	207	215	Pomona	6/25/96	927	4280	2	1	6	1941
$230,000	147	200	Pomona	5/22/97	1567	4000	2	2	7	1988
$247,000	172	220	Pomona	7/12/96	1433	4000	3	1.5	8	1943
$291,000	203	116	Pomona	9/6/96	1432	4000	3	3	8	1950
$262,000	174	138	Pomona	6/6/97	1505	3600	3	1	8	1946
$211,000	198	146	Pomona	4/16/96	1067	4000	2	1	4	1944

Figure 5.10 In this multiple criteria search example, the streets San Carlos *and* Pomona appear. Such searches can handle any number of requests for data in the same field.

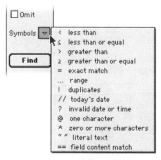

Symbols pop-up menu:

<	less than
≤	less than or equal
>	greater than
≥	greater than or equal
=	exact match
...	range
!	duplicates
//	today's date
?	invalid date or time
@	one character
*	zero or more characters
" "	literal text
==	field content match

Figure 5.11 Click on the Symbols pop-up menu to access 13 choices for fine tuning your search. See Table 5.1 for details.

Refining Searches

Within Find mode, the Symbols pop-up menu in the left-hand status area offers 13 choices for quickly fine tuning your search (**Figure 5.11**). Combined with the status area's *Omit* checkbox (for more information on Omit, see page 62), these tools can be a major help when trying to find a series of records amid hundreds (**Table 5.1**).

Table 5.1

Using Find's Symbols/Operators Pop-up Box

USE	TO FIND	TYPE IN FIELD	NOTES
<	Less than value to right of symbol	<200	
≤	Less than or equal to value to right	≤200	
>	Greater than value to right	>200	
≥	Greater than or equal to value to right	≥200	
=	Exactly value to right	=Pomona	Exact match and other values (e.g., will find Pomona Ave.)
==	Exact value in order & nothing else	==Pomona	Exact match with no other values (e.g., will not find Pomona Ave.)
...	A range of dates, times, numbers, text	... or .. (two periods)	Includes beginning and ending values; displays in A–Z, 1–10 order
!	Duplicate values	!	Finds any duplicate field entries—great for mailing lists
//	Today's date	//	
?	Invalid dates, times, or calculations	?	Finds format errors that can create calculation problems
@	One unknown or variable text character	@omona	A one character search that will find Pomona and Romona
*	Zero or more unknown variable characters	P*a	No character limit: "P*a" finds Pomona but also Pia, Paula
" "	Text exactly as it appears	"Pomona"	Ignores letter case, so it will find "Pomona" and "pomona"
==	Empty fields	==	Useful for finding missing data

To refine a search:

1. Switch to the layout of your database that contains the field or fields you want to search. Choose View > Find Mode, or use your keyboard: [Ctrl][F] (Windows) or [⌘][F] (Mac). A blank version of the selected layout will appear.

2. Click on the field you'll be searching. Now click on the Symbols pop-up menu in the left-hand mode status area and select the appropriate symbol or *operator* (**Figure 5.11**). (See **Table 5.1** for details on how each operator functions.) In this example, we want to find all the homes selling for less than $200,000. Select the first operator in the pop-up list, then type in 200,000 (**Figure 5.12**).

3. Click the *Find* button in the status area or press [Enter] (Windows) or [Return] (Mac). FileMaker will then display all the records meeting that criteria (**Figure 5.13**).

✔ Tips

■ You can use Find's Symbols drop-down menu when making multiple criteria search requests as well as for simple searches.

■ If your search request criteria include finding the current date, time, user name, an item from your index, or the last record, FileMaker's Insert menu can speed your work. Just click on the field you'll be searching, then choose Insert and then any command between *Current Date* and *From Last Record* (**Figure 5.14**). You can also use the Insert menu while creating new records. (For information on indexing, see *Storage options* on page 110.)

Figure 5.12 Combining data you type in directly (200,000) with the pop-up menu's symbols (<) lets you quickly define a search for all entries of less than 200,000.

Sales Price	Cost/ Square'	House Number	Street Name
$183,000	215	11	San Carlos
$166,000	177	12	Carmel
$187,000	174	7415	Fairmont
$152,000	169	227	Carmel
$173,000	207	217	Ashbury
$185,000	155	140	Ashbury
$192,000	207	215	Pomona
$173,000	166	244	Ashbury
$191,000	165	309	Carmel
$100,000	110	225	Ramona

Figure 5.13 After completing the search, FileMaker displays all records matching the <200,000 Find request.

Figure 5.14 The Insert menu includes five items (*Current Date* to *From Last Record*), which can speed creation of Find requests.

Figure 5.15 Commands for altering or modifying your most recent Find request reside under the Requests menu, but can be selected *only* if you're in Find mode.

Figure 5.16 If you want to change a search but already are in Browse mode, choose Records > Modify Last Find.

Modifying Find Requests

FileMaker offers several commands for altering or modifying your most recent Find request. Most reside under the Requests menu: Add New Request, Duplicate Request, Delete Request, and Revert Request (**Figure 5.15**). As long as you are still in Find mode, these commands can be used directly to revise your most recent search. However, if you've already performed the Find and are viewing the found records in Browse mode, you'll need to take an additional step. (See *To modify your previous Find request* below.)

None of these commands can be applied to the previous search once you've done *another* search, which wipes out the previous search's criteria.

To modify your previous Find request:

1. Make sure you've got the layout you want. If necessary, use the layout drop-down menu to select the right one.

2. Make sure you're in Find mode (View > Find Mode).

3. Choose Records > Modify Last Find (Ctrl R in Windows or ⌘ R on the Mac) (**Figure 5.16**).

4. When the form appears, modify your request and click *Find* or press Enter (Windows) or Return (Mac).

Adding a New Request

FileMaker calls this adding a new request because you're adding search criteria to an *existing* request. This differs from simply modifying a Find because it's creating a logical *Or* search, which requires searching *one* field for *two or more* criteria.

To add to a Find request:

1. If you've already performed your first Find and now are in Browse mode, choose Records > Modify Last Find (**Figure 5.16**). Or use your keyboard: Ctrl R (Windows) or ⌘R (Mac). Now choose Requests > Add New Request or use your keyboard: Ctrl N (Windows) or ⌘N (Mac).

   If you're still in Find mode, choose Requests > Add New Request (**Figure 5.17**). Or use your keyboard: Ctrl N (Windows) or ⌘N (Mac).

2. A blank version of the selected layout fields will appear below the ones you previously filled in. Type your additional search criteria into the appropriate fields (**Figure 5.18**). Note: In this example only the street has been changed, but the price could be changed as well.

3. Continue adding requests just as you did in Step 3. When you've added all the requests, click *Find*, or press Enter (Windows) or Return (Mac).

✔ Tip

- This bears repeating because it can be so frustrating if you miss this step: Once you perform a Find (and so have wound up in Browse mode), you cannot modify that Find without first choosing Records > Modify Last Find. Once you do that, you can then choose New, Duplicate, Delete, or Revert Request under the Requests menu without erasing the previous search criteria.

Figure 5.17 To add to a search, choose Requests > Add New Request.

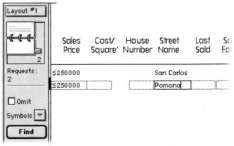

Figure 5.18 When you add a search request to an existing one (what FileMaker calls Add New Request), a blank request form appears below the one you previously filled in.

Figure 5.19 To duplicate a Find request, choose Requests > Duplicate Request.

Sales Price	Cost/ Square'	House Number	Street Name	Last Sold	Square Footage	Lot Size	Bed Rms	Bath Rms	Total Rms	Year Built
≤200000			Pomona	≥1/1/91	≥1200		≥2	≥1.5		≥1960
≤200000			San Carlos	≥1/1/91	≥1200		≥2	≥1.5		≥1960

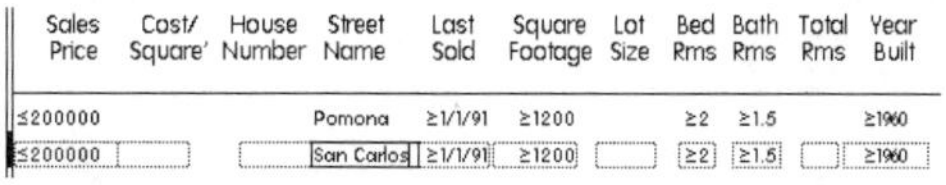

Figure 5.20 The Duplicate Request command saves time if you only need to change a few of the previous Find request's criteria.

To duplicate (and then change) a Find request:

1. Switch to the layout you want.

2. If you've typed in your first request but are still in Find mode, choose Requests > Duplicate Request (Ctrl D in Windows or ⌘ D on the Mac) (**Figure 5.19**).

   If you've already performed the Find and now are in Browse mode, first choose Records > Modify Last Find (Ctrl R in Windows or ⌘ R on the Mac) (**Figure 5.16**), and then choose Requests > Duplicate Request (Ctrl D in Windows or ⌘ D on the Mac) (**Figure 5.19**).

3. A duplicate of your first request will appear (**Figure 5.20**). You can then alter the appropriate fields—saving yourself a bit of time.

4. Repeat the steps until you've duplicated (and then changed) all the requests you need. Click *Find*, or press Enter (Windows) or Return (Mac).

DUPLICATING AND CHANGING A REQUEST

To delete a Find request:

1. Switch to the layout you want.

2. If you've typed in a request but are still in Find mode, use the flipbook icon to click to the Find request you want to delete (**Figure 5.21**).

    If you've already performed the Find and now are in Browse mode, first choose Records > Modify Last Find ([Ctrl][R] in Windows or ⌘[R] on the Mac). Now use the flipbook icon to click to the Find request you want to delete (**Figure 5.21**).

3. Choose Requests > Delete Request (**Figure 5.22**). Or use your keyboard: [Ctrl][E] (Windows) or ⌘[E] (Mac). The selected request will be deleted (**Figure 5.23**).

✔ Tip

■ You can delete as many Find requests as you like—until there's just one left, which you cannot delete.

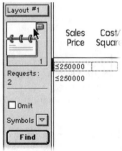

Figure 5.21 If you want to delete a particular request and are still in Find mode, use the flipbook to reach it.

Figure 5.22 Once you find the request, choose Requests > Delete Request.

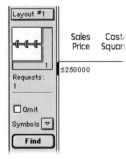

Figure 5.23 Once you delete a request, the status area will reflect the change.

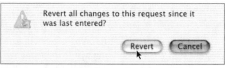

Figure 5.24 If you make a mistake in creating a Find request, choose Requests > Revert Request.

Figure 5.25 Choosing Requests > Revert Request triggers an alert dialog box. Click *Revert* to correct a mistake or *Cancel* to leave things as they are.

Figure 5.26 To find all your records, choose Records > Show All Records if you are in Browse mode (left) or Requests > Show All Records if you're in Find mode (right).

Reverting Requests

This command lets you correct entries *while* you're creating a Find request. It does not return you to where you were before you performed a Find. But it will let you start fresh on building the current Find request—no matter how many fields you've already filled in within that request.

To revert a request:

1. You must be in Find mode, filling out a Find request. When you make a mistake, choose Requests > Revert Request (**Figure 5.24**).

2. When the warning dialog box appears, click *Revert* (**Figure 5.25**). All the fields within that Find request will become blank, allowing you to start fresh.

To find all records:

◆ If you are in Browse mode, choose Records > Show All Records (left, **Figure 5.26**). If you're in Find mode, choose Requests > Show All Records (right, **Figure 5.26**). The keyboard command is the same in either mode: Ctrl J (Windows) or ⌘J (Mac).

Omitting Records

Omitting records does not delete them from your database but simply hides them from view. In that sense, omitted records are the reverse of the *found set* generated by a Find request. When you perform a Find, the records *not* shown are what FileMaker calls the *omitted set*. Used with the Find and Sort commands, the Omit command allows you to quickly make a selection and then *invert* it by finding all the records *not* in that selection.

To omit one record:

1. In Browse mode, select the record you want to omit.

2. Choose Records > Omit Record (**Figure 5.27**). Or use your keyboard: Ctrl M (Windows) or ⌘ T (Mac).

Figure 5.27 To hide a record from view, select it, then choose Records > Omit Record. Omitting records does not delete them but simply tucks them out of sight.

OMITTING RECORDS

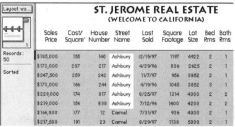

Figure 5.28 Choosing Records > Omit Multiple hides a group of records—starting with the first one you select.

Figure 5.29 In the example, the far-left thin black bar indicates the first of the six Ashbury records that will be omitted.

Figure 5.30 When the Omit dialog box appears, type in the number of records you want to hide, then click *Omit*.

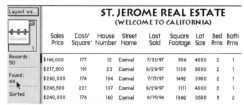

Figure 5.31 All six Ashbury records have been hidden. The *Records: 50* and *Found: 44* in the left-hand status area confirm that six records have been omitted.

To omit more than one record:

1. In Browse mode, select the first record of the group you want to omit.

2. Choose Records > Omit Multiple (**Figure 5.28**). Or use your keyboard: Shift Ctrl M (Windows) or Shift ⌘ T (Mac).

3. A dialog box will appear asking how many records you want to omit. In our real estate example, we sorted the records to place together the six Ashbury records we want to omit (**Figure 5.29**). Since we'd selected the first Ashbury record in Step 1, we enter 6 and click the *Omit* button (**Figure 5.30**). The Ashbury records have been omitted—not deleted, just hidden. The "Records: 50" and "Found: 44" in the left-hand status area confirm that six records have been omitted (**Figure 5.31**).

To bring back omitted records:

- Remember: Omitting a record does not delete it but simply removes it from the found set. To bring it back, choose Records > Show Omitted (**Figure 5.32**). The six records omitted in our previous example appear and are now the found set (**Figure 5.33**). The *previous* found set of 44 records are now omitted. It takes some getting used to, but the Find Omitted command's back-and-forth toggle nature becomes very handy when used with the Find and Sort commands.

Records
New Record ⌘N
Duplicate Record ⌘D
Delete Record... ⌘E
Delete Found Records
Modify Last Find ⌘R
Show All Records ⌘J
Show Omitted
Omit Record ⌘T
Omit Multiple... ⇧⌘T
Sort... ⌘S
Replace... ⌘=
Relookup
Revert Record

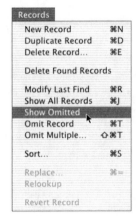

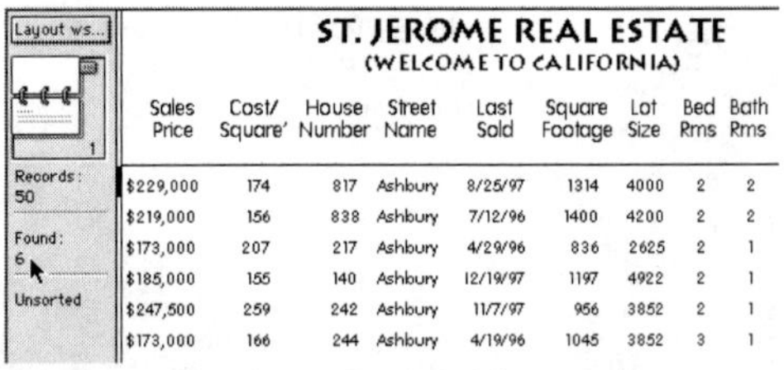

Figure 5.32 Because omitted records are only hidden, choosing Records > Show Omitted restores them to view.

✔ Tip

- Whenever you select the Show Omitted command it will display any records not already on the screen—even if you have every single record displayed. In that case, the Show Omitted command will display *no* records. Choose Show Omitted again and up pop *all* the records. When you think about it, it makes sense.

Layout ws...
Records: 50
Found: 6
Unsorted
ST. JEROME REAL ESTATE
(WELCOME TO CALIFORNIA)
Sales Price | Cost/ Square' | House Number | Street Name | Last Sold | Square Footage | Lot Size | Bed Rms | Bath Rms
$229,000 174 817 Ashbury 8/25/97 1314 4000 2 2
$219,000 156 838 Ashbury 7/12/96 1400 4200 2 2
$173,000 207 217 Ashbury 4/29/96 836 2625 2 1
$185,000 155 140 Ashbury 12/19/97 1197 4922 2 1
$247,500 259 242 Ashbury 11/7/97 956 3852 2 1
$173,000 166 244 Ashbury 4/19/96 1045 3852 3 1

Figure 5.33 The six previously hidden records return to view after choosing Show Omitted.

Figure 5.34 First select the record you want to delete (in this case a blank record on the right), then choose Records > Delete Record.

Figure 5.35 FileMaker presents a warning dialog box to make sure you really want to delete a record. If you're sure, click *Delete*.

ST. JEROME REAL ESTATE
(WELCOME TO CALIFORNIA)

Sales Price	Cost/ Square'	House Number	Street Name	Last Sold	Square Footage	Lot Size	Bed Rms
$185,000	155	140	Ashbury	12/19/97	1197	4922	2
$173,000	207	217	Ashbury	4/29/96	836	2625	2
$247,500	259	242	Ashbury	11/7/97	956	3852	2
$173,000	166	244	Ashbury	4/19/96	1045	3852	3
$229,000	174	817	Ashbury	8/25/97	1314	4000	2
$219,000	156	838	Ashbury	7/12/96	1400	4200	2

Figure 5.36 The blank record disappears after the Delete command is invoked.

Deleting Records

Unlike the Omit command, which just hides records, the Delete command really does zap records and all the data inside them. Once you delete them, they're gone: no undo, no going back. To play it safe, consider making a backup copy of a file before you embark on a record-deleting session.

Think about this for a second. First create a copy of the file—just in case. If you're only looking to start with a fresh empty version of the layout, consider creating a clone of the existing database. Cloning gives you an empty database but does so by copying an existing database's layout without touching the original.

To delete a single record:

1. In Browse mode, select the record you want to delete. In our real estate example, we've selected an unwanted blank record. Choose Records > Delete Record or use your keyboard: Ctrl E (Windows) or ⌘ E (Mac) (**Figure 5.34**).

2. As a safeguard against accidentally deleting a record, FileMaker presents a warning dialog box (**Figure 5.35**). If you're sure, click the *Delete* button. The selected record is then deleted (**Figure 5.36**).

To delete a group of records:

1. Use the Find or Omit Multiple commands to select a group of records to delete.

2. Once you've selected the group of records, choose Records > Delete Found Records (**Figure 5.37**). (To keep you from accidentally invoking the command, it has no keyboard equivalent.) As a second safeguard, FileMaker presents a warning dialog box that notes how many records are about to be deleted (**Figure 5.38**). If you're sure, click the *Delete* button.

To delete all records in a database:

1. If you truly want to delete all the records, choose Show All Records from the Requests or Records menus (Ctrl J in Windows or ⌘ J on the Mac).

2. Choose Records > Delete All Records (**Figure 5.39**).

3. Again, FileMaker presents a warning dialog box asking if you really want to delete that many records (**Figure 5.40**). Remember: There's no undo for this command. If you're sure, click the *Delete* button.

Figure 5.37 To delete a group of records, select them, and then select Records > Delete Found Records.

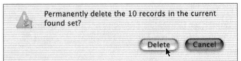

Figure 5.38 To keep you from accidentally deleting a group of records, FileMaker asks for confirmation of the number selected. If you're sure, click *Delete*.

Figure 5.39 To delete all records in a database, choose Records > Delete All Records.

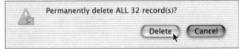

Figure 5.40 To keep you from accidentally wiping out your database, FileMaker presents an alert dialog box.

Table 5.2

How FileMaker Sorts What		
CONTENT	ASCENDING	DESCENDING
Text	A to Z	Z to A
Numbers	1–100	100–1
Time	6:00–11:00	11:00–6:00
Dates	1/1/98–12/1/98	12/1/98–1/1/98
	Jan. 1–Dec. 1	Dec. 1–Jan. 1

Figure 5.41 To run a sort, choose Records > Sort.

Figure 5.42 The Sort Records dialog box allows you to control which fields are sorted, the type of sorting used, and the order in which the sort occurs.

Figure 5.43 After you've selected a field, you can change the *type* of sort by clicking the appropriate radio button (*Ascending*, *Descending*, or *Custom*) in the lower-left area of the Sort Records dialog box.

Sorting Records

FileMaker stores records in the order they were created but that's no reason for you to work with them in that somewhat random order. Using the Sort command, you can rearrange the order for browsing, printing, or updating. FileMaker uses the found set concept discussed on page 50 to search through select fields and then arrange the records as you desire.

FileMaker offers three basic ways of arranging the records: ascending order, descending order, and a custom order based on a list you create. If, like me, you can hardly keep right and left straight, let alone what's ascending and descending, *How FileMaker Sorts What* (**Table 5.2**) should help.

To run a simple sort:

1. Use any combination of the Find, Omit, and Delete commands to first narrow your selection of records for sorting. Of course, you can always sort the entire file.

2. Choose Records > Sort (**Figure 5.41**). Or use your keyboard: Ctrl S (Windows) or ⌘ S (Mac).

3. The Sort Records dialog box will appear (**Figure 5.42**). On the left side is a list of the fields in your file. Select the field you want to sort with by clicking on an item in the left list, then click the *Move* button in the middle to place it in the right-hand window.

   By default, the field will be sorted in ascending order. If you want to change the *type* of sort, first click the field in the right-hand list, then click on the appropriate radio button (*Ascending, Descending,* or *Custom*) in the lower-left area of the Sort Records dialog box (**Figure 5.43**). For more information, see *To set (or reset) a custom sort order* on page 71.

(continued)

4. Click the *Sort* button in the middle of the dialog box or simply press ⟨Enter⟩ (Windows) or ⟨Return⟩ (Mac). If you want to adjust the results, choose Records > Sort again or use your keyboard: ⟨Ctrl⟩⟨S⟩ (Windows) or ⟨⌘⟩⟨S⟩ (Mac).

✔ Tip

■ The Sort order will remain in place until you perform a new sort.

Sort Records options

Whenever you run a sort, the Sort Records dialog box will appear. Most sort actions are controlled by six buttons (only five appear at any one time) running down the middle of the dialog box (**Figure 5.44**).

◆ **Clear All:** Click this button to remove all sort fields in the dialog box's right-side Sort Order list.

◆ **Move:** This button appears only after you click a field name in the dialog box's *left-side* list. Click *Move* to place a field name in the *right-side* Sort Order list.

◆ **Clear:** This button appears only after you click a field name in the *right-side* Sort Order list. Click *Clear* to remove a field name from that list.

◆ **Sort:** Click this button to start the sort itself.

◆ **Unsort:** Click this button to return your file to its status before the sort was performed.

◆ **Done:** Click this button to close the Sort Records dialog box without performing another sort.

Figure 5.44 The Sort Records dialog box's six buttons (*Move* and *Clear* never appear at the same time) control most Sort actions.

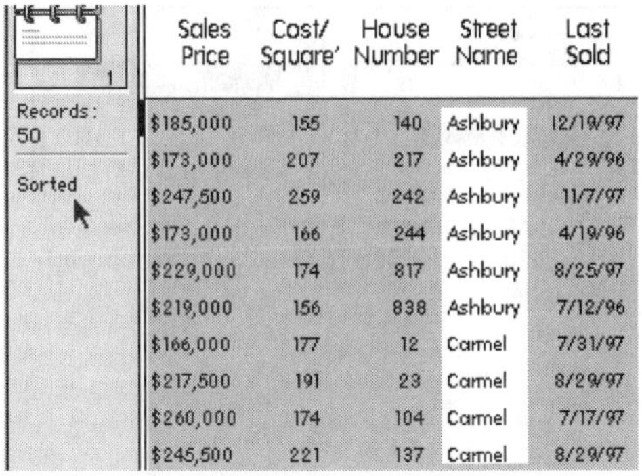

Sales Price	Cost/ Square'	House Number	Street Name	Last Sold
$185,000	155	140	Ashbury	12/19/97
$173,000	207	217	Ashbury	4/29/96
$247,500	259	242	Ashbury	11/7/97
$173,000	166	244	Ashbury	4/19/96
$229,000	174	817	Ashbury	8/25/97
$219,000	156	838	Ashbury	7/12/96
$166,000	177	12	Carmel	7/31/97
$217,500	191	23	Carmel	8/29/97
$260,000	174	104	Carmel	7/17/97
$245,500	221	137	Carmel	8/29/97

Records: 50

Sorted

Figure 5.45 By controlling the sort order within the Sort Records dialog box, all Ashbury homes appear first (with their house numbers in ascending order), followed by all the Carmel homes.

Running Multiple Sorts

A multiple sort allows you to precisely arrange the order of your database records. When you sort more than one field at once, the precedence is based on the order in the Sort Records dialog box. Fields listed first in the box's right-side list will take precedence over fields listed later. Looking at our real estate example, if the Street field is listed before the Number field the records will be first sorted by the street name (A to Z) and then by the address number (1 to 100) (**Figure 5.45**).

To run a multiple sort:

1. Use any combination of the Find, Omit, and Delete commands to first narrow your selection of records to sort. Of course, you can always sort the entire file.

2. Choose Records > Sort (**Figure 5.41**). Or use your keyboard: Ctrl S (Windows) or ⌘ S (Mac).

3. The Sort Records dialog box will appear (**Figure 5.42**). Select the left-side field name you want to first sort by. Click the *Move* button in the middle to place the field name in the right-hand *Sort Order* list.

(continued)

RUNNING MULTIPLE SORTS

4. Continue selecting field names on the left side and placing them in the right side by using the *Move* button. Remember: Their relative precedence is set top to bottom. If you need to change the right-side order, click and hold your cursor over the double-arrow just left of the field name and then drag up or down. The field name will move, altering the sort order precedence (**Figure 5.46**).

5. Pick the *type* of sort (*Ascending*, *Descending*, or *Custom*) for each right-side field name by clicking on the name, then clicking on the appropriate radio button in the lower-left area of the Sort Records dialog box.

6. When you're ready, click the *Sort* button or simply press [Enter] (Windows) or [Return] (Mac). The records will then appear in the sorted order. If you need to adjust the sort order, choose Records > Sort again or use your keyboard: [Ctrl][S] (Windows) or [⌘][S] (Mac).

Since you can unsort with the click of a button, feel free to experiment a bit to get a full sense of how different sorts work.

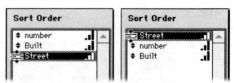

Figure 5.46 To change the sort order, use your cursor to drag the selected field name up or down in the order.

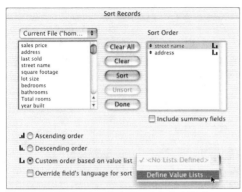

Figure 5.47 Click the radio button labeled *Custom order based on value list*, wait for the pop-up menu to appear, and choose *Define Value Lists*.

Figure 5.48 When the Define Value Lists dialog box appears, click *New*.

Setting Sort Orders

The Custom sort order is determined by a *value list*. Such lists—and their order—are typically created when fields are first being defined (see *Defining Fields* on page 99). However you can change the order of a value list—and thereby the Custom sort order—any time.

To set (or reset) a custom sort order:

1. Choose Records > Sort or use your keyboard: Ctrl S (Windows) or ⌘ S (Mac).

2. The Sort Records dialog box will appear (**Figure 5.47**). If the field name for which you want to create a custom sort order is already listed in the right-side list, click on it there and go to step 3.

   If the field name for which you want to create a custom sort order has not yet been selected and moved to the right side, click on its name in the left-side list. Now click the *Move* button, which will place the field's name in the right-side list.

3. By default, the field's sort type is Ascending. To change the type to a Custom order, click the radio button labeled *Custom order based on value list*, wait for the pop-up menu to appear, and choose *Define Value Lists* (**Figure 5.47**).

4. When the Define Value Lists dialog box appears, click *New* (**Figure 5.48**).

(continued)

5. When the Edit Value List dialog box appears, type an easy-to-recognize name into the Value List Name box, then type each of your custom values into the right-side box in the exact order you want them sorted (**Figure 5.49**). When you're done, click *OK*.

6. When the Define Value Lists dialog box reappears, click *Done*.

7. When the Sort Records dialog box reappears, click Sort to apply your Custom order. The records will sort out in the order of the names in the Streets value list (**Figure 5.50**).

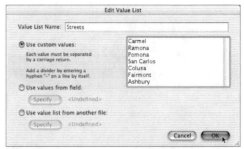

Figure 5.49 Use an easy-to-recognize word for your Value List Name, then type your custom values in the right-side box in the exact order you want them sorted. When you're done, click *OK*.

Sales Price	Cost/ Square'	House Number	Street Name	Last Sold	Square Footage	Lot Size
$152,000	169	227	Carmel	1/20/95	898	
$191,000	165	309	Carmel	10/15/97	1160	4000
$225,000	174	120	Ramona	5/31/96	1295	4000
$270,000	205	237	Ramona	9/26/97	1315	6000
$269,000	210	314	Ramona	8/29/97	1280	4000
$228,500	101	11	Pomona	8/15/97	2265	4280
$291,000	203	116	Pomona	9/6/96	1432	4000

Figure 5.50 Once you run the Custom sort, the record sequence mirrors the order of the value list.

Using Spell Check and Dictionaries

Each FileMaker record can be spell checked by FileMaker's built-in *main dictionary*, which contains an impressive 100,000 words, and by a special *user dictionary* of up to 32,000 words. If you frequently use special terms not commonly found in a dictionary—medical terms or irregular trademarks like FileMaker—you'll want to create one or more user dictionaries.

By default the main dictionary checks all FileMaker files, while you select which files are checked by a user dictionary. In fact, each FileMaker database can be linked to its own user dictionary. This allows you to link a medical database to a user medical dictionary or link a music-oriented database to a user dictionary of performing artists' names. Once that file-to-dictionary link is made, you need not specify it again.

In any case, *you* create the user dictionaries, either by importing an existing text file of your own special terms or by adding words one by one to an empty user dictionary created by FileMaker.

One more thing: FileMaker gives you the option to check your spelling as you type. For more information, see *Setting FileMaker's Preferences* on page 301.

To check spelling:

1. When you have a record or layout to spell check, choose Edit > Spelling. The submenu will then offer you the choice of checking the spelling of only what you've already highlighted (*Check Selection*), the entire record currently on your screen (*Check Record*), or the records browsed in the current session (*Check All*) (**Figure 6.1**). Choose one and release your cursor and the Spelling dialog box will appear.

2. If the dictionary says the selection is spelled correctly, click *Done* (top, **Figure 6.2**). If FileMaker suspects that the word is misspelled, it will display one or more possible replacement words (bottom, **Figure 6.2**). Click the one you prefer—or type in your own choice—then click the *Replace* and *Done* buttons.

3. If the word isn't in FileMaker's dictionary because it's a formal name or special term, you can click *Skip* or *Learn*, and then click *Done* when that button appears. Clicking *Learn* will add the word to the current *user dictionary*. If you have not created a special dictionary for this file, FileMaker will automatically create one named USER.UPR and place it in the System folder (Windows) or the FileMaker Extensions folder (Mac).

✔ Tip

■ If the field or file you're spell checking is password protected or access to it is otherwise restricted, you won't be able to change a misspelling.

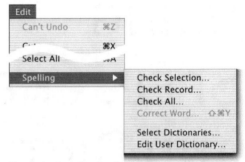

Figure 6.1 Found under the Edit menu, the Spelling submenu offers you three spelling selection choices.

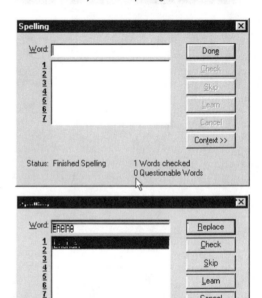

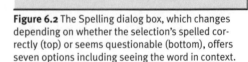

Figure 6.2 The Spelling dialog box, which changes depending on whether the selection's spelled correctly (top) or seems questionable (bottom), offers seven options including seeing the word in context.

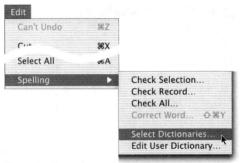

Figure 6.3 To create or select a dictionary, choose Edit > Spelling > Select Dictionaries.

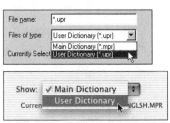

Figure 6.4 Use the *Files of type* drop-down menu (top, Windows) or the *Show* pop-up menu (bottom, Mac) to choose the *Main Dictionary* or a specially created *User Dictionary*.

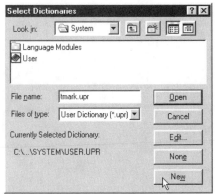

Figure 6.5 Ⓦ Give your new user dictionary an easy to remember name, such as tmark for a special trademark dictionary. Be sure to include the suffix .upr before clicking *New*.

To create a user dictionary:

1. Choose Edit > Spelling > Select Dictionaries (**Figure 6.3**).

2. In the dialog box that appears, click your cursor on the *Files of type* drop-down menu (Windows) or the *Show pop-up menu* (Mac) and choose *User Dictionary* (**Figure 6.4**).

   Ⓦ Within the Select Dictionaries dialog box's *File name* text box, type what you want to call your new user dictionary. Make it something recognizable, such as *tmark* for a special trademark dictionary. Be sure to include .upr at the end of the file name (**Figure 6.5**). When you're done, click *New*. Once the new dictionary appears in the main list, close the dialog box.

   Ⓜ Within the Open dialog box, click *New* (top, **Figure 6.6**). When the New User Dictionary dialog box appears (bottom, **Figure 6.6**), navigate to the FileMaker Extensions folder and type a name for your new user dictionary in the Save As text window. Use an easy to remember name, such as *tmark* for a special trademark dictionary. Once you're done, click *Save*.

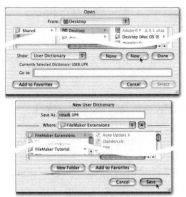

Figure 6.6 Ⓜ In the Open dialog box, click *New* (top). Use the New User Dictionary dialog box (bottom) to navigate to the FileMaker Extensions folder, name the new dictionary, and click *Save*.

Selecting dictionaries

Once you've created more than one *user* dictionary, you'll need to select which one—if any—you want to apply to any new FileMaker databases. You can also use these steps to switch your *main* dictionary from US English to UK English.

To select or switch dictionaries:

1. Choose Edit > Spelling > Select Dictionaries (**Figure 6.3**).

2. In the dialog box that appears, click your cursor on the *Files of type* drop-down menu (Windows) or the *Show pop-up menu* (Mac) (**Figure 6.4**). When the choices—*Main Dictionary* and *User Dictionary*—appear, choose *User Dictionary*. (When you want to change your main dictionary, choose *Main Dictionary*.)

3. Pick which *user* dictionary you want assigned to the current FileMaker database by double-clicking its name in the dialog box, or by highlighting the name and clicking Select (**Figure 6.7**). If you've stored the dictionary in another folder, navigate your way there and double-click it.

    This also is where you can switch your *main* dictionary. If necessary, use the dialog box's main window to navigate to the dictionary you're seeking.

✔ Tip

■   Occasionally, you may want to check words only against the *main* dictionary and not use any *user* dictionaries. To do so, choose Edit > Spelling > Select Dictionaries. Within the dialog box that appears, click the *None* button (**Figure 6.5**, Windows; top, **Figure 6.6**, Mac).

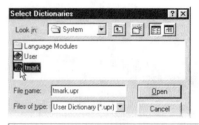

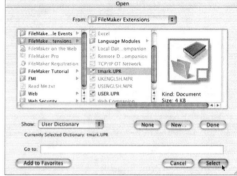

Figure 6.7 Pick a dictionary by double-clicking its name within the main window of the Select Dictionaries dialog box (top, Windows; bottom, Mac).

Figure 6.8 To change dictionary entries, choose Edit > Spelling > Edit User Dictionary.

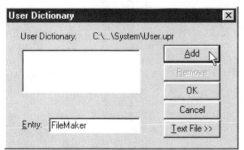

Figure 6.9 Within the User Dictionary dialog box, type in the word you want, then click *Add*. Click *Remove* to delete words from the text window.

Editing user dictionaries

Editing a dictionary allows you to add and remove words one by one or import an existing text file of special terms you've created in another application.

To edit a user dictionary:

1. First make sure you've selected the right dictionary to edit. (For more information, see *To select or switch dictionaries* on the previous page.) Choose Edit > Spelling > Edit User Dictionary (**Figure 6.8**).

2. When the dictionary's dialog box appears, type the word you want to add into the *Entry* text box, then click *Add* (**Figure 6.9**). To remove words, navigate through the list within the top text box, click on the word you want removed, and click *Remove*. You can continue adding or removing words one by one until you're done. If you've already built a list of special terms in another application, you can use this dialog box to import them as a text file (see *To import or export a text file* on the next page.)

3. When you're done editing the dictionary, click *OK* to close the dialog box.

To import or export a text file:

1. You must first convert your original special-terms file to plain text so that FileMaker can recognize it. For example, if you created the list in Microsoft Word use that application's export feature to convert it to a text file.

2. Within FileMaker, choose Edit > Spelling > Edit User Dictionary (**Figure 6.8**).

   ▣ When the dictionary's dialog box appears, click *Text File* and then click *Import* or *Export* when the buttons appear (**Figure 6.10**). (You can use this same process to export a user dictionary you've built within FileMaker to use in another application.)

   ◉ When the dictionary's dialog box appears, click the triangle just to the right of *Text File* (**Figure 6.11**). Click the *Import* or *Export* button.

3. Use the dialog boxes to navigate your way to the file you want to import. Once you find it, click *Open*, then *OK* (Windows) or *Save* (Mac).

4. When you're done importing or exporting, click *OK* to close the dictionary dialog box.

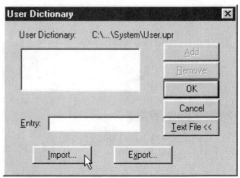

Figure 6.10 ▣ To import (or export) a file of special terms, click *Text File*, and then click the *Import* or *Export* button within the dictionary dialog box.

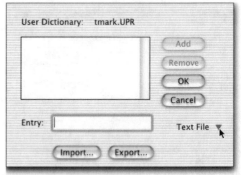

Figure 6.11 ◉ To see the *Import* and *Export* buttons, click the triangle to the right of *Text File* within the dictionary dialog box.

CONVERTING FILES

No software program is an island. This chapter focuses on using FileMaker to build bridges by converting files from older FileMaker versions, bringing data from other application files into FileMaker (importing), and formatting FileMaker data so that other programs can use it (exporting). The chapter also discusses the unspeakable: how to recover data if a FileMaker file should ever become damaged. For information on importing graphics and scripts into files, see *Formatting and Graphics in Layouts* on page 175 and *Using Templates and Scripts* on page 199. For information on using FileMaker's ODBC (Open Database Connectivity) features, see *Exchanging Data via ODBC* on page 259.

To convert files from earlier FileMaker versions:

1. While running FileMaker version 5.5, choose File > Open (⌈Ctrl⌉⌈O⌉ in Windows/ ⌘⌈O⌉ on the Mac) and navigate to the file created using an earlier version of FileMaker. Once you find it, click *Open*.

2. A dialog box will appear, alerting you that the older *original* file will be converted and automatically renamed by adding *Old* to its name (**Figure 7.1**). (By default, the new FileMaker 5.5 version of the file will be given the original file's name.) Unless you want to type in another name, click *OK*. A new version of the data will appear in Browse mode.

✔ Tip

■ Converting older version FileMaker files to version 5.5 is a one-way trip: Only FileMaker 5 and 5.5 will be able to read the converted file, which can be a problem if not all your co-workers have upgraded to at least version 5.

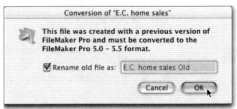

Figure 7.1 A warning dialog box asks you to rename older FileMaker databases you convert to version 5.5.

Importing Data into FileMaker

Moving data into FileMaker boils down to converting your original source document to a file format that FileMaker can handle. (See **Table 7.1**, *Using FileMaker with Other File Formats*, below.) When importing, you have two basic choices: move the data into a *new* FileMaker database (sometimes called *converting* data) or move it into an *existing* FileMaker base. If your destination file is an existing FileMaker database, you'll also need to decide whether to add to the existing records, replace all the records, or just update any changed records.

Table 7.1

Using FileMaker with Other File Formats

File Extension	Format	What FileMaker Can Do With Format
.FP5, .FP3, or .FM	FileMaker	Import data from FileMaker (v2, 2.1, 3, or 4) Export only to FileMaker 5 or 5.5
.TAB or .TXT	Tab-separated text	Exchange data with almost any application, including Claris Impact
.CSV or .TXT	Comma-separated values; Comma-separated text	Exchange data with BASIC programs and dBASE
.SLK	SYLK	Exchange data with spreadsheet applications
.DIF	DIF	Exchange data with spreadsheet applications, such as VisiCalc
.WK1 or .WKS	WKS	Exchange data with Lotus 1-2-3. FileMaker can import both formats but only exports .WK1
.BAS	BASIC	Exchange data with Microsoft BASIC programs
.MER	Merge	Combine Merge file data with main file text to create form letters
.CWK or .CWS	ClarisWorks	Import data from ClarisWorks 2.0–4.0 (Mac) and ClarisWorks 4.0 (Windows) database files
.HTM or .HTML	HyperText Markup Language table	Export FileMaker data as an HTML table for Web use
.DBF	DBF	Exchange data with dBASE III and dBASE IV
.XLS	Excel	Import data from Microsoft Excel
	ODBC	Import from other data sources, serve FileMaker data

To import data for a *new* FileMaker database:

1. First make a copy of your original data. Now, open your source file using its original application and save it in one of the formats listed in **Table 7.1** on page 81. Close the source file and quit the original application.

2. Launch FileMaker and choose File > Open (⌃O in Windows/⌘O on the Mac).

3. When the Open File dialog box appears, use the *Show* pop-up menu to select the format in which you saved the source file (**Figure 7.2**).

4. Navigate to the folder where the source file is stored, select it, and click *Open* (**Figure 7.3**).

5. If you're converting an Excel file that contains more than one worksheet (spreadsheet), FileMaker will ask you which one to use (**Figure 7.4**). Select the worksheet you want and click *OK*.

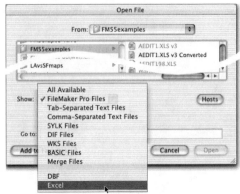

Figure 7.2 Use the Open File dialog box's *Show* pop-up menu to pick a format for the incoming data.

Figure 7.3 Navigate to the folder where the source file is stored, select it, and click *Open*.

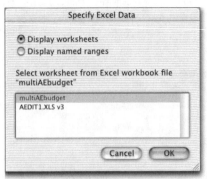

Figure 7.4 If an Excel file contains more than one worksheet (spreadsheet), FileMaker will ask you to choose one.

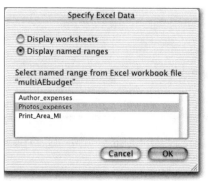

Figure 7.5 New in version 5.5: You can now select and convert named ranges within the spreadsheet.

Figure 7.6 If you're converting a spreadsheet, FileMaker will ask whether you want to treat the column headings as *Field Names* or *Data*.

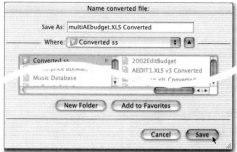

Figure 7.7 Give the converted data a clear name and click *Save*.

6. If the spreadsheet includes named ranges, FileMaker also will let you specify which one you want to use (**Figure 7.5**). Select the range you want and click *OK*. Another dialog box will ask whether you want to treat the spreadsheet's column headings as *Field names* or *Data* (**Figure 7.6**). Make your choice—in most cases, *Field names*—and click *OK*.

7. A dialog box will appear and automatically add *Converted* to the file's name (**Figure 7.7**). Change the name as you wish, navigate to the folder where you want it stored, and click *Save*.

8. Once the new file opens (the time required depends on the file's size), the original source data will appear in the FileMaker database (**Figure 7.8**).

✔ Tip

■ If there's lots of data within the other application document that you won't need in the FileMaker database, it's easier to weed it out using the original application *before* you import it into FileMaker.

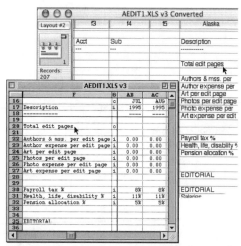

Figure 7.8 The data, and even some of the layout, of the Excel spreadsheet (lower left) ported cleanly over to FileMaker (upper right).

To import data into an *existing* FileMaker database:

1. Make backup copies of your original data *source* file (the one you're importing data from) and the FileMaker *destination* file (the one you're importing the data into).

2. Open your source file using its original application and save it in one of the formats listed in **Table 7.1** on page 81. Close the source file and quit the application.

3. Launch FileMaker and make sure you're in Browse mode (Ctrl B in Windows/⌘ B on the Mac). Open the FileMaker data-

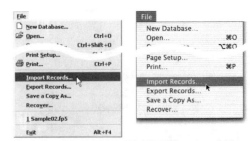

Figure 7.9 To import data into FileMaker, choose File > Import Records.

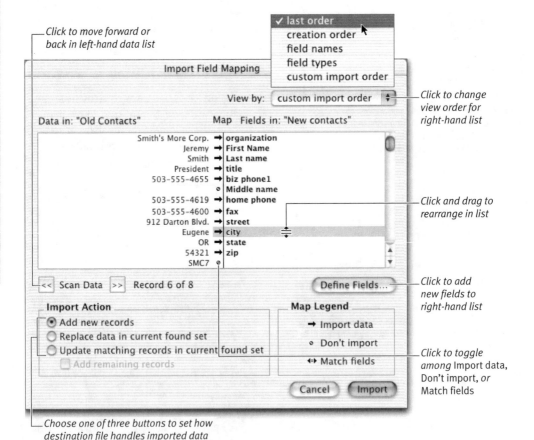

Figure 7.10 The Import Field Mapping dialog box gives you precise control over the data imported—and its order.

Table 7.2

Import Field Mapping Symbols		

SYMBOL	ACTION	EXPLANATION
➡	Import data	Left-side data placed in right field
⊘	Don't import	Importing blocked
◀=▶	Match fields	Occurs only if data in source and destination fields match

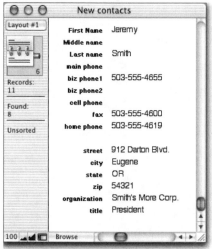

Figure 7.11 Once you've finished matching up the data fields, FileMaker displays the newly imported records in Browse mode.

base into which you want to import data (Ctrl O in Windows/⌘ O on the Mac). If you'll be replacing particular records, use FileMaker's Find, Omit, and Sort commands to expand or narrow the Found Set to only the records you'll be replacing.

4. Now, choose File > Import Records (**Figure 7.9**).

5. When the Import Field Mapping dialog box appears (**Figure 7.10**), check to see if the data listed in the left-side window is properly matched with the field names on the right side. Many times, a few things will need fixing: In **Figure 7.10**, for example, the *City* field was moved up in the right-hand list to match the left-hand data. Click the name of a mismatched field and use the double-arrow to drag it until it's matched with the correct field. You also can use the *Scan Data* << and >> buttons to make sure the left-side data is matched with the correct right-side fields.

6. To activate individual field imports, click the center column to turn the slashed zero into a single-headed arrow to import data or a double-headed arrow to match fields. For details, see **Table 7.2**.

7. To add a new field to the FileMaker database, click the lower right *Define Fields* button and create the needed field.

8. Decide whether you want the source data to *add*, *replace* or *update* the records already in the FileMaker database. Click the appropriate radio button in the lower left of the dialog box.

9. Once you've tweaked the source-to-database mapping to your satisfaction, click *Import*. FileMaker will display the newly imported records in Browse mode (**Figure 7.11**).

To import records from another FileMaker 5 or 5.5 database:

1. Before you import the FileMaker *source* records, use FileMaker's Find and Omit commands to expand or narrow the Found Set to just the records you'll want. Use Sort to put them in the order you want. They'll appear in that same order in the new FileMaker file.

2. Open the FileMaker *destination* database (the one you'll be importing records into). If you'll be replacing particular records, use FileMaker's Find, Omit, and Sort commands to expand or narrow the Found Set to only the records you'll be replacing.

3. Make sure you're in Browse mode (Ctrl B in Windows/⌘B on the Mac) and choose File > Import Records (**Figure 7.9**).

4. When the Open File dialog box appears, use the *Show* pop-up menu to select the type of file you want to open. (See **Table 7.1**, *Using FileMaker with Other File Formats*, on page 81.)

5. Click *Open*.

6. When the Import Field Mapping dialog box appears (**Figure 7.10**), check to see if the data listed in the left-side window is properly matched with the field names on the right side and tweak as necessary.

7. Click *Import*.

Figure 7.12 To export data out of FileMaker, choose File > Export Records.

Figure 7.13 Use the *Save as type* pop-up menu within the Export Records to File dialog box to pick a format accepted by your target application.

Exporting FileMaker Data

It's easy to export FileMaker records into another application—just as long as the receiving application can read one of the formats listed in **Table 7.1** on page 81. FileMaker's layouts can't be exported, but you can use FileMaker to arrange the record fields in the same order as a particular layout, as well as select exactly which records are exported.

To export FileMaker records:

1. Before you export the FileMaker database, use FileMaker's Find and Omit commands to expand or narrow the Found Set to just the records you'll want. Use FileMaker's Sort command to then put the records in the order you want them to appear within the receiving document.

2. In Browse mode ($\boxed{\text{Ctrl}}\boxed{\text{B}}$ in Windows/$\boxed{\mathcal{H}}\boxed{\text{B}}$ on the Mac), choose File > Export Records (**Figure 7.12**).

3. When the Export Records to File dialog box appears, type in a name for the file and navigate to the folder where you want to store it. Use the *Save as type* pop-up menu to select a file format accepted by the application you're exporting to and click *Save* (**Figure 7.13**).

(continued)

4. When the Specify Field Order for Export dialog box appears (**Figure 7.14**), select fields in the left-side list you want to export, and click the center *Move* button to place them in the right-side list of fields to be exported. To export all the fields, click *Move All* (**Figure 7.15**). If you change your mind and want to remove a field from the right-side list, select it and click *Clear*.

5. Once you've moved all the fields you want to export into the right-side list, click and drag the double-arrows next to each field to rearrange the list's export order.

6. Choose one of two format options listed in the dialog box's lower-left corner. Use the *Format output using current layout* button to export, for example, commas and dollar signs along with the numbers in any fields you've formatted that way. Use *Don't format output* if you just want to export the raw, unformatted data.

7. Click *Export*. FileMaker will then place the data into a file based on your chosen format, which you can now open in your other application (**Figure 7.16**).

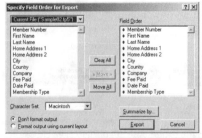

Figure 7.14 Use the Specify Field Order for Export dialog box to pick and order the FileMaker fields you're exporting.

Figure 7.15 Use the Specify Field Order for Export dialog box's four buttons (*Move* and *Clear* never appear at the same time) to control which fields appear in the right-side list.

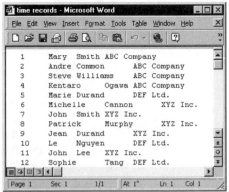

Figure 7.16 Once the data is exported as tab-separated text, it can be opened in other applications, such as Word.

EXPORTING FILEMAKER DATA

Figure 7.17 Use the *Character Set* drop-down menu to ease font mapping problems when exporting to other platforms.

✔ Tips

W The Specify Field Order for Export dialog box includes an option to ease cross-platform exports. Click the *Character Set* drop-down menu and choose the platform on which the exported data will be used (**Figure 7.17**).

■ If you're exporting records containing subsummary data, other applications may not be able to handle FileMaker's summary fields directly. You'll need to take the extra step of clicking on any summary fields among those fields you've moved into the Specify Field Order for Export dialog box's right-side list (**Figure 7.14**). Once you highlight the summary field, click the *Summarize by...* button and use the dialog box that appears to choose the field or fields used by the summary field. (See *Using Calculation and Summary Fields* on page 123.)

■ Not every export format can handle the multiple values contained in FileMaker's repeating fields. Work around this by cloning the original file that contains the repeating fields (see *To save a copy of a database file* on page 37). Then divide the repeating field data into separate records by selecting *Splitting them into separate records* within the Import Options dialog box. (See *Using Repeating Fields* on page 116.)

EXPORTING FILEMAKER DATA

Recovering Damaged Files

A file can become damaged from any number of causes: a sudden power loss, a disk drive crash, a corrupted bit of software. Most of the time, if you close and reopen the file, FileMaker will perform what it calls a consistency check and everything will be fine. If that doesn't work, you can try to rescue the file with FileMaker's Recover command.

To recover a damaged file:

1. If you suspect that the file's been damaged, close it immediately (Ctrl W in Windows/⌘W on the Mac).

2. Choose File > Recover (**Figure 7.18**).

3. Use the Open Damaged File dialog box when it appears to navigate your way to the damaged file. Click *Open*.

4. By default, FileMaker will add the word *Recovered* to the end of the file's old name (**Figure 7.19**). If you like, type in another name. Click *Save*.

5. As it runs through a number of steps to recover the file, FileMaker will display a series of status dialog boxes (**Figure 7.20**). When FileMaker's done, a status report dialog box appears—hopefully with good news (**Figure 7.21**). Click *OK*.

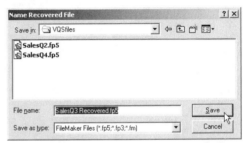

Figure 7.18 Make sure to first close a possibly damaged FileMaker file, then choose File > Recover.

Figure 7.19 When it opens a damaged file, FileMaker automatically adds *Recovered* to its previous name. Change the name if you wish, then click *Save*.

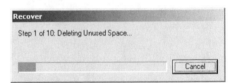

Figure 7.20 While FileMaker's trying to recover a file, it will display a series of status dialog boxes.

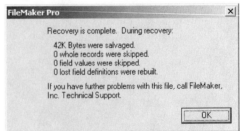

Figure 7.21 May the news always be this good: FileMaker provides a detailed report on how many records, fields, and values were recovered.

PART III

CREATING & DESIGNING DATABASES

PLANNING
DATABASES

If you're building a database from scratch, congratulations. You're free to do it right. Of course, you still have to start from scratch. It's a bit like building a new house versus restoring an old one. The new house gets a new foundation using the latest materials but it also starts as a clean—and very blank—sheet on the drafting table. With renovation, if the foundation's crumbling, you have a big old house to somehow hold in place while you do the repairs.

No matter where you start, however, you won't be entirely free of constraints. If you're building a database for your department, at some point, you'll probably need to share some data with another department. Even the home office worker will want, from time to time, to share information with others. In either case, you may have to export your FileMaker data to another format. By planning carefully, you can make even that task relatively easy.

How about a SlowStart?

You know the saying: Hurry now, wait later. The time you spend in this little chapter with nothing more than a notepad and your thoughts will save you hours of frustration later at the keyboard. This is the secret to successful databases: they're not really about data, they're about people and how they work together. As odd as it might seem initially, the data itself doesn't dictate the database design. Instead, the processes and procedures among people within an organization's various groups drive the design. The very same data in a different organization might need a completely different design.

Any time you build a database, you inevitably face questions about the group it's intended for: Where does this information come from? Who knows this? Who needs this? Why do we do it that way? Before you veer into an existential thicket, here's the point: Take time to understand the users' needs—along with their organization's structure and information flow—and you'll build a better database.

That, of course, means talking to people about how they use information. Even organizations that don't already have a database still have information flows, whether it's hidden in memos, spreadsheets, or the brains of those folks you find in every office who know where everything's kept and who did what, when, and why. Talk to them. Not just at the beginning of the design process, but at every step. They know more about their needs than you do. Unless, you are the user. In that case, have a little heart-to-heart with your own self. You'll probably learn something.

Follow the paper

Paper can be an important clue to how people use data in any organization. Look for
which reports get printed out regularly and
what overhead slides get used in meeting
after meeting. Both are signs of what people
find useful. Examine not just what they *contain* but what *form* they take. You'll find great
ideas for what should be in the database and
what layouts will be most useful. Don't just
mimic the hard copy, of course, but those
papers will help you more than pushing people to jump feet first into an electronic
approach.

The same go-slow, pay-attention approach
applies in looking at your organization's
existing databases. Likely, you'll find them
everywhere: inventories, billings, and mailing
lists. Some will still be in use, others long
dormant. Almost any database older than
seven years is going to be full of overlapping,
redundant information. Don't slight them,
however. Even if they're a bit creaky, they
may contain useful data that you can import
once you've built a new database.

In puzzling all this through, you may have
some false starts. Don't worry. Unlike some
database programs that force you to anticipate all your needs up front, FileMaker is
very forgiving: You can always go back and
add fields, layouts, scripts, or even new databases as you need them.

You must remember this...

- Once you've done the planning, start listing the fields you'll need for all the information you'll want to track. If you're building a customer database, for example, you'll want the obvious fields for names, addresses, and phone numbers. You may also want a field or two or three for things like a customer's email address, pager number, and weekend message service. Don't forget that you're not limited to just fields for text and numbers. How about a picture field in the product catalog? And while you can't predict the future, the best databases anticipate growth and change. Need a crystal ball? Talk to those users again. To get started on using fields, see *Defining Fields* on page 99.

- Next, list the possible layouts you'll need. Assign a separate layout to each task: mailing labels gets its own layout, so do order invoices, summary reports, etc. You should also consider creating a different layout for each type of user. The sales folks, for example, probably need to see different data than the accountants.

  All the action won't be on the screen, so you'll also need to think about layouts for printed reports, again using the layout-per-task rule of thumb. For more information, see *Creating Layouts* on page 129. To make layouts easy on the eyes and easy to understand, see *Formatting and Graphics in Layouts* on page 175. By the way, thanks to FileMaker's lookups and portals, layouts aren't confined to showing data from just one database. For help, see *Creating Relational Databases* on page 221.

- You don't have to start from scratch in building your layouts. *Using Templates and Scripts* on page 199 shows you how to customize the many templates built into FileMaker. The chapter also shows you how to use scripts to automate multi-step actions, which makes it easier on the user. Creating scripts can also be a great way, for example, to find, sort, and highlight a group of records that show a pattern only FileMaker-savvy users could unearth without a script.

- Finally, list the various databases you'll need, creating a separate database for each major category of information. For example, it's much better to create one database for products and another database for vendors rather than combine all that information in a single database. That's where FileMaker's relational abilities come in. Again, take your time. Building relational databases calls on everything else you'll learn in this section: defining fields, creating and formatting layouts, and using scripts. For more information, take a look at *Creating Relational Databases* on page 221.

PLANNING DATABASES

DEFINING FIELDS

Creating records in FileMaker is a multi-step process of defining fields, setting entry options for those fields, and setting relationships among the fields. This chapter covers each step in turn.

Controlling the *appearance* of your database and its records is covered separately in *Creating Layouts* starting on page 129.

Choosing a Field Type

FileMaker's eight different types of fields are assigned via the Type radio buttons within the Define Fields dialog box (**Figure 9.1**). For step-by-step instructions on using this dialog box, see *To define a field* on page 102. But first, here's a quick rundown on the best uses for each field type:

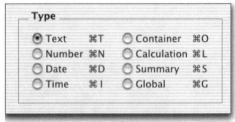

Figure 9.1 Choose your field type via the *Type* radio buttons in the Define Fields dialog box.

◆ **Text:** A text field can contain up to 64,000 characters (letters, symbols, and numbers as text). Text fields can be sorted (usually A–Z or Z–A) and used in formulas. Even items that might not at first blush seem to be text sometimes should be placed in text fields. For example, telephone numbers usually contain non-numeric hyphens or slashes, and, so, are best made into text fields.

◆ **Number:** A number field can contain up to 255 characters (numbers or other characters, which will not be treated as numbers). Number fields can be sorted (1–100 or 100–1) and used in formulas for calculations and summary fields.

◆ **Date:** Date fields must contain at least the day and month of a date. Date fields can be sorted (earliest-latest or latest-earliest) and used in formulas for calculations and summary fields. To avoid any Y2K problems, be sure to use FileMaker's new option for entering four-digit years. For more, see *Validation options* on page 108.

◆ **Time:** Time fields can only contain the hours, minutes, and seconds of a time. Time fields can be sorted (earliest-latest or latest-earliest) and used in formulas for calculations and summary fields.

◆ **Container:** Container fields hold graphics, sounds, QuickTime movies, or Object Linking and Embedding (OLE) objects (Windows only), or PDF files (Mac OS X only). Container fields cannot be sorted, but can be used in formulas for calculations and summary fields. While container fields cannot contain text or numbers, you can create—and sort—related text or number fields to describe a container field's contents. For more information, see *Understanding Formulas* on page 118 and *Using Calculation and Summary Fields* on page 123.

◆ **Calculation:** Calculation fields display the results of calculations made using other fields and, so, cannot have values typed directly into them. The result can be text, a number, date, time, or container. With the exception of summary functions, calculation fields operate on data *within single records*. For more information, see *Using Calculation and Summary Fields* on page 123.

◆ **Summary:** Like calculation fields, summary fields cannot have values entered directly into them. Instead, they display summary values based on other fields in the database. In general, summary fields operate on data *from a group of records*. For more information, see *Using Calculation and Summary Fields* on page 123.

◆ **Global:** Global fields display the same value in every record within a database. That value can be text, a number, date, time, or container. Typical uses include displaying boilerplate text or a company logo within each record. Global field values can be used in formulas for calculations and scripts. Since global fields appear in every record, they cannot be used to find records within a database.

CHOOSING A FIELD TYPE

Defining and Changing Fields

As you create fields for your database, you'll need to assign names and field types (for example, text or number), then choose how they will be displayed. The following steps cover most field types. For information on defining calculation and summary fields, see pages 123 and 128.

To define a field:

1. To create a field, choose File > Define Fields (**Figure 9.2**). Or use your keyboard: Ctrl Shift D (Windows) or Shift ⌘ D (Mac).

2. When the Define Fields dialog box appears (**Figure 9.3**), type the name of your first field in the *Field Name* text box.

3. Choose the type of field you want from the lower-left section of the dialog box (**Figure 9.4**). For more on deciding which field type best suits your needs, see *Choosing a Field Type* on page 100.

4. Once you click the *Create* button, the name of your new field will appear in the center window of the Define Fields dialog box (**Figure 9.5**).

5. At this point, you can repeat the steps to create another field. Or you can further define your field by highlighting its name in the center window of the Define Fields dialog box and then clicking the *Options* button. For more information, see *Setting Field Entry Options* on page 104.

6. When you've finished creating fields (you can always add more later), click *Done*. FileMaker will then display the created fields in Browse mode. To dress up a field's appearance and layout, see *Creating Layouts* on page 129.

Figure 9.2 To create a field, choose File > Define Fields.

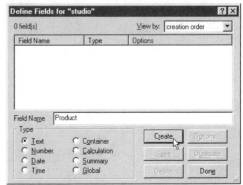

Figure 9.3 Assign a name to a new field within the Define Fields dialog box.

✔ Tips

- In naming your fields, FileMaker prevents you from using any of the symbols or words it needs to calculate functions: , (comma), +, *, /, ^, &, =, >, <, (,), ", ;, :, AND, OR, XOR, NOT. You also cannot use words that are the names of FileMaker functions, such as *Status*, *Count*, or *Sum*. One last thing: Don't start a file name with a period or a number.

- When defining a Global field, you'll need to take an extra step once you're back in Browse mode: Enter your desired information into the Global field in any record. Now select a new record—presto, the Global field is filled in.

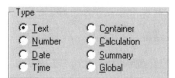

Figure 9.4 The lower-left section of the Define Fields dialog box offers a choice of eight field types.

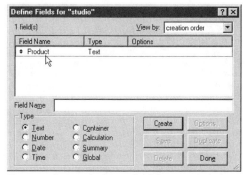

Figure 9.5 Once you create a field, its name appears in the list of fields within the Define Fields dialog box.

To delete or add a field:

1. Choose File > Define Fields ([Ctrl][Shift][D] in Windows, [Shift][⌘][D] on the Mac) to open the Define Fields dialog box (**Figure 9.3**).

2. To *delete* a field, click on its name in the center window, then click the *Delete* button. When the warning dialog box appears, again click *Delete*.

   To *add* a field, type the new field's name into the Field Name text box, check one of the radio buttons in the lower left *Type* area, and click the *Create* button.

3. When you're ready, click the *Done* button.

To change a field's name or type:

1. Choose File > Define Fields ([Ctrl][Shift][D] in Windows, [Shift][⌘][D] on the Mac) to open the Define Fields dialog box (**Figure 9.3**).

2. To change the *name* of a field, click on its name in the center text window and type in a new name.

   To change a field's *type*, highlight the field in the center text window, then find and select your new type choice among the eight radio buttons in the lower left *Type* area.

3. Click the *Save* button, then click the *Done* button.

DEFINING AND CHANGING FIELDS

Setting Field Entry Options

FileMaker's Entry Options dialog box offers several powerful tools for speeding data entry and ensuring it meets certain standards. If more than one person will be entering data into the database, these options can reduce keyboard mistakes and problem-generating format variations. The options can be set while you're defining fields—or added later.

FileMaker lets you customize your field entries for four general areas: Auto-Enter, Validation, Repeating fields, and Storage options. For more information, see page 106 (Auto-Enter), page 108 (Validation), page 116 (Repeating fields), and page 110 (Storage options).

To set field entry options:

1. Whether you want to set entry options for a new field or add them to an existing field, the steps are the same: Choose File > Define Fields. Or use your keyboard: [Ctrl][Shift][D] (Windows) or [Shift][⌘][D] (Mac).

2. In the center window of the Define Fields dialog box, select a field, then click the *Options* button (**Figure 9.6**). Or use the shortcut: double-click in the list on the field you want.

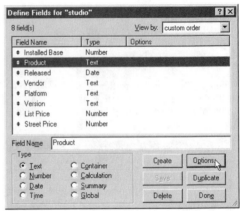

Figure 9.6 Double-click the field whose entry options you want to modify or click the *Options* button.

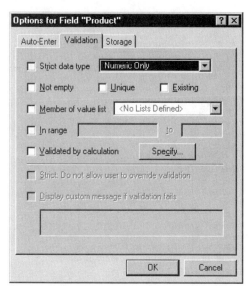

Figure 9.7 The tabs in the Entry Options dialog box control the Auto-Enter, Validation, and Storage settings.

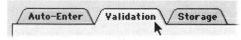

Figure 9.8 To switch among the Auto-Enter, Validation, and Storage settings, just click a tab.

3. When the options dialog box appears, make your selections. Of the three functions handled by the dialog box (*Auto-Enter*, *Validation*, and *Storage*), only one appears at a time (**Figure 9.7**). Click the tab to reach the desired function (**Figure 9.8**). Once you're done, click *OK*.

4. The Define Fields dialog box reappears. If you want to set entry options for another field, repeat steps 2 and 3. Once you're ready, click *Done*.

5. Though you've changed the entry options for a field, its *display* remains the same until you change the layout. For more information, see *To format a repeating field* on page 117, *To format a value list field* on page 114, and *Creating Layouts* on page 129.

Auto-Enter options

Follow steps 1–3 in *To set field entry options* on page 104 to reach the Auto-Enter options (**Figure 9.9**). Here's how each functions:

◆ **Creation Date, Time, Name:** Use the first checkbox and its related drop-down menu (**Figure 9.10**) to have the date or time when a record is created or modified entered automatically. It can also auto-matically enter the name of the person who originally created the record or the name of the person who most recently changed the record. Your choice here must conform with the type of field you've created: If you've already defined the field type as Date, the *Creator Name* and *Modifier Name* choices won't be available.

◆ **Serial number, next value, increment by:** Use these checkboxes to generate a unique number for every record in a data-base. It's particularly useful for invoices and other records that need one-of-a-kind identifiers. Once you've checked the *Serial number* box, you can then use the *next value* box to set the starting number for the next record. Starting numbers can include text at the front, such as A100 or Bin10. Use the *increment by* box to con-trol whether the serial numbers increase in steps of 1, 2, 5, 10, or whatever.

◆ **Value from previous record:** This checkbox can save you a bit of keyboard-ing if you're creating a series of records where some of the fields need to contain the same value.

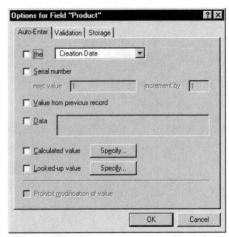

Figure 9.9 The Auto-Enter panel's seven check-boxes control the automatic entry of values into selected fields.

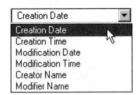

Figure 9.10 The Auto-Enter pop-up menu triggers the entry of times, dates, or names related to when a field is created or modified.

- **Data:** Use this checkbox and the related text window to have a bit of text or a number automatically appear in a particular field.

- **Calculated value:** Use this checkbox and the *Specify* button to automatically enter the results of any formula you choose. For more information, see *Using Calculation and Summary Fields* on page 123.

- **Looked-up value:** Use this checkbox and the *Specify* button to enter a value from another database. For more information, see *Creating Relational Databases* on page 221.

- **Prohibit modification of value:** This checkbox only becomes active if you've checked one of the previous boxes. Use it to ensure that a field's data isn't improperly changed. For more information, see the *Strict, Display custom message* choices under Validation options.

AUTO-ENTER OPTIONS

Validation options

Follow steps 1–3 in *To set field entry options* on page 104 to reach the Validation options (**Figure 9.11**). These options ensure that data entered in the fields you select is correctly formatted.

◆ **Strict data type:** Use this checkbox and its related drop-down menu to automatically create a Numeric, 4-Digit Year Date, or Time of Day type of field. The 4-Digit Year Date choice, which uses the format 2000 instead of 00, is intended to avoid Y2K problems.

◆ **Not empty, Unique, Existing:** Use the first checkbox to make sure a field isn't skipped during data entry. The other two checkboxes work in opposing ways— *Unique* ensures that a record contains a one-of-a-kind value while *Existing* ensures that the value is the *same* as that of another field.

◆ **Member of value list:** Use this checkbox and its related drop-down menu to present the user with a predefined list of entry choices. Value lists may be the single best tool in speeding data entry and preventing typos in records. For more information, see *Using Value Lists* on page 111.

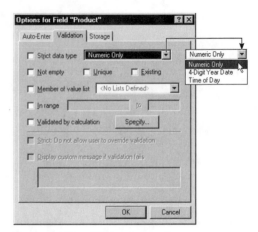

Figure 9.11 The Validation panel's nine checkboxes ensure that data entered into selected fields is correctly formatted.

- **In range:** Use this checkbox to ensure that the data entered falls within the range of the text, numbers, dates, or times you specify in the two entry boxes.

- **Validated by calculation:** Use this checkbox and the *Specify* button to double-check a value against a chosen formula.

- **Strict, Display custom message:** These two checkboxes control what users see if the data they enter doesn't meet the criteria you've already set in the Validation dialog box. By checking *Strict: Do not allow user to override validation*, you prevent users from simply clicking *OK* and ignoring warning dialog boxes. This can be necessary if, for example, the field's value is used in a calculation and must be in one form only. If you check *Strict*, however, it's always good to also check the *Display custom message if validation fails* box and write a message that will explain why the entry was not accepted—and what users might do to conform to the field's requirements. The message can contain up to 255 characters.

VALIDATION OPTIONS

Storage options (indexing)

FileMaker's Entry Options include setting storage options (indexing) for any text, number, date, time, and calculation field. Indexing creates an alphabetical (or numeric) list of all the values in the selected field, greatly speeding any search for records—once the index is created. But indexing also increases your database's size and can slow down running large files. For that reason, FileMaker gives you field-by-field control of which, if any, fields are indexed. Indexing can also be used to store results for calculation fields. (See *To store calculation results* on page 127.)

To set indexing:

1. Select a field to index by following steps 1–3 in *To set field entry options* on page 104 to reach the Storage options (**Figure 9.12**).

2. The lower half of the dialog box offers three index settings: *On*, which creates an index for the selected field; *Off*, which blocks FileMaker from indexing the field; and *Automatically turn indexing on if needed*. The third choice, which becomes available when you check the *Off* radio button, allows indexing only if you later use the field in a search or as part of a relational database. Make your choices, and if necessary, reselect which language the index will use by using the bottom pop-up menu.

3. Click *OK*. The Define Fields dialog box reappears. If you want to set indexing for another field, repeat steps 1 and 2. When you're finished, click *Done*.

✔ Tip

■ For information on using the *Repeating* panel at the top of the Storage options dialog box, see *Using Repeating Fields* on page 116.

Figure 9.12 Check the *On* radio button in the *Indexing* panel to set indexing for a selected field.

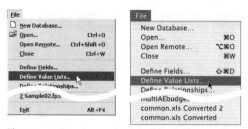

Figure 9.13 To create a value list directly, choose File > Define Value Lists.

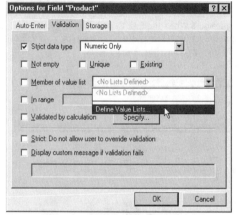

Figure 9.14 To create a value list while defining a field, press your cursor on the drop-down menu next to the *Member of value list* checkbox, then select *Define Value Lists*.

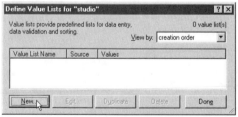

Figure 9.15 When the Define Value Lists dialog box appears, click *New* to create a new list or *Edit* if you want to change an existing value list.

Using Value Lists

By offering users a predefined list of field entry choices, value lists save lots of time and aggravation. The more people you have entering data into a database, the more important value lists become in maintaining record consistency and accuracy. Don't worry about locking yourself in: Like so many things in FileMaker, value lists can be altered any time. A quick-and-dirty explanation for formatting value lists is included in this section, but you'll want to read *Creating Layouts* on page 129 to get a fuller sense of your formatting options for value lists. While value lists often are created at the same time you create a field, they exist independently of any particular field and can be created at any time.

To define a custom value list:

1. Choose File > Define Value Lists (**Figure 9.13**).

   or

   Follow steps 1–3 in *To set field entry options* on page 104. When you reach the Validation panel, select the *Member of value list* checkbox, then click the adjacent drop-down menu and select Define Value Lists (**Figure 9.14**).

2. When the Define Value Lists dialog box appears, click *New* to create a new list or *Edit* if you want to change an existing value list (**Figure 9.15**).

   (continued)

3. When the Edit Value List dialog box appears, a generic name will appear in the *Value List Name* text box and the *Use custom values* radio button will be selected. Type in a distinctive name for your new value list, then click inside the blank right-hand text box to enter the custom values you want (**Figure 9.16**). (You can also create a value list using values from an existing field. See the following steps, *To define a value list using another field.*)

4. Type in your first value, then press [Enter] (Windows) or [Return] (Mac) to begin a new value. When you're done adding values to the list, click *OK*. To create another value list, repeat steps 2 and 3.

5. When you've finished creating lists, click *Done* (**Figure 9.17**). Though you've made the field into a value list, its *display* will not change until you change the layout. See *To format a value list field* on page 114 for a quick rundown. For more information, see *Creating Layouts* on page 129.

✔ Tip

■ If you have a long list of entries for a Value List, you can make it easier to read by typing in some hyphens, *, # (or whatever) on a line of their own, then pressing [Enter] (Windows) or [Return] (Mac) to start a new line with a new value.

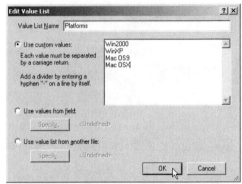

Figure 9.16 When the Edit Value List dialog box appears, choose *Use custom values*, type your values into the right-side box, and click *OK.*

Figure 9.17 When you've finished defining your value lists, click *Done* to close the dialog box.

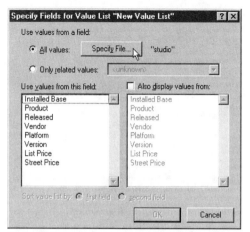

Figure 9.18 If you want to use values from the *current* database's fields, double-click the entry in the left list. To reach a field in *another* database, click the *Specify File* button.

To define a value list using another field:

1. Choose File > Define Value Lists.

2. When the Define Value Lists dialog box appears, click *New* to create a new list or *Edit* if you want to change an existing value list (**Figure 9.15**).

3. When the Edit Value List dialog box appears, select the second radio button, *Use values from field*, and click *Specify*.

4. The Specify Fields for Value List dialog box appears listing all the fields within your current database (**Figure 9.18**). If one of these suits your purposes, select it in the left-side list, and click *OK*. More likely, you'll want to use values from a field in another FileMaker record, so click the *Specify File* button.

5. Navigate your way to the FileMaker database file you want and open it. A new dialog box will appear listing all of that database's fields. Select the one you want to use and click *OK*. Those values will now be used in your pop-up list.

   Again, you'll need to switch to Layout mode to format how you want the value list to appear. See the following steps, *To format a value list field*, for a quick rundown. For more information, see *Creating Layouts* on page 129.

DEFINING A VALUE LIST USING ANOTHER FIELD

To format a value list field:

1. If you haven't already defined your value list, see *To define a custom value list* on page 111. When you're ready to format a field, switch to Layout mode (Ctrl L for Windows, ⌘L on the Mac). Select the field you want to format by clicking on it.

2. Choose Format > Field Format (**Figure 9.19**). The Field Format dialog box will appear (**Figure 9.20**).

3. Choose the second radio button, which will activate the adjacent *Pop-up list* menu, as well as the adjacent *using value list* pop-up menu (**Figure 9.21**).

4. Select which style you want for your value list: *Pop-up list, Pop-up menu, Check boxes,* or *Radio buttons* (**Figure 9.22**). Also select from the second pop-up menu the value list you created for the field when you defined it earlier.

5. The *Style* section of the Field Format dialog box includes three other checkboxes to make your value list formatting more flexible for the user (**Figure 9.20**). The last two checkboxes can work as double-edged swords so consider whether you want to give users that flexibility or whether you'd prefer to limit entries to what's in the value list.

   Choose *Include "Other..." item to allow entry of other values* if you want to let users enter a value that's *not* in your value list. This formatting option can be added to every value list format except the Pop-up list. If the user picks the *Other...* choice, a dialog box will open, allowing the user to add another value (**Figure 9.23**).

   Choose *Include "Edit..." item to allow editing of value list* if you want to let users change the choices in your value list. This choice can only be used for the Pop-up list and Pop-up menu formats. If the user

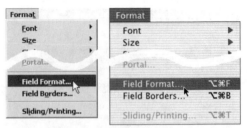

Figure 9.19 To format a field, switch to Layout mode, then choose Format > Field Format.

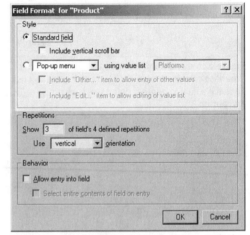

Figure 9.20 The highlighted *Style* section controls the *appearance* of the value list.

Figure 9.21 Clicking on the *Style* section's second radio button allows you to choose a format for your value list.

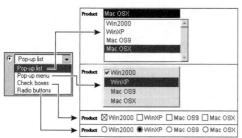

Figure 9.22 From top to bottom: The same field's value list formatted as a pop-up list, a pop-up menu, a series of checkboxes, and a series of radio buttons.

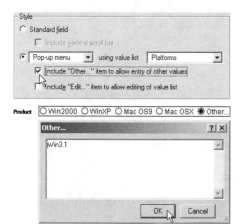

Figure 9.23 Checking *Include "Other..."* (top) allows users to *add* items not already in the value list (bottom).

picks the *"Edit..."* choice, a dialog box will open allowing the user to change an existing value or add more values to the list (**Figure 9.24**).

6. When you're done making your selections, click *OK* at the bottom of the Field Format dialog box. Switch to Browse mode (Ctrl B for Windows, ⌘ B on the Mac) and your field will appear with its new formatting.

✔ **Tip**

■ Which value list style best suits your needs? The Pop-up list and Pop-up menu options simply show a blank field—with no clue that it holds multiple choices— unless the user clicks on it. That's handy if you don't have much screen space or want a clean, simple look. The checkbox and radio button options let the user immediately see all the choices for the field. Checkboxes allow multiple selections, while radio buttons only allow one selection at a time.

Figure 9.24 Checking *Include "Edit..."* (top) allows users to *change* an existing value list any way they like (bottom).

Using Repeating Fields

Repeating fields let you create a single field that accommodates more than one value—saving you the trouble of creating multiple fields that might not always be needed. A quick-and-dirty explanation for formatting repeating fields is included in this section. But to get a fuller sense of your formatting options see *Creating Layouts* on page 129.

To define a repeating field:

1. Choose File > Define Fields (⌃Ctrl ⇧Shift D in Windows, ⇧Shift ⌘ D on the Mac). When the Define Fields dialog box appears, double-click the name of the field you want to define as repeating (**Figure 9.25**).

2. When the Options for Field dialog box appears, click the *Storage* tab, and choose the *Repeating field with a maximum of __ repetitions* checkbox (**Figure 9.26**). Fill in the blank with the number of repetitions you want and click *OK*.

3. The Define Fields dialog box will reappear; click *Done*. Though you've now defined the field as repeating, its *display* will not change until you change the layout. See *To format a repeating field* on the next page for a quick rundown. For more information, see *Creating Layouts* on page 129.

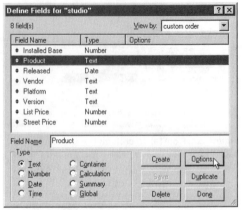

Figure 9.25 To *define* a repeating field, double-click the field's name in the Define Fields dialog box or select it and click *Options*.

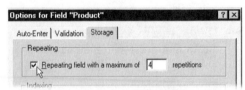

Figure 9.26 Within the Options for Field dialog box, click the Storage tab, check *Repeating field...*, and type in how many times you want the field repeated.

Figure 9.27 The Field Format dialog box lets you choose how many times you want the field to appear and its orientation.

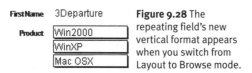

Figure 9.28 The repeating field's new vertical format appears when you switch from Layout to Browse mode.

To format a repeating field:

1. Switch to Layout mode ([Ctrl][L] for Windows, [⌘][L] on the Mac). Select the field you want to format by clicking on it.

2. Choose Format > Field Format and the Field Format dialog box will appear. Within the box's *Repetitions* section, enter how many times you want the field to appear and choose its orientation (**Figure 9.27**). Choosing *vertical* will stack the fields; *horizontal* will place them side by side. Click *OK*.

3. FileMaker will return you to the Layout view of the field and the rest of the record. Switch to Browse mode ([Ctrl][B] for Windows, [⌘][B] on the Mac) to see the new format (**Figure 9.28**).

✔ Tip

■ In the above example, the repeating fields appear as Pop-up lists, but you can use the Style section's pop-up menu to have them appear in any of the other three formats. The two pop-up formats work best for repeating fields, however, since the checkbox and radio button options will produce a blizzard of boxes and circles.

FORMATTING REPEATING FIELDS

Understanding Formulas

Formulas are used in two kinds of FileMaker fields: calculation fields and summary fields. For the most part, formulas used in calculation fields operate on data in the *current* record. Formulas used in summary fields operate on data from *more than one* record.

Beneath a sometimes confusing raft of terms and definitions, formulas are simple. Using a set of specific instructions, formulas take data from one or more fields, calculate or compare or summarize it, and then display the results. That's it. The twist comes in that word *specific*: Formulas must be constructed in a set order, or syntax. Mess up the syntax and the formula won't work properly, if at all.

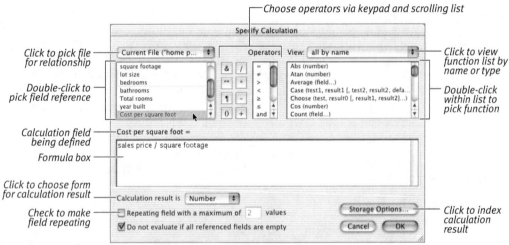

Figure 9.29 Within the Specify Calculation dialog box, formulas are built in the center formula box using pieces taken from (upper left to right) the field reference list, the keypad and scrolling list of operators, and the functions list.

Syntax and the parts of a formula

You'll build most of your formulas within the Specify Calculation dialog box (**Figure 9.29**), which will go a long way in helping keep your syntax straight. The dialog box works like a construction kit with tools to let you assemble the necessary field references, constants, operators, and functions. Once the formula is run, it spits out results, whose form you also control. Before you start, however, take a moment to understand some of the key terms used in formulas.

Field References: A field reference directs a formula to use the value in the field it's named after. The left-hand list within the Specify Calculation dialog box displays all the field references in the selected database.

Constants: As the name implies, a constant is a *fixed* value used in a formula. It remains the same from record to record. A string of text, a number, a date, or a time can all be constants. Each of these types of constants must be typed in a particular format for the formula to recognize which type of constant it represents. For more on the required formats, see **Table 9.1**, *Constants*.

Table 9.1

Constants		
FOR THIS TYPE DATA	**REMEMBER TO**	**EXAMPLES**
Text	Enclose text in quotes (")	"Welcome to FileMaker" "94530-3014"
Number	Do not include currency symbols or thousand separators (, or ;)	80.23 450000
Date	Use the value as parameter of the Date function or the TextToDate function. See *Date functions*, on page 309.	Date(3,13,1998) TextToDate("03/13/1998")
Time	Use the value as parameter of the Time function or the TextToTime function. See *Time functions*, on page 309.	Time(10,45,23) TextToTime ("10:45:23")

UNDERSTANDING FORMULAS

Expressions: An expression is simply a value or any computation that produces a value. Expressions can contain field references, constants, and functions, and can be combined to produce other expressions. For more information, see **Table 9.2**, *Expression Examples*.

Operators: Operators enable a formula to compare the contents of two (or more) fields. Insert operators into your formulas using your keyboard or the keypad and scrolling list within the Specify Calculation dialog box (**Figure 9.30**). Operators combine expressions and resolve what operation should be performed on the expressions. For example, the addition sign, +, is simply an operator that combines the value appearing before it with the value appearing after it: Subtotal + Tax.

Mathematical and text operators are used with—surprise—numbers and text. Comparison operators compare two expressions and return a result of True or False, in what is known as a Boolean expression. Logical operators compare two or more conditions, such as whether the Cost field is more than $200,000 (the first condition) *and* the Square footage field is less than 1,000 (the second condition). For more information, see **Tables 9.3–9.6**.

Table 9.2

Expression Examples	
TYPE OF EXPRESSION	EXAMPLE
Text constant	"FileMaker"
Number constant	80.23
Field reference	Cost per square foot
Function	TextToDate
Combination of expressions	(Price/House Size)*0.10

Formula Operators

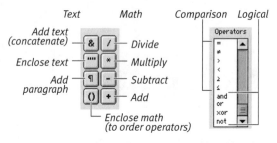

Figure 9.30 Build formulas using the keypad and scrolling list, which contain text, math, comparison, and logical operators.

Table 9.3

Mathematical Operators (see Figure 9.30)			
SYMBOL	NAME	DEFINITION	EXAMPLES
+	Addition	Adds two values	2+2, Subtotal+Sales Tax
-	Subtraction	Subtracts second value from first	2-1, Total-Discount
*	Multiplication	Multiplies value	Subtotal*Sales Tax
/	Division	Divides first value by second	Total/Units
^	Exponentiation	Raises first value to power of second	(A2 + B2) returns A^2B^2

Note: Exponentiation (^) symbol not part of operators keypad, use regular keyboard (Shift 6)

Table 9.4

Text Operators (see Figure 9.30)

Symbol	Name	Definition	Examples
&	Concatenation	Appends the text string on right to end of text string on left	"AAA" & "BBB" returns "AAABBB"
" "	Text constant	Marks beginning and end of text constant. Quotes with no text between them indicate a blank space. Text in formula without quotes is interpreted as a field name or function name. To mark a quote mark within a text constant, precede it with another quote mark.	"Welcome to FileMaker" returns as Welcome to FileMaker " " returns an empty (null) value "Welcome to our "favorite" place" returns as Welcome to our "favorite" place
¶	Return marker	Inserts a paragraph return in a text constant	"Welcome to¶FileMaker" returns Welcome to FileMaker

Table 9.5

Comparison Operators (see Figure 9.30)

Symbol	Name	Definition	Examples
=	Equal to	True when both items are equal	4=5 returns False 4=4 returns True
≠ or <>	Not equal to	True when the items are not equal	4≠5 returns True 4≠4 returns False
>	Greater than	True when value on left exceeds value on right	4>5 returns False 5>4 returns True
<	Less than	True when value on left is less than value on right	4<5 returns True 5<4 returns False
≥ or >=	Greater than or equal to	True when value on left is greater than or equal to value on right	4≥5 returns False 5≥5 returns True
≤ or <=	Less than or equal to	True when value on left is less than or equal to value on right	5≤4 returns False 4≤4 returns True

Table 9.6

Logical Operators (see Figure 9.30)

Symbol	Definition	Examples
AND	True only when both values are true: True when true AND true False when true AND false False when false AND false	Cost per square foot <200 AND Bedrooms≥2
OR	True when either value is true: True when true OR true True when true OR false False when false OR false	Cost per square foot <200 OR Bedrooms≥2
XOR	True when either, but not both, of values is true: False when true AND true True when false AND true False when false AND false	Cost per square foot <200 XOR Bedrooms≥2
NOT	Changes value within parentheses from false to true, or true to false: False when NOT (true) True when NOT(false)	NOT Cost per square foot >200

Using predefined formulas (functions)

A function is simply a *predefined* formula with a set name, such as TextToDate. Functions perform a particular calculation and return a single value. FileMaker comes with more than 150 functions, all of which are listed in *Functions* on page 307. All those functions are available via the right-hand list within the Specify Calculation dialog box, but scrolling through the whole list for one function would be a bother. Instead, use the top-right pop-up menu to display handier portions of the list (**Figure 9.31**). By toggling among the options, you can zero in on the function you need (**Figure 9.32**).

Functions have three parts: the predefined function, the parameters used by the function, and a set of parentheses enclosing the parameter. In almost all cases, FileMaker functions follow this syntax, or order:

Function name(*parameter*)

For example: TextToDate(*time*) or Average(*field*)

The parameter (the value within the parentheses) can be a field reference, a constant, an expression, or another function. Sometimes a function needs more than one parameter, in which case separate each parameter from the next parameter with a comma or semicolon:

Average (*field1, field2, field3*). In this example, field1, field 2, and field3 are just placeholders for the actual field reference you'd place into the formula.

Calculation Results: Once the formula runs, it displays the calculation as a result. The result can take several forms—text, number, date, time, or container—which you control via the Specify Calculation dialog box. For more information, see *To change the display of calculation results* on page 126.

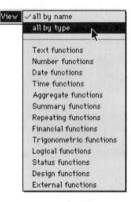

Figure 9.31 Use the Specify Calculation dialog box's *View* pop-up menu to fine tune your view of FileMaker's 150+ built-in functions.

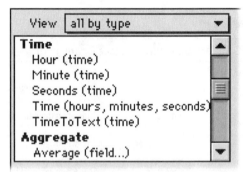

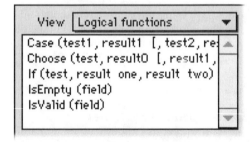

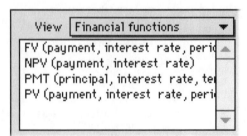

Figure 9.32 The View pop-up menu helps you quickly find the function you need.

Figure 9.33 Once you create a new field, select the *Calculation* radio button within the *Type* area and click *Create*.

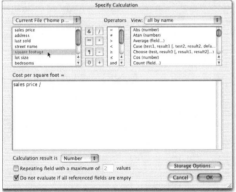

Figure 9.34 Use the Specify Calculation dialog box to create your formula, then click *OK*.

Figure 9.35 The Specify Calculation dialog box's formula operators are controlled by the keypad and the scrolling window.

Using Calculation and Summary Fields

You cannot enter anything directly into a calculation or summary field. Instead, the fields store and display the results of calculations you build via the Specify Calculation dialog box or the Options for Summary Field dialog box.

Formulas used to define a calculation field can be as basic or as complex as you need and will seldom use every tool available in the Specify Calculation dialog box. Our first example walks through a very simple formula.

To define a calculation field:

1. To create a calculation field, choose File > Define Fields ((Ctrl)(Shift)(D) in Windows or (Shift)(⌘)(D) on the Mac).

2. When the Define Fields dialog box appears, type into the Field Name text box the name of your field.

3. Select the *Calculation* radio button within the Type area of the dialog box, then click *Create* (**Figure 9.33**).

4. The Specify Calculation dialog box, where you define a formula for the selected field, appears (**Figure 9.34**). The simple *Cost per square foot* example uses just two field references and a single symbol: (*sales price/square footage*).

   Add the *Price* field reference by double-clicking its name within the list, click the division symbol (/) in the symbols keypad (**Figure 9.35**), then double-click the *House Size* field reference in the left-side list. (For information on using the *Storage Options* button in the Specify Calculation dialog box, see *To store calculation results* on page 127.)

   (continued)

5. Once you're finished building the formula, click *OK*.

6. When the Define Fields dialog box reappears, click *Done*.

✔ Tips

■ Instead of mouse-clicking on the symbols keypad within the Specify Calculation dialog box, you can use their equivalents on your keyboard.

■ Selecting the *Do not evaluate if all referenced fields are empty* checkbox will keep FileMaker from performing a calculation unless the field referenced by the formula has a value—saving some otherwise wasted time.

To edit a formula:

1. To reach the Specify Calculation dialog box and edit a formula, choose File > Define Fields ([Ctrl][Shift][D] in Windows, [Shift][⌘][D] on the Mac). When the Define Fields dialog box appears, double-click on the name of the calculation field whose formula you want to change.

2. The Specify Calculation dialog box will show the formula in the center box. If you want to start fresh, double-click on the formula, then press [Delete] or simply click on the first piece of the new formula (usually a field reference).

   To edit individual parts of the formula, highlight that piece, and then click the replacement field reference, operator, or function.

3. When you've finished editing the formula, click *OK*, then click *Done* when the Define Fields dialog box reappears.

✔ Tip

- If you ever change the name of a field, you don't need to manually edit the formulas that reference that field. FileMaker automatically updates the field references in formulas to reflect any field name changes.

EDITING FORMULAS

To change the display of calculation results:

1. First create a calculation field and build a formula for it. (See *To define a calculation field* on page 123.) Now click the *Calculation result is* pop-up menu (**Figure 9.36**).

   By default, FileMaker displays the results of a calculation as a number, which is what's needed in most cases. However, there are formulas that may need to be displayed as text, a time, or even a container. Make your selection among the five choices and release the cursor.

2. Click *OK*. When the Define Fields dialog box reappears, click *Done*.

To repeat a calculation field:

1. Choose File > Define Fields ([Ctrl][Shift][D] in Windows, [Shift][⌘][D] on the Mac).

2. Within the Define Fields dialog box, double-click on the name of the calculation field you want to repeat. When the Specify Calculation dialog box appears, click the checkbox in the lower left labeled *Repeating field with a maximum of __ values*. Fill in the blank with the number of repetitions you want. Click *OK*.

3. When the Define Fields dialog box reappears, click *Done*. Remember: The appearance of a repeating field doesn't change until you format it. See *To format a repeating field* on page 117.

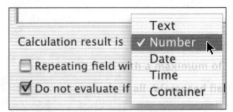

Figure 9.36 Use the *Calculation result is* pop-up menu in the Specify Calculation dialog box to control how the results are displayed.

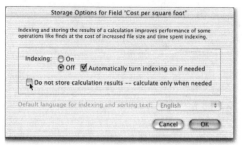

Figure 9.37 Use the checkbox in the Storage Options dialog box to control whether to store a calculation result or calculate it only when needed.

Storing calculation results

Storing calculation results carries the same tradeoffs as indexing any other field: It speeds finding records but also increases your database's size. FileMaker offers a decent compromise, however, by giving you the option of only performing a calculation (and, so, storing the result) when it's needed, such as when you're printing or browsing that particular field and record.

Unless you tell it otherwise, FileMaker automatically stores calculations except those from summary and global fields, as well as those that depend on another calculation already marked as unstored.

To store calculation results:

1. First create a calculation field and build a formula for it. (See *To define a calculation field* on page 123.) If you already have a calculation field defined, choose File > Define Fields (Ctrl Shift D in Windows, Shift ⌘ D on the Mac).

2. When the Define Fields dialog box appears, double-click on the name of the calculation field whose results you want to store or index. The Specify Calculation dialog box will appear with the formula in the center box. Click the *Storage Options* button.

3. The Storage Options dialog box will appear (**Figure 9.37**). To keep a result from being stored, select the *Do not store calculation results—calculate only when needed* checkbox.

4. Click *OK*. When the Define Fields dialog box reappears, click *Done*.

STORING CALCULATION RESULTS

To define a summary field:

1. Choose File > Define Fields ([Ctrl] [Shift] [D] in Windows, [Shift][⌘][D] on the Mac).

2. When the Define Fields dialog box appears, type into the *Field Name* text box the name of your summary field. Select *Summary* within the *Type* panel in the lower-left section of the dialog box. Click the *Create* button (**Figure 9.38**).

3. When the Options for Summary Field dialog box appears, choose which type of summary you want performed from the left-hand list, and select which field you want summarized from the scrolling list in the center (**Figure 9.39**, **Table 9.7**). You can also modify several of the summary types by selecting the checkbox just below the scrolling list, whose function varies in response to which type you've chosen. For more information, see **Table 9.7**, *Summary Field Types*.

4. Click *OK*. When the Define Fields dialog box reappears, click *Done*.

✔ Tip

■ Formatting summary fields varies depending on which summary part you use to display them. See *Creating Layouts* on page 129.

Figure 9.38 To define a Summary field, click that choice in the *Type* area of the Define Fields dialog box, then click *Create*.

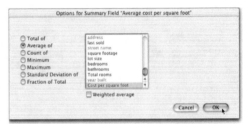

Figure 9.39 Use the Options for Summary Field dialog box to select a summary action. The *Weighted average* checkbox modifies many of the left-hand options.

Table 9.7

Summary Field Types (see Figure 9.39)

NAME	DEFINITION	OPTION VIA CHECKBOX	TO FINE TUNE OPTION:
Total of	Totals values in selected field	Running total	
Average of	Averages values in selected field	Weighted average	Pick a field for averaged values
Count of	Counts how many records contain a value for field	Running total	
Minimum	Finds lowest number, or earliest time or date, for field	none	
Maximum	Finds highest number, or latest time or date, for field	none	
Standard Deviation of	Calculates standard deviation from mean of values in field	by population	
Fraction of Total of	Calculates the ratio of field's value to total for all values in field	Subtotaled	Pick a field for subtotaled values

CREATING LAYOUTS

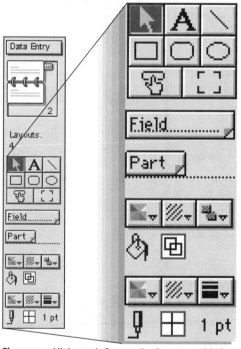

Figure 10.1 All the tools for creating layouts reside in the left-hand status area whenever you're in Layout mode.

FileMaker's layouts allow you to vary the *appearance* of your data without changing the data itself. This gives you the freedom to create layouts tailored to specific tasks and users. Workers entering orders into a database, for example, probably will find it easier to use a layout that mirrors the sequence of information they get from customers. Sales managers, on the other hand, may need layouts that help them spot what's selling well. Day-to-day tasks need a different layout than big-picture analysis demands. Remember: You need not show all of a database in a layout. In fact, the more you can pare down a layout to just the essential information, the easier it will be to use.

The Layout status area (**Figure 10.1**), runs down the left side of your screen when you're in Layout mode. The status area includes all the tools you'll need for adding text, graphics, fields, and parts to a layout and then applying colors, patterns, and lines to make them attractive.

You don't necessarily need to start from scratch in creating layouts: FileMaker includes dozens of built-in templates. Some you may want to use as is, others may provide a starting point for creating your own custom layouts. For more information, see *Using Templates and Scripts* on page 199.

Choosing a Layout Type

When you first define fields in a database, FileMaker by default generates a *standard* layout, which lists the fields and their labels in the order they were created (**Figure 10.2**). You're free to modify that default layout any way you like. Or you may save yourself some trouble in generating a new layout by choosing from the predefined layout types built into FileMaker.

Use the New Layout command for creating standard, columnar, table, label, envelope, and blank layouts. For information on label and envelope layouts, see *Using Label and Envelope Layouts* on page 141.

Here's a quick comparison of each layout type:

Standard: Nothing fancy here. This layout displays all the database's fields in the order they were created. The field labels for each field appear just *left* of the fields (**Figure 10.3**). It includes a blank header and footer.

Columnar list/report: This layout places the database's fields in a row across a single page. The labels for the fields appear in the header *above* the body of the record (**Figure 10.4**). (The footer is blank.) You determine the order of the fields when creating the layout or you can go back and rearrange them any time. Columnar lists and reports make it easier to compare one record to another or to squeeze multiple records onto the same screen.

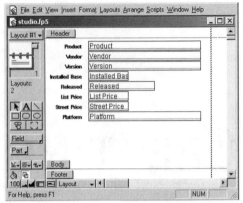

Figure 10.2 When you first define fields, FileMaker by default generates a standard layout with fields and labels listed in the order they were created.

Figure 10.3 The Standard layout displays fields and their labels in the order they were created.

Figure 10.4 The Columnar list/report layout places fields in a single row across the page.

Figure 10.5 The Table view is automatically generated and helps you inspect multiple records on a single screen.

Figure 10.6 The Labels layout will handle dozens of preset mailing label styles.

Figure 10.7 The Envelope layout takes the hassle out of generating addressed envelopes.

Figure 10.8 The Blank layout is exactly that—a blank slate if you want to start from scratch.

Table view: This isn't actually a layout as FileMaker usually defines the term. Instead it (**Figure 10.5**) is an automatically generated view of your data, though a very useful one for seeing and sorting multiple records on a single screen. For details on using tables, see pages 44 and 46. For details on controlling the layout setup for tables, see page 140.

Labels: Use this layout only for labels: you can't enter data into it directly (**Figure 10.6**). The dialog box that appears lets you choose from dozens of pre-set Avery label styles. For more information, see *To create a label layout* on page 141.

Envelope: This layout is tailored for printing on regular business envelopes and includes main and return address areas (**Figure 10.7**). Like the labels layout, it's not used for entering data directly. It includes a header and body but no footer. For more information, see *To create an envelope layout* on page 143.

Blank: This layout is entirely blank—nothing appears in the header, body, or footer (**Figure 10.8**). If you want to start with a clean slate and only add fields as you're ready, this is the layout for you.

Working with Layouts

Because label and envelope layouts behave a tad differently than most layouts, they're covered separately on pages 141–144.

To switch to layout mode:

◆ Choose View > Layout Mode (**Figure 10.9**).

or

◆ Use your keyboard: Ctrl L, in Windows, ⌘ L on the Mac.

or

◆ Click your cursor on the status mode pop-up at the bottom left of your screen (**Figure 10.10**).

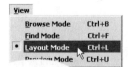 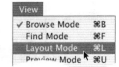

Figure 10.9 To switch to Layout mode, choose View > Layout Mode.

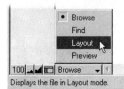

Figure 10.10 You also can switch to Layout mode by clicking the pop-up at the bottom of the status area.

Figure 10.11 The New Layout/Report command can be found within the Layouts menu. The command also is used to *add* a layout.

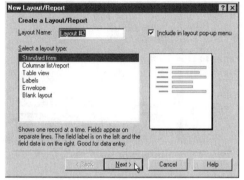

Figure 10.12 In the Create a Layout/Report portion of the New Layout/Report dialog box, give your layout a name, choose one of six types, and click *Next*.

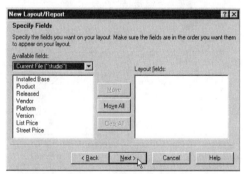

Figure 10.13 Highlight the fields in the left-hand list that you want to appear in the layout and use the *Move* or *Move All* buttons to place them in the right-hand list.

Creating a new layout

FileMaker now includes a set of three screens within the New Layout/Report dialog box that walk you through the process. For Windows users, this Wizard-style guide will be old hat.

To create a new layout:

1. Switch to Layout mode (Ctrl L in Windows, ⌘L on the Mac). Choose Layouts > New Layout/Report (Ctrl N in Windows, ⌘N on the Mac) (**Figure 10.11**).

2. When the Create a Layout/Report portion of the New Layout/Report dialog box appears, type a name into the *Layout Name* text box (**Figure 10.12**). By default, FileMaker assigns each new layout a generic name (e.g., *Layout #2*), but it's best to give it an easy to recognize name. Choose one of the six layouts in the left-side *Select a layout type* text box (a preview will appear to the right), and click *Next*.

3. When the Specify Fields screen appears (**Figure 10.13**), highlight the fields in the left-hand list that you want to appear in the layout and use the *Move* or *Move All* buttons to place them in the right-hand list. Or double-click on fields in the left list and they will automatically appear to the right. When you're done, click *Next*.

(continued)

CREATING NEW LAYOUTS

4. When the Select a Theme screen appears, make a choice in the left-side *Layout themes* list and a preview will appear to the right (**Figure 10.14**). When you're done, click *Finish*.

The new layout will appear on your screen (**Figure 10.15**). If you're happy with the layout, switch to Browse (Ctrl B in Windows, ⌘ B on the Mac) and begin entering data. More likely, however, you'll want to further format the layout. For more information, see *Formatting Fields or Objects* on page 181.

✔ Tips

- By default, FileMaker activates the *Include in layout pop-up menu* checkbox in the New Layout/Report dialog box (**Figure 10.12**). It's best to leave it checked to ensure that this layout appears in your layouts pop-down menu.

- FileMaker's layout themes, new in version 5, offer a quick way to apply colors and formatting consistently. Depending on the complexity of your choices, FileMaker will offer you the option of creating a script for applying the very same steps in the future (**Figure 10.16**). For more on scripts, see *Using Templates and Scripts* on page 199.

- As you create more layouts, click on the pop-down menu above the flipbook icon to quickly switch to the layout you need to use (**Figure 10.17**).

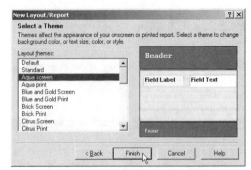

Figure 10.14 Pick a theme on the left and a preview appears on the right.

Figure 10.15 Once you make your choices in a series of dialog boxes, the new layout appears on your screen.

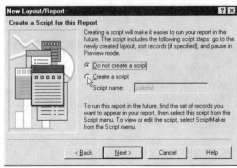

Figure 10.16 FileMaker now offers you the option of generating a script to help you replicate complex layouts.

Figure 10.17 To switch to another layout, click on the pop-down menu above the flipbook.

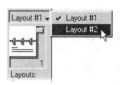

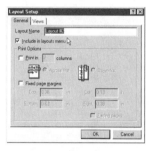

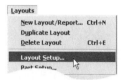

Figure 10.18 Select the layout you want by clicking it in the pop-down menu just above the flipbook icon.

Figure 10.19 Choose the Layout Setup command from the Layouts menu.

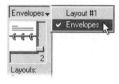

Figure 10.20 Type the new layout name inside the *Layout Name* text box and click *OK*.

Figure 10.21 The new name will appear in the pop-down menu of available layouts.

Figure 10.22 Use the Delete Layout command in the Layouts menu ([Ctrl][E] in Windows, [⌘][E] on the Mac) to eliminate the layout on your screen.

Figure 10.23 Still sure you want to get rid of the layout? Then click *Delete*.

To rename a layout:

1. Make sure you're in Layout mode ([Ctrl][L] in Windows, [⌘][L] on the Mac), then select the layout you want to rename by clicking it in the pop-down menu just above the flipbook icon (**Figure 10.18**).

2. Choose Layouts > Layout Setup (**Figure 10.19**).

3. When the Layout Setup dialog box appears, make sure the *General* tab is selected, type in the new name, and click *OK* (**Figure 10.20**). The layout pop-down menu now displays the renamed layout (**Figure 10.21**).

To delete a layout:

1. Make sure you're in Layout mode ([Ctrl][L] in Windows, [⌘][L] on the Mac), then select the layout you want to rename by clicking it in the pop-down menu just above the flipbook icon (**Figure 10.18**).

2. Once the layout appears onscreen, choose Layouts > Delete Layout (**Figure 10.22**) or use your keyboard: ([Ctrl][E] in Windows, [⌘][E] on the Mac).

3. A warning dialog box will appear. If you're sure, click *Delete* (**Figure 10.23**). The layout will disappear onscreen, replaced by the next layout listed in the pop-down menu.

RENAMING AND DELETING LAYOUTS

Duplicating a layout

This procedure will save you some time if you want to design a new layout based on elements in an existing layout.

To duplicate a layout:

1. Make sure you're in Layout mode ((Ctrl)(L) in Windows, (⌘)(L) on the Mac). Select the layout you want to duplicate by clicking on it in the pop-down menu just above the flipbook icon.

2. Choose Layouts > Duplicate Layout (**Figure 10.24**). (There are no keyboard equivalents.) The duplicate layout will appear onscreen and will be listed in the layout pop-down menu as a copy of the layout you selected. If you want to give the duplicate layout a more distinctive name, see *To rename a layout* on the previous page.

To choose a layout view:

◆ Make sure you're in Layout mode ((Ctrl)(L) in Windows, (⌘)(L) on the Mac). Click on the pop-down menu just above the left-hand flipbook and release your cursor on the layout of your choice (**Figure 10.25**).

Figure 10.24 Use the Duplicate Layout command in the Layouts menu to copy an existing layout.

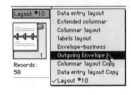

Figure 10.25 To choose among your existing layouts, use the pop-down menu just above the flipbook icon.

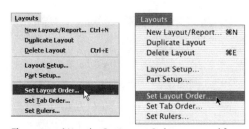

Figure 10.26 Use the Set Layout Order command from the Layouts menu to reorder the pop-down menu of layouts.

Figure 10.27 Click and drag to reorder layouts listed within the Set Layout Order dialog box.

To reorder the layout pop-down menu:

1. Make sure you're in Layout mode (Ctrl L in Windows, ⌘L on the Mac). Choose Layouts > Set Layout Order (**Figure 10.26**).

2. When the Set Layout Order dialog box appears, click on the layout name you want to reorder. Keep your cursor down and a double arrow will appear (**Figure 10.27**). While holding down the cursor, drag the layout name to the place you want it listed in the order. Release the cursor. Repeat this step to further rearrange the layout order.

3. Once you're satisfied with the order, click *OK*. The layout pop-down menu will now reflect the new order.

✔ Tip

■ If you've set up a database for multiple users, only the host will be able to reorder the list—and only when filesharing for the database is turned off. For more information, see *Networking* on page 243.

REORDERING LAYOUTS

Putting layouts in the pop-down menu

FileMaker's default is to automatically include layouts in the pop-down menu via the checkbox within the New Layout/Report dialog box (**Figure 10.28**). If you want to tidy up the list by excluding some layouts—or you mistakenly excluded a layout from the list—the steps are the same.

To exclude or include layouts in the layout pop-down menu:

1. Make sure you're in Layout mode ([Ctrl][L] in Windows, [⌘][L] on the Mac). Choose Layouts > Set Layout Order (**Figure 10.26**).

2. When the Set Layout Order dialog box appears, there will be a column of checkmarks just left of the list of layouts. To *exclude* a layout from the pop-down menu, move your cursor over the layout item's checkmark and click. The checkmark will disappear. To *include* a layout, move your cursor to the blank area just left of the layout's name and click the cursor. A checkmark will appear (**Figure 10.29**).

3. When you're satisfied, click *OK*.

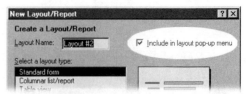

Figure 10.28 So easy to miss: The *Include in layout pop-up menu* checkbox within the New Layout/Report dialog box determines which layouts *initially* appear in the pop-down menu.

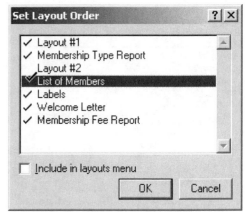

Figure 10.29 Use your cursor to control which layouts appear in the revised pop-down menu of layouts. Checked layouts will appear; unchecked will not.

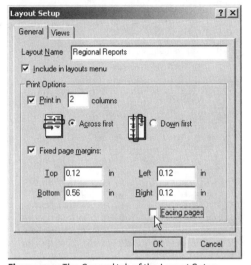

Figure 10.30 Choose Layouts > Layout Setup to reach the Layout Setup dialog box.

Figure 10.31 The *General* tab of the Layout Setup dialog box lets you set how the layout prints (across or down the page), its page margins, and whether it accommodates facing pages.

Changing the general layout setup

Use this to change how layout columns print and to change a layout's page margins.

To change the general layout setup:

1. Pick the layout you want to change by selecting it via the pop-down menu just above the left-hand flipbook.

2. Choose Layouts > Layout Setup (**Figure 10.30**).

3. Within the Layout Setup dialog box (**Figure 10.31**), click the *General* tab and you'll have three options for controlling how the layout prints out:

   ◆ You can have your layout print in columns—even if it's not a columnar-type layout. Select the *Print in* check-box, then fill in how many columns you want. The *Across first* option works well for mailing labels; use *Down first* for directory-style print-outs.

   ◆ Use the *Fixed page margins* checkbox and the four number-entry boxes if you want to use different margins from your printer's default settings.

   ◆ Use the *Facing Pages* checkbox if you'll be printing on both sides of the page. This will place the narrower, inside margin on the left of odd-numbered pages and on the right of even-numbered pages.

4. When you're done, click *OK* and switch to Browse mode to see the effects of your choices.

Changing the table view setup

Use this to change the setup of the table view. You also can use it to limit a user's view of the database as a list, form, or table.

To change the table view:

1. Pick the layout you want to change by selecting it via the pop-down menu just above the left-hand flipbook.

2. Choose Layouts > Layout Setup (**Figure 10.30**).

3. When the Layout Setup dialog box appears, click the *Views* tab, and then click the *Properties* button (**Figure 10.32**).

4. When the Table View Properties dialog box appears, use the checkboxes to set whether the table will display a grid, a header or any other parts, and column headers (**Figure 10.33**). You also can use the *Rows* checkbox and its adjacent text windows to fine-tune the height of the table rows.

5. Once you've made your choices, click *OK* and switch to Browse mode to see the effects of your choices.

✔ Tips

■ In step 3, if you uncheck any of the three views, that choice will be dimmed (and, so, not available) in the View menu within the Browse mode (**Figure 10.34**).

■ In step 4, if you check *Sort data when selecting column*, you can then resort columns within the Browse mode just by clicking any column header (**Figure 10.35**).

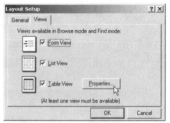

Figure 10.32 Use the *Views* tab of the Layout Setup dialog box to control which views are available in Browse mode or click *Properties* to set the details of the *Table View*.

Figure 10.33 The Table View Properties dialog box offers precise control over how the table appears.

Figure 10.34 Based on your choices in step 3, some choices will be dimmed in the View menu.

MyTable ▼	sales price	address	last sold	street name
	152000	227	1/20/95	Carmel
	218000	145	3/6/96	Pomona
	211000	146	4/16/96	Pomona
	173,000	244	4/19/96	Ashbury
	173000	217	4/29/96	Ashbury
Records: 32	192000	215	6/25/96	Pomona
	247000	220	7/12/96	Pomona
Sorted	219000	838	7/12/96	Pomona

MyTable ▼	sales price	address	last sold	street name
	173000	217	4/29/96	Ashbury
	185000	140	12/19/97	Ashbury
	173,000	244	4/19/96	Ashbury
	247500	242	11/7/97	Ashbury
Records: 32	229000	817	8/25/97	Ashbury
	219000	838	7/12/96	Ashbury
	166000	12	7/31/97	Carmel
Sorted	152000	227	1/20/95	Carmel

Figure 10.35 By checking *Sort data when selecting column* in step 4, you can then resort data by clicking any column header.

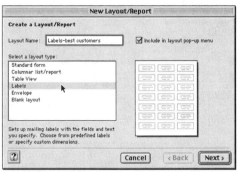

Figure 10.36 When the New Layout/Report dialog box appears, choose *Labels* in the left-side list and click *Next*.

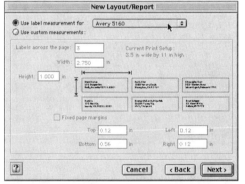

Figure 10.37 Use the label setup screen to choose a preset Avery-based label size or create a custom size.

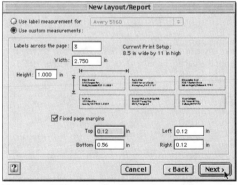

Figure 10.38 Choosing the *Use custom measurements* button lets you adjust the label's width and height, and set how many labels fit across the page.

Using Label and Envelope Layouts

This section only covers label and envelope layouts. For more information on using standard layouts, see *Working with Layouts* on page 132.

To create a label layout:

1. Switch to Layout mode (Ctrl L in Windows, ⌘ L on the Mac), then choose Layouts > New Layout/Report (Ctrl N in Windows, ⌘ N on the Mac).

2. When the Create a Layout/Report screen of the New Layout/Report dialog box appears, type a name into the *Layout Name* text box. Choose *Labels* in the left-side *Select a layout type* text box and click *Next* (**Figure 10.36**).

3. The next dialog box gives you the choice of using one of several dozen preset Avery-based label sizes or creating a custom-size label (**Figure 10.37**).

4. To use an Avery-based label, leave the *Use label measurement for* radio button selected and use the pop-down menu to choose the appropriate Avery size based on the labels you're using. By the way, even non-Avery label packages usually list an Avery-equivalent stock number.

5. To create a custom size, select the *Use custom measurements* radio button, then use the *Labels across the page*, *Width*, and *Height* boxes to configure your label's size (**Figure 10.38**).

6. Click *Next*.

(continued)

CREATING LABEL LAYOUTS

7. When the Specify Label Contents screen appears, double-click in the upper-left list the fields you want displayed or select a field in the list and click the *Add Field* button (**Figure 10.39**). Selected fields will appear in the lower window surrounded by « » brackets. The brackets act as placeholders for data.

8. To place a field on a new line, press (Enter) (Windows) or (Return) (Mac). To insert punctuation marks, space between the fields, or additional text just use your keyboard.

9. To remove a mistake, select the entry in the lower box and press (Delete). To start over, click on the dialog box's *Clear All* button. To further format the layout, see *Formatting Fields or Objects* on page 181.

10. When you're done, click *Next*. One final dialog box will appear (**Figure 10.40**), giving you a choice of switching to Preview mode to see how the labels will print or staying in Layout mode to continue tweaking its appearance. Make your choice and click *Finish*. The chosen view will appear, which in our example is the Layout view (**Figure 10.41**).

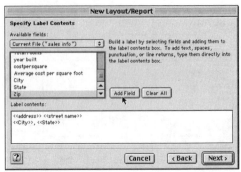

Figure 10.39 Use the Specify Label Contents screen to choose the fields you want displayed.

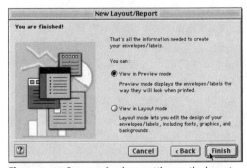

Figure 10.40 Once you're done setting up the layout, you can switch to Preview mode to see how the labels will print, or stay in Layout mode.

Figure 10.41 The layout for the label appears once you close the Specify Label Contents screen. Click on and drag the vertical marker to adjust the label's width.

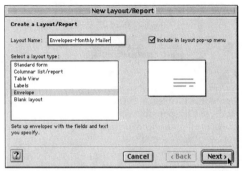

Figure 10.42 When the New Layout/Report dialog box appears, name the layout and choose *Envelope* in the left-side list.

To create an envelope layout:

1. Switch to Layout mode (⌃L in Windows, ⌘L on the Mac), then choose Layouts > New Layout/Report (⌃N in Windows, ⌘N on the Mac).

2. When the Create a Layout/Report dialog box appears, type a name into the *Layout Name* text box. Choose *Envelope* in the left-side *Select a layout type* text box and click *Next* (**Figure 10.42**).

3. When the Specify Label Contents dialog box appears, double-click on the fields in the upper-left list that displayed or select each one in the list and click the *Add Field* button (**Figure 10.39**). Selected fields will appear in the lower window surrounded by « » brackets. The brackets act as placeholders for data.

   To place a field on a new line, press Enter (Windows) or Return (Mac). To insert punctuation marks, space between the fields, or additional text just use your keyboard.

   To remove a mistake, select the entry in the lower box and press Delete. To start over, click on the dialog box's *Clear All* button. To further format the layout, see *Formatting Fields or Objects* on page 181.

4. When you're done, click *Next*. One final dialog box will appear (**Figure 10.40**), giving you a choice of switching to Preview mode to see how the envelopes will print or staying in Layout mode to continue tweaking its appearance. Make your choice, click *Finish* and the layout will appear in the chosen mode. For more information on printing, see *Printing* on page 237.

To create an envelope return address:

1. Once you've created an envelope layout, be sure you're still in Layout mode. Select the layout using the pop-down menu just above the flipbook icon (**Figure 10.43**).

2. Select the Type tool from within the Layout mode's status area, then click within the envelope layout's *header*.

3. Type in the return address, using the text options under the Format menu. For more on formatting *individual* blocks of text, see *Formatting Fields or Objects* on page 181. For more on *database-wide* text defaults, see *To set formatting defaults* on page 178.

4. Click on and drag the double arrow between the header and body to close up the empty space around the return address (**Figure 10.44**).

5. Choose Preview from the Mode menu (Ctrl U in Windows, ⌘U on the Mac) to double-check your envelope layout before you print it (**Figure 10.45**).

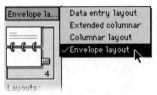

Figure 10.43 While still in Layout mode, use the pop-down menu above the flipbook icon to select the layout you want to change.

Figure 10.44 After creating a return address for an envelope, drag the double arrow to close up empty space around the return address.

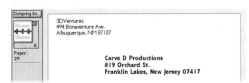

Figure 10.45 Use the Preview command (Ctrl U in Windows, ⌘U on the Mac) to double-check the envelope's appearance before printing.

Creating Form Letter Layouts

Form letters—standard letters containing bits of customized information—are easy to create using FileMaker's merge fields. By creating a layout that's mostly text with a few judiciously placed merge fields, you can create a customized letter for your customers:

> Dear Ms. Rose,
>
> Spring is in the air and as a long-time customer, you'll want to take advantage of our annual spring flower sale.
>
> All bedding plants are 20 percent off, garden tools are discounted by 15 percent, and turf builders are reduced by 30 percent. But the savings don't stop there! You'll find hundreds of items on sale.
>
> For preferred customers like yourself, the doors open at 10 a.m. on Thursday, Feb. 21. The sale starts for the general public at 10 a.m. on Friday, Feb. 22.
>
> Sincerely,
>
> James Green

In FileMaker, which uses << and >> to mark merge fields, the letter looks like this:

> Dear <<courtesy title.>> <<last name>>,
>
> Spring is in the air and as a long-time customer, you'll want to take advantage of our annual spring flower sale.
>
> All <<spring purchase #1>> are <<discount-spring purchase #1>> off, <<spring purchase #2>> are discounted by <<discount-spring purchase #2>>, and <<spring purchase #3.> are reduced by <<discount-spring purchase #3>>. But the savings don't stop there! You'll find hundreds of items on sale.
>
> For preferred customers like yourself, the doors open at 10 a.m. on Thursday, Feb. 21. The sale starts for the general public at 10 a.m. on Friday, Feb. 22.
>
> Sincerely,
>
> <<sales staff name>>

If you resist the urge to drown customers with frequent mailings, form letters with merge fields can be a powerful tool.

To create a form letter with merge fields:

1. Open the database from which the data will be drawn and switch to Layout mode (Ctrl L in Windows, ⌘ L on the Mac).

2. Choose Layouts > New Layout/Report (Ctrl N in Windows, ⌘ N on the Mac). When the New Layout/Report dialog box appears (**Figure 10.46**), type a name into the *Layout Name* text box, choose *Blank layout* within the *Select a layout type* area, and click *Finish*.

3. When the new layout appears, select the Type tool from the left-hand Layout status area and begin typing in your letter. When you reach the spot where you want the first merge field to appear (**Figure 10.47**), choose Insert > Merge Field (**Figure 10.48**). Or use your keyboard: Ctrl M in Windows, ⌘ M on the Mac.

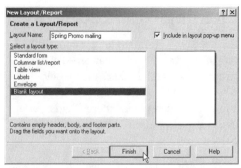

Figure 10.46 To create a form letter, choose *Blank layout* when selecting a new layout.

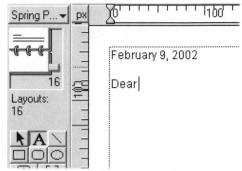

Figure 10.47 Click your cursor where you want a merge field to appear, then...

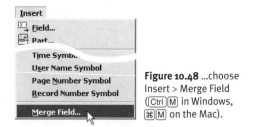

Figure 10.48 ...choose Insert > Merge Field (Ctrl M in Windows, ⌘ M on the Mac).

Figure 10.49 When the Specify Field dialog box appears, double-click on the field you want as a merge field.

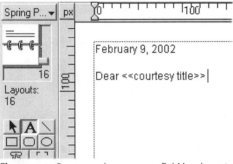

Figure 10.50 Once you place a merge field in a layout, a pair of << >> will mark its boundaries.

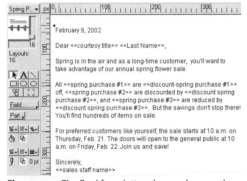

Figure 10.51 The final form letter shows where each merge field's contents will be inserted once you switch to Browse mode.

4. When the Specify Field dialog box appears, double-click on the field you want to appear in the letter (**Figure 10.49**). A merge field will appear within the form letter layout (**Figure 10.50**).

Continue typing the letter, adding additional merge fields as you need them until you're done (**Figure 10.51**). To see what the form letter will look like, switch to Browse mode. To format the letter's fonts and other text attributes, see *Formatting Fields or Objects* on page 181. To set the letter's margins and prepare it for printing, see *Printing* on page 243.

Using Variable Fields

FileMaker's Insert menu includes a great feature that lets you insert field data that is automatically updated. There are two types of fields in the Insert menu: fixed and variable (**Figure 10.52**). Fixed data fields—Current Date, Current Time, and Current User Name—paste information that is current *at the time it is entered*. Once pasted into a file, the data remains fixed and is not updated. In contrast, the variable fields—Date Symbol, Time Symbol, User Name Symbol, Page Number Symbol, and Record Number Symbol—are updated *when the file is viewed or printed*.

These variable fields are particularly handy for form letters because a letter can be prepared in advance, yet contain the dates and times reflecting the time when it's actually printed out. This trick, by the way, need not be confined to form letters. Use it in any layout where you need updated information to appear—including onscreen forms.

To insert a variable field:

1. Make sure you're in Layout mode (Ctrl L in Windows, ⌘L on the Mac), select the Type tool from within the Layout mode's status area, and click in the layout where you want the variable data to appear.

2. Choose Insert and then the variable field type you want: Date Symbol, Time Symbol, User Name Symbol, Page Number Symbol, or Record Number Symbol (**Figure 10.52**). Release your cursor and a placeholder symbol will be inserted (**Figure 10.53**). For more on what will appear in the layout, especially the placeholder symbols, see **Table 10.1**.

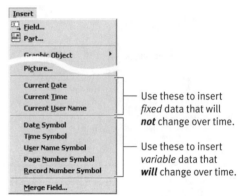

Figure 10.52 The Insert menu contains two types of fields: fixed and variable.

> //
>
> Dear <<courtesy title>> <<Last Name>>,
>
> Spring is in the air and as a long-time custom take advantage of our annual spring flower s

Figure 10.53 When you choose Insert > Date Symbol, a double forward slash (//) acts as a placeholder within the layout.

Table 10.1

Variable Field Symbols		
TO USE	CHOOSE INSERT AND:	INSERTS (SYMBOL
Fixed date	Current Date	Date at time field created
Fixed time	Current Time	Time at time field created
Fixed user name	Current User Name	Name of person creating field
Variable date	Date Symbol	Placeholder (//)
Variable time	Time Symbol	Placeholder (::)
Variable name	User Name Symbol	Placeholder (||)
Variable page	Page Number Symbol	Placeholder (##)
Variable record	Record Number Symbol	Placeholder (@@)

USING VARIABLE FIELDS IN LAYOUTS

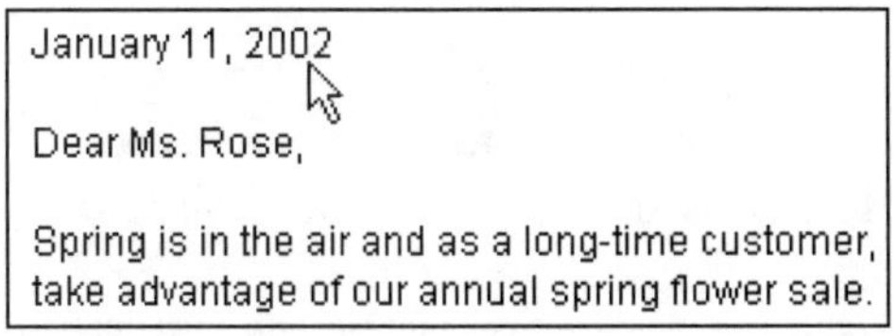

January 11, 2002

Dear Ms. Rose,

Spring is in the air and as a long-time customer, take advantage of our annual spring flower sale.

Figure 10.54 When you switch from Layout to Browse mode, the date symbol is replaced by the *current* date, which will be continually updated.

3. Return to Browse mode and the place-holder is updated to reflect the most current data (**Figure 10.54**).

✔ Tip

■ The formatting for dates, times, and numbers inserted with variable fields is controlled like any other date, time, or number field. For example, you can have dates appear as 5/6/2002 or May 6, 2002. For more information, see *Formatting and Graphics in Layouts* on page 175.

USING VARIABLE FIELDS IN LAYOUTS

Working with Parts

In most cases, the function of the various layout parts are obvious from their names: header, body, and footer. Summary parts work a bit differently than other layout parts. Since summary fields gather information from across several records, they cannot appear within the body of an individual record. That's where the various kinds of summary parts come in by providing a way to display this cross-record data. *Grand summary* parts summarize information for all the records being browsed. *Subsummary* parts do the same for a group of records, based on the break field you designate within the Part Definition dialog box.

Title header: This special type of header appears only at the top of the page or first screen. It can also be used as a title page. Each layout can only contain one title header.

Header: Use for field titles or column headings in columnar layouts (**Figure 10.55**). It appears at the top of every page or screen. Each layout can only contain one header.

Leading grand summary: Use this type of summary part to display summary information at the *beginning* of the group of the records being browsed.

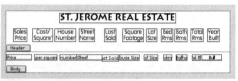

Figure 10.55 Used in a columnar layout, a header part enables you to run field titles across the top for more than one row of records.

Body: Use for the bulk of your data, including graphics. The body will appear for each record in the database. Each layout can only contain one body.

Subsummary: Use this type of summary part to display summary information for the group of the records specified by the break field.

Trailing grand summary: Use this type of summary part to display summary information at the *end* of the group of the records being browsed.

Footer: Use for dates or page numbers. The footer will appear at the bottom of each page or screen. Each layout can contain only one footer.

Title footer: This special type of footer appears only at the bottom of the *first* page or screen. Each layout can only contain one title footer.

To add a layout part:

1. Make sure you're in Layout mode ([Ctrl][L] in Windows, [⌘][L] on the Mac). Choose Layouts > Part Setup (**Figure 10.56**).

2. When the Part Setup dialog box appears, click *Create* (**Figure 10.57**).

3. Within the Part Definition dialog box, select the type of part you want to create from the eight choices (**Figure 10.58**).

4. If you're creating a subsummary part, you'll also need to select from the right-hand list which field (also known as a break field) you'd like the records to sort by.

5. The Part Definition dialog box also allows you to control where and how pages will break. Check the appropriate box or boxes. Click *OK*.

6. When the Part Setup dialog box reappears, click *Done* and the new part appears in the layout.

✔ Tip

- If you're clear about the purpose and placement of layout parts, you can add a part directly by clicking on the Part button in the left-hand Layout status area and dragging the resulting part to where you want it (**Figure 10.59**).

Figure 10.56 Add a part to your layout by choosing Layouts > Part Setup.

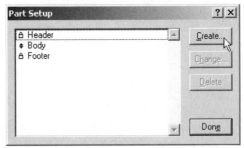

Figure 10.57 Click *Create* when the Part Setup dialog box appears.

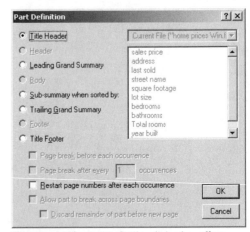

Figure 10.58 The Part Definition dialog box offers eight type choices.

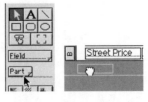

Figure 10.59 The *Part* button within the Layout status area lets you add a part by clicking and dragging directly within the layout.

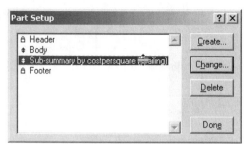

Figure 10.60 Reorder parts by clicking and dragging them within the Part Setup dialog box.

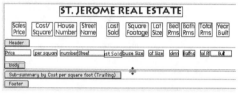

Figure 10.61 To resize a part, click and drag on the dotted line separating one part from another.

To delete a part:

1. Make sure you're in Layout mode ([Ctrl][L] in Windows, [⌘][L] on the Mac). Choose Layouts > Part Setup.

2. Within the Part Setup dialog box, select the part you want eliminated and press [Delete]. If you've selected a part that contains objects, you'll get a warning dialog box. If you're sure, click Delete.

To reorder parts:

1. Make sure you're in Layout mode ([Ctrl][L] in Windows, [⌘][L] on the Mac). Choose Layouts > Part Setup.

2. Click on the part you want to move, hold the cursor down, and drag the part to a new position in the order (**Figure 10.60**).

3. Click Done. The part appears in the new position.

To resize a part:

◆ Make sure you're in Layout mode ([Ctrl][L] in Windows, [⌘][L] on the Mac). Click on the dotted line separating one part from another and drag it to make the part larger or smaller (**Figure 10.61**).

✔ Tip

■ Resizing one part doesn't change the size of any other parts in the layout. Instead, the size of the entire layout will grow or shrink accordingly.

DELETING, REORDERING, AND RESIZING PARTS

153

Changing a Part's Type and Options

FileMaker's Part Definition dialog box (**Figure 10.62**) does more than simply let you change a part's type. It also gives you control over where a page breaks in relation to a particular part and whether the pages are renumbered after that part. The page break and renumbering options are particularly useful when creating forms from which you may want to print out one record per page (**Table 10.2**). Here's a quick rundown of these options:

Page break before each occurrence: Choosing this checkbox will place a page break right before the selected part. Examples might include using it for a Trailing Grand Summary, Title Header, Header, or Body.

Page break after every __ occurrences: Choosing this checkbox will place a page break after x instances of the selected header. You set the number of instances. Examples might include selecting a body or footer part where you've created a layout in which x records will fit on a page.

Restart page numbers after each occurrence: Use this checkbox if, for example, you want to group a subsummary of records together and restart the page numbers after each subsummary.

Allow part to break across page boundaries: By default, FileMaker will try to keep a part on a single page. Use this checkbox if you do *not* want to keep a part on the same page or when the body is simply too large to fit on a single page.

Discard remainder of part before new page: This option can only be used if you've also checked *Allow part to break across page boundaries*.

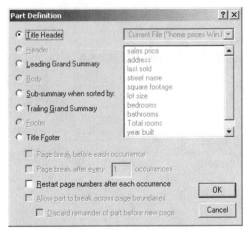

Figure 10.62 The Part Definition dialog box lets you change a part's type, plus control page breaks and numbering related to that part.

Table 10.2

Page Break and Numbering Options	
IN THE PART DEFINITION DIALOG BOX	
CHOOSE	FOR USE WITH THESE LAYOUT PARTS
Page break before each occurrence	Subsummary (if sorted by body) Trailing subsummary Trailing grand summary
Page break after every x occurrences	Leading grand summary Subsummary (if sorted by body) Trailing grand summary
Restart page numbers after each occurrence	Title header Header Leading grand summary Subsummary (if sorted by body) Footer
Allow part to break across page boundaries	Leading grand summary Subsummary (if sorted by body) Trailing grand summary
Discard remainder of part before new page	Leading grand summary Subsummary (if sorted by body) Trailing grand summary

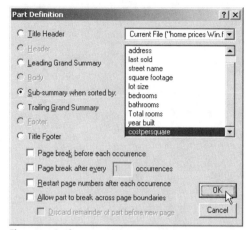

Figure 10.63 If you create a subsummary part, use the right-hand list to pick a field and click *OK*.

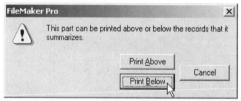

Figure 10.64 You can elect to have the subsummary part printed above or below the records it summarizes.

To change a part type or break field:

1. Make sure you're in Layout mode ([Ctrl][L] in Windows, [⌘][L] on the Mac). Double-click on the label of the part you want to change.

2. When the Part Definition dialog box appears, make your new part type choice from the eight left-side choices.

   If you want to change the field used by a subsummary part (called a break field by FileMaker), click the *Sub-Summary when sorted by* button and then make a new field selection in the right-hand list (**Figure 10.63**).

3. Click *OK*. The part type will now change.

To paginate layout parts:

1. Make sure you're in Layout mode ([Ctrl][L] in Windows, [⌘][L] on the Mac). Double-click on the label of the part you want to change.

2. When the Part Definition dialog box appears, select the appropriate checkbox among the five in the lower part of the dialog box. See **Table 10.2** for more information on which page breaks and numbering schemes work best with various layout parts.

3. When you're done making your changes, click *OK*.

4. If you chose a summary part, a dialog box may appear asking whether you want the part printed above or below the records it's summarizing (**Figure 10.64**). Click on your choice.

Working with Fields in Layouts

When you're working with layouts remember: *Adding* a field to a *layout* isn't the same thing as *creating* a field for the *database*. Layouts are simply differing views of the same data. Add a layout or delete a layout—either way the database itself isn't changed. The same notion applies when adding a field to a layout: It's just a view of a field that's already been created within the database.

For information on how to create a brand new field, see *To define a field* on page 102. Once you've created a field, you can easily add it to a new layout directly without having to define it again. In fact, however, it's common while designing a layout to discover that you need to define a new field. Just keep straight the difference between defining fields for the database versus adding a field to a layout and you'll be fine.

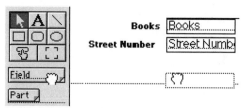

Figure 10.65 To add an already defined field to a layout, click on the status area's *Field* button and drag the resulting field to where you want it.

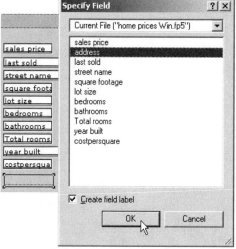

Figure 10.66 Selecting the *Field* button will open the Specify Field dialog box, allowing you to select a field definition (and add its name if you leave the bottom box checked).

To add a field to a layout:

1. To add *already defined* fields to a layout, click on the *Field* button in the left-hand Layout status area and drag the resulting field where you want it within the layout (**Figure 10.65**).

2. When the Specify Field dialog box appears, click on a name for the new field (**Figure 10.66**). You can add a field defined in another database by clicking on the *Current File* pop-down menu above the field list and navigating to the database with the desired field.

3. If you want a field label to appear in the layout, also check the *Create field label* box below the list.

4. Click *OK*. The layout will reappear with the added field. If you want to further format the field, see *Formatting Fields or Objects* on page 181.

✔ Tip

■ If you want to redefine the just-added field, stay in Layout mode and just double-click on the field. The Specify Field dialog box will reappear, allowing you to pick another field definition.

To delete a field from a layout:

1. Make sure you're in Layout mode ((Ctrl)(L) in Windows, (⌘)(L) on the Mac). Select the field you want to delete by clicking it.

2. Press (Delete).

✔ Tip

■ Remember: Deleting a field from a layout merely removes it from that layout. The data and field still exist in the *database* and, so, can be used in other layouts as you need them.

Resizing fields

Sometimes you create a field and only later realize that it is too small for the intended text. (**Figure 10.67**). In that case, the text will be cut off. Resizing solves the problem.

To resize a field:

1. Switch to Layout mode (Ctrl L in Windows, ⌘ L on the Mac).

2. Click on the field you want to resize and hold down your cursor. The corners of the field will become small black boxes, known as handles.

3. Drag the handles to make the field larger or smaller. When it reaches the size you want, release the cursor.

4. Switch back (Ctrl B in Windows, ⌘ B on the Mac) and you'll see that all the field's text now shows. Getting the field big enough may require some toggling between Layout and Browse modes to check your progress.

✔ Tip

■ To cleanly enlarge a field horizontally or vertically, click on the field and press Shift just before you drag the handle. The field will then only expand in the direction you first drag it, whether it's horizontal or vertical.

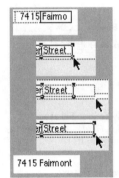

Figure 10.67 To resize a field in Layout mode, click on the field and drag a corner. Once back in Browse mode (bottom), the field's text is no longer cut off.

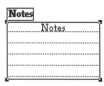

Notes
+Roof replaced in 95.
+Stem wall not working and
drainage in general a problem.
+Pest report OK
+Kitchen OK but could use come

Figure 10.68 Consider adding a scroll bar when a field has too much text to fit within your layout.

Figure 10.69 Switch to Layout mode, then click on the field to select it.

Figure 10.70 Choose Format > Field Format to open the Field Format dialog box.

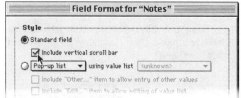

Figure 10.71 Within the Field Format dialog box, choose the *Standard field* radio button, check *Include vertical scroll bar*, and click *OK*.

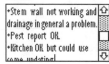

Notes
+Stem wall not working and
drainage in general a problem.
+Pest report OK
+Kitchen OK but could use
come updating

Figure 10.72 The field after a scroll bar is added.

Adding scroll bars to large text fields

Sometimes enlarging a field isn't practical, either because your layout doesn't have the room or because the field has so much text that it would overwhelm the rest of the layout (**Figure 10.68**). In such cases, adding a scroll bar to the text field is the best approach.

To add a scroll bar:

1. Switch to Layout mode (Ctrl L in Windows, ⌘ L on the Mac) and click on the field to select it (**Figure 10.69**).

2. Choose Format > Field Format (**Figure 10.70**). The Field Format dialog box will appear.

3. Inside the Field Format dialog box, choose the *Standard field* radio button, and then check *Include vertical scroll bar*. Click *OK* (**Figure 10.71**).

4. Back in Layout mode, the field now has a scroll bar. Switch to Browse mode and you'll see that the scroll bar not only allows you to scroll through all the text but also offers an immediate visual cue that there's more text than what shows (**Figure 10.72**).

ADDING SCROLL BARS TO FIELDS

To set the field tab order:

1. Switch to Layout mode (Ctrl L in Windows, ⌘L on the Mac), then choose Layouts > Set Tab Order (**Figure 10.73**).

2. The Set Tab Order dialog box appears, along with a series of numbered arrows indicating the current tab order for your fields.

   If you want to just slightly alter the order, click on the tab number you want to change and type it in. If you assign No. 1 to an arrow, you'll also need to renumber the original No. 1 arrow (**Figure 10.74**).

   If you want to completely change the order, click on the *Create new tab order* radio button in the dialog box, which will eliminate all the tab numbers. Then just click on the arrows in the order you want the tab order set (**Figure 10.75**).

3. When you're done, click *OK*. The new tab order is now set.

✔ Tip

■ Each layout can have its own tab order, allowing you to customize each layout for its intended users.

Figure 10.73 To change the entry order for your fields, choose Layouts > Set Tab Order from the menu.

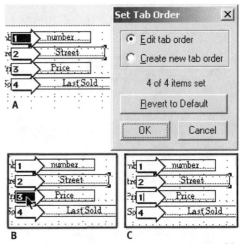

Figure 10.74 To slightly alter the existing tab order (**A**), click on the arrow you want to change (**B**), and type in the new number (**C**).

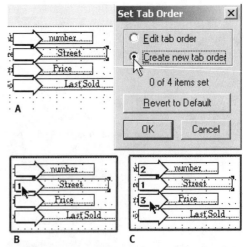

Figure 10.75 To completely change the tab order, click on the *Create new tab order* radio button, which will erase all the previous numbers (**A**). Then click on the arrows in the order you want the tab order set (**B, C**).

WORKING WITH OBJECTS IN LAYOUTS

Whether it's text, a field, a field name, or a graphic, FileMaker treats them all as separate objects that can be selected, moved, rearranged, and grouped. Most of these functions reside under the Arrange menu, which appears only when you're in Layout mode. These objects also can be graphically embellished with shading, borders, and fills via the tools in the Layout status area. For more information on using graphics with objects, see *Working with Graphics* on page 190.

While FileMaker makes it easy to move individual objects around a layout, it also allows you to *group* objects and then treat them as a single object. By creating groups of groups, you can organize pieces of a layout into units that speed your work.

By default, FileMaker displays objects in the order they were created, with the most recent atop (or in front of) the earlier objects. Sometimes in designing a layout, it's useful to stack objects atop each other to create a special effect, such as the appearance of a three-dimensional object. While each object remains a separate object, rearranging the stack order changes the overall appearance.

To make it easier to build layouts, FileMaker comes with built-in rulers, T-Squares, and grids. For more information, see *Using Layout Guides* on page 170.

✔ Tip

■ You may find it faster when arranging and grouping objects to use FileMaker's Arrange toolbar (**Figure 11.1**). To turn it on, choose View > Toolbars > Arrange.

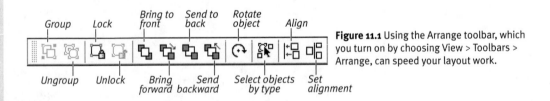

Figure 11.1 Using the Arrange toolbar, which you turn on by choosing View > Toolbars > Arrange, can speed your layout work.

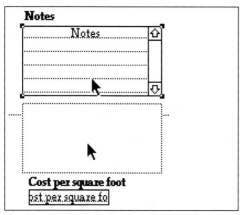

Figure 11.2 To move an object within a layout, click on it and drag it. A dotted outline of the object appears as you move the object.

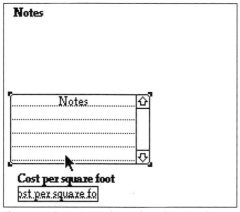

Figure 11.3 Once you've dragged an object to where you want it, release the cursor.

To move an object within the same layout:

1. Switch to Layout mode ([Ctrl][L] in Windows, [⌘][L] on the Mac), then select the object by clicking on it with your cursor. Keep pressing your cursor and drag the object to its new location in the layout. A set of dotted lines marks the object's position as you drag it (**Figure 11.2**).

   If you want to ensure that the object only moves horizontally (or vertically), hold down [Shift] as you drag it.

2. Once you put the object where you want it, release the cursor (**Figure 11.3**). The object will now appear in the new location within the layout.

✔ Tip

■ While the field moved in the above example, the "Notes" field label did not. That's because the label is a separate object. While you can move more than one object at a time by [Shift]-clicking on several objects before dragging them, *grouping* such objects often makes more sense because things like field labels automatically tag along when you move a field. See *To group objects* on page 165.

To move an object to another layout:

1. Switch to Layout mode ([Ctrl][L] in Windows, [⌘][L] on the Mac), then select the object by clicking on it with your cursor.

2. Choose Edit > Cut ([Ctrl][X] in Windows, [⌘][X] on the Mac).

3. Switch to the other layout and choose Edit > Paste ([Ctrl][V] in Windows/[⌘][V] on the Mac).

4. Once the object appears in the layout, use your cursor to move it exactly where you want it.

MOVING OBJECTS WITHIN LAYOUTS

To copy an object:

1. Switch to Layout mode ((Ctrl)(L) in Windows, (⌘)(L) on the Mac), then select the object by clicking on it with your cursor.

2. Choose Edit > Duplicate ((Ctrl)(D) in Windows, (⌘)(D) on the Mac).

3. Use your cursor to move the duplicated object to where you want it.

To delete an object:

1. Switch to Layout mode ((Ctrl)(L) in Windows, (⌘)(L) on the Mac), then select the object by clicking on it with your cursor.

2. Press (Delete). If you deleted the wrong object, choose Edit > Undo ((Ctrl)(Z) in Windows, (⌘)(Z) on the Mac).

COPYING AND DELETING OBJECTS

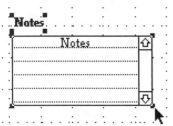

Figure 11.4 To select a field and its label for grouping, press (Shift) and click on both objects.

Figure 11.5 After you've selected several objects, choose Arrange > Group.

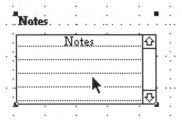

Figure 11.6 Once they're grouped, the field and its label become one object, as indicated by the single set of handles at the object's corners.

Grouping objects

By default, FileMaker treats each item added to a layout as a separate object. But sometimes there can be great advantage to having multiple objects treated as a single object (grouping). For example, if you use labels for fields, grouping the label with the field ensures that they stay together when you move a field within a layout. Similarly, it can speed up your layout work to group related topic fields and then move them to a new spot with a single click-and-drag.

To group objects:

1. Switch to Layout mode ((Ctrl)(L) in Windows, (⌘)(L) on the Mac), then select the first object by clicking on it with your cursor.

2. Hold down (Shift) while you continue clicking on the objects you want to group together (**Figure 11.4**).

3. Choose Arrange > Group or use your keyboard: (Ctrl)(G) in Windows, (⌘)(G) on the Mac (**Figure 11.5**). The previously individual objects now become a single object (**Figure 11.6**).

✔ Tip

■ You can create subgroups within larger groupings. For example, create a group of just two objects (a field label with its field) before grouping that field with other fields. That way, if you later decide to ungroup the fields, you'll still have the field name grouped with its field.

GROUPING OBJECTS

To ungroup objects:

1. Make sure you're in Layout mode (Ctrl L in Windows, ⌘L on the Mac), then select the objects you no longer want grouped by clicking on each as you hold Shift.

2. Choose Arrange > Ungroup (**Figure 11.7**) or use your keyboard: Ctrl Shift G in Windows, Shift ⌘G on the Mac. The selected objects will no longer be grouped (see *Tip* for exceptions).

✔ Tip

■ If you have created subgroups within a group, you'll have to repeat the Ungroup command at each level to fully break up those groupings.

To lock layout objects:

1. Make sure you're in Layout mode (Ctrl L in Windows, ⌘L on the Mac), then select the pieces of the layout you want to protect from accidental changes by holding down Shift as you click on each object.

2. Choose Arrange > Lock (**Figure 11.8**) or use your keyboard: Ctrl H in Windows, ⌘H on the Mac.

To unlock layout objects:

1. Make sure you're in Layout mode (Ctrl L in Windows, ⌘L on the Mac), then hold down Shift as you click on the objects you want to unlock.

2. Choose Arrange > Unlock (**Figure 11.9**) or use your keyboard: Ctrl Shift H in Windows, Shift ⌘H on the Mac.

✔ Tip

■ When creating groups, if one object is locked, all the grouped objects will become locked as well.

Figure 11.7 To break a grouped object back into individual objects, select it and choose Arrange > Ungroup.

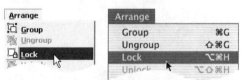

Figure 11.8 To protect against accidental changes to a layout, select the objects and choose Arrange > Lock.

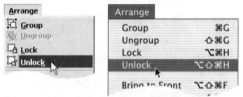

Figure 11.9 To unlock a layout object—enabling others to easily change it—choose Arrange > Unlock.

1.

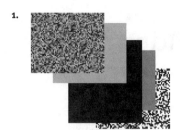

2.

3.

4.

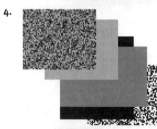

5.

Figure 11.10 1. Initially, the black square lies in the middle of the stack order. **2.** Brought to the front. **3.** Brought forward one layer from its initial position. **4.** Sent back one layer from its initial position. **5.** Sent to the back.

To change the stack order of objects:

1. Switch to Layout mode (Ctrl L in Windows, ⌘ L on the Mac), then select the object you want to move by clicking on it with your cursor.

2. From the Arrange menu, choose one of four commands: Bring to Front, Bring Forward, Send to Back, or Send Backward. The closer an object lies to the front (or top) of the stack, the more of it will be visible. By selecting and moving various objects, you can manipulate the arrangement to your satisfaction (**Figure 11.10**).

- ◆ **Bring to Front** (no Windows keyboard equivalent, Shift Option ⌘ F on the Mac): Use this command to bring the selected object to the very front (or top) of the stack.

- ◆ **Bring Forward** (Ctrl Shift F in Windows, Shift ⌘ F on the Mac): Use this command to bring the selected object forward one layer.

- ◆ **Send to Back** (no Windows keyboard equivalent, Shift Option ⌘ J on the Mac): Use this command to send the selected object to the very back (or bottom) of the stack.

- ◆ **Send Backward** (Ctrl Shift J in Windows, Shift ⌘ J on the Mac): Use this command to send the selected object back one layer.

CHANGING THE OBJECT STACKING ORDER

Rotating objects

Because every field, label, and graphic within FileMaker is treated as an object, you're free to rotate them to make a layout more compact, less cluttered, or just more eye-grabbing. FileMaker limits you to rotating objects in 90-degree increments. If you need more precise control, create the object within a true graphics program and then import it into FileMaker.

To rotate an object:

1. Switch to Layout mode ((Ctrl)(L) in Windows, (⌘)(L) on the Mac), then select the object you want to rotate by clicking on it with your cursor (**Figure 11.11**).

2. Choose Arrange > Rotate (**Figure 11.12**) or use your keyboard: no Windows keyboard equivalent, (Option)(⌘)(R) on the Mac. The Rotate command moves an object 90 degrees clockwise (**Figure 11.13**).

✔ Tips

■ Repeat the Rotate command to continue spinning an object in 90-degree increments until it reaches the position you want.

■ If you prefer, press and hold your cursor on the selected object's "handles"—the small black squares on its periphery—then rotate it directly.

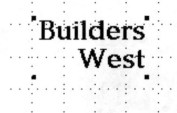

Figure 11.11 To rotate an object, first select it while in Layout mode ...

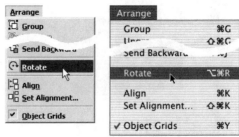

Figure 11.12 ... then choose Arrange > Rotate.

Figure 11.13 The Rotate command spins the object clockwise in 90-degree increments. Repeat the command to spin the object 180 and 270 degrees.

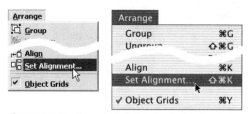

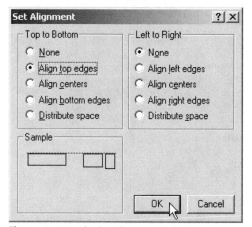

Figure 11.14 To align selected objects, choose Arrange > Set Alignment.

Figure 11.15 Use the Set Alignment dialog box to control the top-to-bottom and left-to-right relationships among several selected objects. The lower-left panel displays a sample of the chosen setting.

Aligning objects

Your layout will be easier to read and look more professional if you vertically or horizontally align fields, labels, and groups of fields as much as possible.

To align objects:

1. Switch to Layout mode (⌘Ctrl⌘L⌘ in Windows, ⌘⌘⌘L⌘ on the Mac), then select the objects you want to align by holding down ⌘Shift⌘ and clicking on them with your cursor.

2. Choose Arrange > Set Alignment or use your keyboard: ⌘Ctrl⌘⌘Shift⌘⌘K⌘ in Windows, ⌘Shift⌘⌘⌘⌘⌘K⌘ on the Mac (**Figure 11.14**).

3. When the Set Alignment dialog box appears, you can control the top-to-bottom and the left-to-right alignment of the selected objects (**Figure 11.15**). The *Sample* area in the window's lower-left corner lets you see the effect of each combination.

4. When you're satisfied with the alignment, click *OK*.

✔ Tip

■ If you're happy with the choices you've made in the Set Alignment dialog box, you can apply them to any selected objects without having to reopen the window simply by using the align command: ⌘Ctrl⌘⌘K⌘ in Windows, ⌘⌘⌘⌘K⌘ on the Mac.

ALIGNING OBJECTS

Using Layout Guides

FileMaker's various layout guides are strictly optional but you'll find that they make it much easier to create professional layouts. You can use them while you're creating a layout or to go back and tidy up previous work. Here's a quick rundown on how each guide functions:

Text Ruler: Provides a horizontal measure in inches, pixels, or centimeters (**Figure 11.16**).

Graphic Rulers: Provides horizontal and vertical rulers in inches, pixels, or centimeters (**Figure 11.17**).

Ruler Lines: Provides a matrix of horizontal and vertical dotted lines to help position layout objects. The matrix can be set in inches, pixels, or centimeters (**Figure 11.18**).

T-Squares: Provides an intersecting horizontal line and vertical line, which can be moved to guide the positioning of layout objects (**Figure 11.19**).

Object Grids: Provides an invisible grid whose measurement units can be adjusted. When Object Grids is on, layout objects "snap" to the nearest grid line.

Size Palette: Provides a set of number entry boxes that help you precisely position layout objects (**Figure 11.20**).

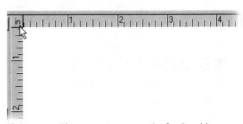

Figure 11.16 The Text Ruler lets you choose your measurement units and includes icons for choosing fonts, alignments, and tabs.

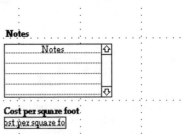

Figure 11.17 The measurement units for Graphic Rulers, which aid horizontal and vertical placement of the selected object, can be changed via the Layouts menu.

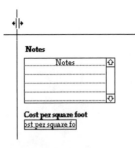

Figure 11.18 The Ruler Lines provide a visible matrix to help position layout objects.

Figure 11.19 The T-Squares option provides a horizontal and a vertical line that extends across the entire layout—easing alignment of multiple objects.

Size		×
←	1.917	in
↑	0.667	in
→	5.431	in
↓	1.250	in
↔	3.514	in
↕	0.583	in

Figure 11.20 The Size Palette allows you to precisely position layout objects via the numeric entry boxes.

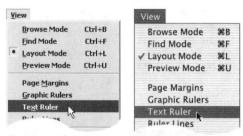

Figure 11.21 If you're in Layout mode, you can turn on the Text Ruler by choosing View > Text Ruler.

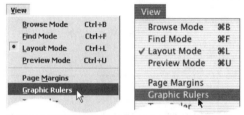

Figure 11.22 Once you're in Layout mode, turn on the Graphic Rulers by choosing View > Graphic Rulers.

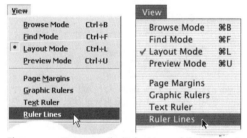

Figure 11.23 To turn on the Ruler Lines while in Layout mode, choose View > Ruler Lines.

To use the Text Ruler:

1. Make sure you're in Layout mode (Ctrl L in Windows, ⌘ L on the Mac), then choose View > Text Ruler (**Figure 11.21**).

2. Use the ruler or, if you have it turned on, the various text icons in the Text Formatting toolbar to adjust selected text as you desire. For more information on text formats, see *Formatting Fields or Objects* on page 181.

3. To hide the ruler, choose View > Text Ruler again.

To use the Graphic Rulers:

1. Make sure you're in Layout mode (Ctrl L in Windows, ⌘ L on the Mac), then choose View > Graphic Rulers (**Figure 11.22**). To adjust the measurement units used, click the upper-left corner where the horizontal and vertical rulers meet to cycle through the choices: inches, centimeters, or pixels. For more information, see *To change ruler and grid units* on page 174.

2. To hide the graphic rules, choose View > Graphic Rulers again.

To use Ruler Lines:

1. Make sure you're in Layout mode (Ctrl L in Windows, ⌘ L on the Mac), then choose View > Ruler Lines (**Figure 11.23**). To adjust the measurement units used, see *To change ruler and grid units* on page 174.

2. To hide the rulers, choose View > Ruler Lines again.

USING LAYOUT RULERS

To use T-Squares:

1. Make sure you're in Layout mode (Ctrl L in Windows, ⌘ L on the Mac), then choose View > T-Squares (**Figure 11.24**). To adjust the placement of the T-Square lines, click and hold your cursor, then drag the line where you want it (**Figure 11.25**).

2. To hide the T-Squares, choose View > T-Squares again.

To use Object Grids:

1. Make sure you're in Layout mode (Ctrl L in Windows, ⌘ L on the Mac), then choose Arrange > Object Grids. (There's no Windows keyboard equivalent, use ⌘ Y on the Mac, **Figure 11.26**). To adjust the measurement units used and the fineness of the grid, see *To change ruler and grid units* on page 174.

2. To turn off Object Grids, choose Arrange > Object Grids again.

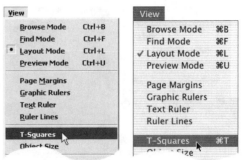

Figure 11.24 To turn on the T-Squares, choose View > T-Squares.

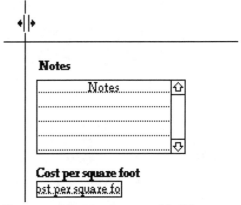

Figure 11.25 Adjust the placement of the T-Square lines by clicking on a line and dragging it.

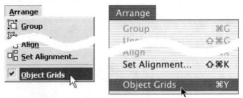

Figure 11.26 Choosing Arrange > Object Grids turns on an invisible set of lines to which new layout objects will "snap."

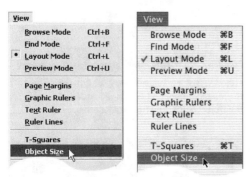

Figure 11.27 While in Layout mode, choose View > Object Size to reach the Size Palette.

To use the Size Palette:

1. Make sure you're in Layout mode (Ctrl L in Windows, ⌘L on the Mac), then select the object you want to position by clicking on it with your cursor.

2. Choose View > Object Size (**Figure 11.27**).

3. Once the Size Palette appears (**Figure 11.28**), make sure you're working in the measurement units you prefer: inches, pixels, or centimeters. To adjust the palette's measurement units, see *To change ruler and grid units* on the next page.

4. Type in the measurements you want in the Size Palette's number entry boxes. When you're done, press Enter in Windows, Return on the Mac. The object will be resized based on your entry.

✔ Tip

- Use the Size Palette while click-dragging an object to position a layout object *exactly* where you want it. Just select your object, open the Size Palette, and click-drag the object while keeping an eye on the palette's measurements.

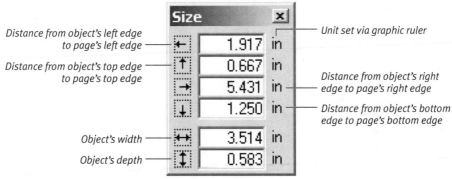

Distance from object's left edge to page's left edge

Distance from object's top edge to page's top edge

Unit set via graphic ruler

Distance from object's right edge to page's right edge

Distance from object's bottom edge to page's bottom edge

Object's width

Object's depth

Figure 11.28 The Size Palette provides details on the position—and dimensions—of a selected object.

Changing ruler and grid units

FileMaker lets you set the ruler and grid to measure the layout and its items in inches, pixels, or centimeters.

To change ruler and grid units:

1. To change the units, choose Layouts > Set Rulers (**Figure 11.29**).

2. The Set Rulers dialog box includes two pop-down menus (**Figure 11.30**). The top one sets the *Units* used by the Graphic rulers, Ruler lines, the Object Grids, and the Size Palette. The second pop-down menu, *Grid Spacing*, controls the fineness of the Object Grids' mesh of horizontal and vertical lines. Make your adjustments to one or both pop-down menus and click *OK*.

Figure 11.29 Choose Layouts > Set Rulers to adjust the measurement units of Graphic rulers, Ruler lines, the Object Grids, and the Size Palette.

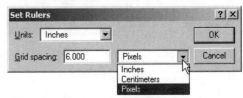

Figure 11.30 The Set Rulers dialog box includes two pop-down menus: one for ruler units and one for controlling the fineness of the Object Grids' mesh.

FORMATTING AND GRAPHICS IN LAYOUTS

12

Once you've done the basic construction for a layout—the parts, fields, and objects covered in the previous chapter—you're ready to start the formatting and graphics detailing that will make your database visually inviting. Whether it's choosing suitable fonts or adding a color graphic, this often time-consuming work can spell the difference between a so-so database that's little used or a professional-grade product with immediate appeal.

Working with Text

Quite often you'll find yourself working with text in a two-step process: You'll add text for the information it provides and then later go back to style the text by choosing special fonts or colors. This section deals with the first step. For information on styling *individual* blocks of text, see *Formatting Fields or Objects* on page 181. To set *database-wide* text defaults, see *To set formatting defaults* on page 178.

To add text to a layout:

1. Make sure you're in Layout mode ([Ctrl][L] in Windows, [⌘][L] on the Mac), then click the Text tool in the left-hand status area (**Figure 12.1**).

2. Click in the layout where you want the text and start typing. An I-beam cursor marks your progress (**Figure 12.2**).

✔ Tip

■ Because creating a text label for a field has no effect on the actual field name, you can create different labels in different layouts for the same field. The sales force, for example, may have an in-house name for something that the accounting folks call something else entirely. By creating a sales layout and an accounting layout—each with its own labels—everyone's happy, even though the field's *actual* name remains the same.

Figure 12.1 Click on the Text tool in the Layout status area to add text.

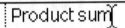

Figure 12.2 An I-beam cursor marks your text-insertion spot.

To select text:

1. In either Layout mode (Ctrl L in Windows, ⌘ L on the Mac) or Browse mode (Ctrl B in Windows, ⌘ B on the Mac), click on the text you want to select. If you want to select an entire word, double-click. To select a full line of text, triple-click on it.

2. Once you've selected the text, you can:

   ◆ Delete it (press Delete).

   ◆ Cut it for pasting elsewhere (Ctrl X in Windows, ⌘ X on the Mac).

   ◆ Replace it with other text (type in the new text or paste selected text from elsewhere).

   ◆ Change its attributes, such as its font, size, or style (see following pages).

SELECTING TEXT

Setting Format Defaults

Default formats apply to fields and objects across the *entire* database. (To set attributes for *individual* fields and objects, see *Formatting Fields or Objects*, on page 181.) At times, you may want to set format defaults up front to save you the bother of formatting every time you create a new field. Other times, setting formats field by field may be exactly what you want to do. FileMaker, as usual, lets you do either.

Setting some basic *database-wide* defaults early on, however, gives you a foundation to build on. As you work along and find you want to change the format for an *individual* field or object differently, you can then use specific choices within the Format menu (**Figure 12.3**).

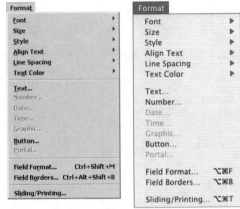

Figure 12.3 Depending on what you've selected, you can use the Format menu to set individual fields or database-wide defaults.

To set formatting defaults:

1. Make sure you're in Layout mode (Ctrl L in Windows, ⌘L on the Mac) with *nothing* selected (otherwise some of the Format menu's choices will be unavailable, signified by them being grayed out).

2. Under the Format menu, choose any of the five middle items (Text, Number, Date, Time, Graphic) to set the default formatting. Examples of each of your selections will appear in that dialog box's sample area. (For information on Button and Portal, see pages 218 and 233.) Here's the rundown on each:

Figure 12.4 Use the Text Format dialog box to set the font, text size, color, and style. Click the *Paragraph* button to set text alignment, indents, and line spacing.

Figure 12.5 The Paragraph dialog box, reached via the Text Format dialog box, lets you set text alignment, indents, and line spacing.

![Default Number Format dialog box showing options: General format, Leave data formatted as entered, Format as Boolean, Format as decimal. Fixed number of decimal digits: 2. Use notation: Currency (leading). Currency symbol: $. Separators, Negative format as -1234. Sample: -$70,123.56]

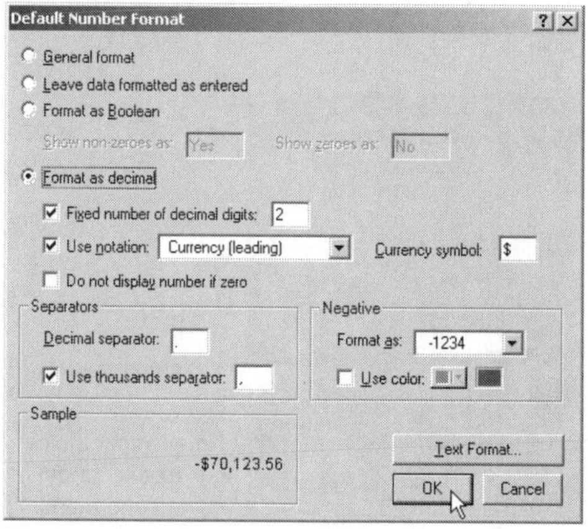

Figure 12.6 Use the Number Format dialog box to control the appearance of field numbers.

Text Format: With this dialog box (**Figure 12.4**), you can set the default *Font*, *Size*, *Color*, and *Style*. By clicking on the lower-left *Paragraph* button, you'll reach the Paragraph dialog box (**Figure 12.5**) where you can set the default alignment, indents, and line spacing for text. Finally, by clicking on the *Tabs* button in the Paragraph dialog box, you'll reach the Tabs dialog box. See *To set text tabs* on page 182.

Number Format: Within this dialog box (**Figure 12.6**), you can set the default to *General Format*, *Leave data formatted as entered*, *Format as Boolean* (Yes-No, True-False), plus control how many decimals you want showing, set a currency symbol to precede numbers (an unlikely database-wide choice unless every number field in the database deals with money), what sort of decimal separator you want (if any), and how negative numbers are displayed. The lower-right *Text Format* button, by the way, takes you back to the Text Format dialog box. Sorry, you can't use it to set a different font for numbers only: If you go back and change the text settings, they'll change in all default fields.

(continued)

Date Format: Within this dialog box (top, **Figure 12.7**), you can choose to *Leave date formatted as entered*, *Format as* (with six different date formatting options) (**Figure 12.8**), or click the *Custom* radio button to reach still more choices (bottom, **Figure 12.7**).

Time Format: Within this dialog box (**Figure 12.9**), you've got another zillion choices on time formats. Who knew there were so many?

Graphic Format: Within this dialog box (**Figure 12.10**), you can use the three pop-up menus to control how graphics are cropped and fitted within your field's frame. Use the *Sample* window to see how the various options will be displayed.

3. When you're done making your default choices, click *OK*. Repeat to set other format defaults.

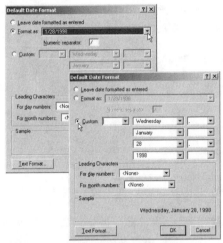

Figure 12.7 Use the Date Format dialog box to choose six standard options (top) or click *Custom* for even more choices (bottom).

Figure 12.8 The *Format as* pop-up menu offers six date format choices.

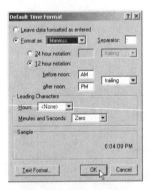

Figure 12.9 Use the Time Format dialog box to select from a myriad of options.

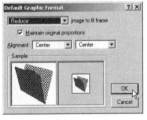

Figure 12.10 Use the Graphic Format dialog box to control cropping and fitting. The sample window previews the options.

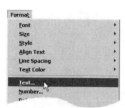

Figure 12.11 Choose Format > Text to reach the Text Format dialog box.

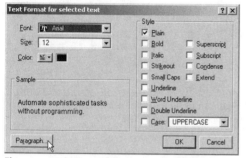

Figure 12.12 The Text Format dialog box lets you set multiple text attributes, including paragraph formatting via the lower-left button.

Figure 12.13 The Paragraph dialog box lets you set text alignment, indentation, and line spacing.

Figure 12.14 Use the Text Formatting toolbar for quick access to most of the text formatting controls.

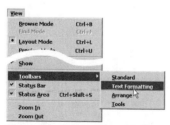

Figure 12.15 Choose View > Toolbars > Text Formatting to turn on the Text Formatting toolbar.

Formatting Fields or Objects

This section shows you how to change *individual* fields or objects. If you're looking to set format defaults for the entire database, see *To set formatting defaults*, on page 178.)

You can, by the way, format several fields at the same time—as long as you're setting the same attribute in each field, such as text.

Setting multiple text attributes

This approach can save you time if you want to change, say, a font's size and style at the same time.

To set several text attributes at once:

1. Select your text and choose Format > Text (**Figure 12.11**).

2. When the Text Format dialog box appears (**Figure 12.12**), use the drop-down menus to select the *Font, Size, Color*, and *Style* of your text. To set the alignment, indentation, or line spacing of text, click the *Paragraph* button in the lower left.

3. Once the Paragraph dialog box appears (**Figure 12.13**), you can set the text *Alignment, Indent*, and *Line Spacing*.

4. When you're done, click *OK*.

✔ Tip

■ It's often quicker to format text via the Text Formatting toolbar (**Figure 12.14**). Just choose View > Toolbars > Text Formatting (**Figure 12.15**).

To set text tabs:

1. Select the text for which you want to set tabs and choose Format > Text (**Figure 12.11**).

2. When the Text Format dialog box appears (**Figure 12.12**), click the *Paragraph* button in the lower left. When the Paragraph dialog box appears (**Figure 12.13**), click the *Tabs* button.

3. When the Tabs dialog box appears (**Figure 12.16**), the current tab settings, if there are any, appear in the upper-left window. To change them, select one with your cursor and type in a new position number, and click *Set*.

   ◆ To create a new tab, choose a *Type* in the upper-right panel, type in the position number, and click *New*.

   ◆ To start over, click *Clear*.

   ◆ To set a decimal tab, click the *Align On* radio button. If you want to use something other than a period, type it into the adjacent entry box.

   ◆ Fill characters appear between tabbed items (usually dashes or periods). Type in your choice.

4. When you're done, click *OK*.

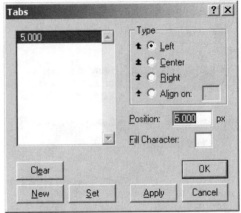

Figure 12.16 The Tabs dialog box lets you change existing tabs or create new ones.

Figure 12.17 Choose Format > Font to quickly apply any font to your selected text.

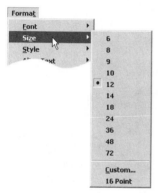

Figure 12.18
Choose Format > Size to gain quick access to all the point sizes in the current font.

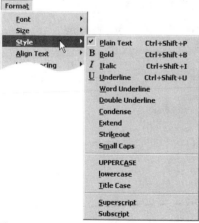

Figure 12.19 Choose Format > Style to change text you've selected.

To choose a font:

1. Select the text to which you want to apply another font. To select multiple fields or objects, just press (Shift) as you click on each field or object.

2. Choose Format > Font (**Figure 12.17**). When the drop-down menu of fonts appears, drag your cursor to the font you want and release the cursor. The selected text will change to the newly selected font.

To choose a text size:

1. Select the text or field containing text you want to change. To select multiple fields or objects, just press (Shift) as you click on each field or object.

2. Choose Format > Size (**Figure 12.18**). When the drop-down menu of text sizes appears, drag your cursor to the size you want and release the cursor. The selected text will change size.

To choose a text style:

1. Select the text or field containing text you want to change. To select multiple fields or objects, just press (Shift) as you click on each field or object.

2. Choose Format > Style (**Figure 12.19**). When the drop-down menu of text styles appears, drag your cursor to the style you want and release the cursor. Since text can have multiple styles (bold with italic with underline), continue using the drop-down menu until you've applied all the desired styles.

SETTING FONTS, TEXT SIZES, AND STYLES

To align text:

1. Select the text or field containing text you want to change. To select multiple fields or objects, just press (Shift) as you click on each field or object.

2. Choose Format > Align Text (**Figure 12.20**). When the drop-down menu of alignment choices appears, drag your cursor to the alignment you want and release the cursor. The alignment of the selected text will reflect your new choice.

To choose line spacing:

1. Select the text or field containing text you want to change. To select multiple fields or objects, just press (Shift) as you click on each field or object.

2. Choose Format > Line Spacing (**Figure 12.21**). When the drop-down menu of spacing choices appears, drag your cursor to the one you want and release the cursor.

   If single or double line spacing won't do, choose Custom, which opens the Paragraph settings dialog box (**Figure 12.22**).

3. Use the Line Spacing section to set your line *Height* and the spacing *Above* and *Below* the line. The drop-down menus for each allow you to make your spacings based on the number of lines, inches, pixels, or centimeters.

4. Once you're ready, click *Apply*, then click *OK*.

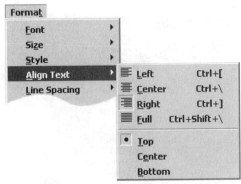

Figure 12.20 Choose Format > Align Text for quick access to alignment options without having to open a dialog box.

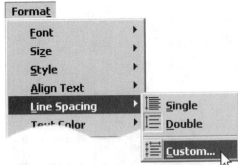

Figure 12.21 Choose Format > Line Spacing to apply single, double, or custom spacing.

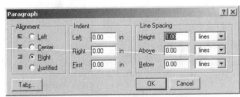

Figure 12.22 Custom line spacing is handled within the Paragraph dialog box.

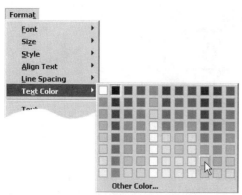

Figure 12.23 Choose Format > Text Color to quickly apply color to selected text.

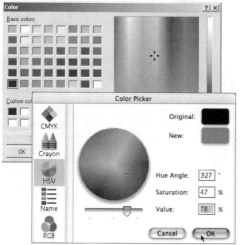

Figure 12.24 Use Windows' Color dialog box (top) or the Mac's Color Picker (bottom) to choose a custom text color.

To choose a text color:

1. Select the text or field containing text you want to change. To select multiple fields or objects, just press (Shift) as you click on each field or object.

2. Choose Format > Text Color (**Figure 12.23**). When the drop-down menu of colors appears, drag your cursor to the one you want, and release the cursor. The text will change to the color you've chosen.

✔ Tip

■ If you want to use a custom color, choose *Other Color* in step 2, and use the dialog boxes that appear to pick your color (**Figure 12.24**). When you're done, click *OK* and the new color will be applied.

To format a number field:

1. Make sure the field you want to format is, in fact, a number-type field. (You can check via the Define Fields dialog box: Ctrl Shift D in Windows, Shift ⌘ D on the Mac.)

2. Choose Format > Number (**Figure 12.25**), which will open the Number Format dialog box (**Figure 12.26**).

3. Make your choices (for specifics on the dialog box, see step 2 of *To set formatting defaults*, on page 178). Click *OK*.

Figure 12.25 To format a number-type field only, choose Format > Number.

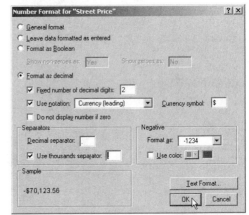

Figure 12.26 The Number Format dialog box's settings are applied to number fields you've selected or used to set *default* number settings if no field is selected.

Figure 12.27 To format a date-type field only, choose Format > Date.

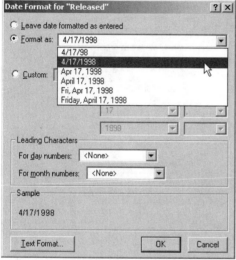

Figure 12.28 The Date Format dialog box's settings are applied to selected date fields or used to set *default* date settings if no field is selected.

To format a date field:

1. Make sure the field you want to format is a date-type field. You can do this by checking the Define Fields dialog box: [Ctrl][Shift][D] in Windows, [Shift][⌘][D] on the Mac.

2. Choose Format > Date (**Figure 12.27**), which will open the Date Format dialog box (**Figure 12.28**).

3. Make your choices (for specifics on the dialog box, see step 2 of *To set formatting defaults*, on page 178). Click *OK*.

✔ Tip

■ While the *Format as* pop-up menu still includes a two-digit year choice, it's best to use the four-digit year formats to avoid any Y2K problems.

To format a time field:

1. Make sure the field you want to format is a time-type field. You can do this by checking the Define Fields dialog box: Ctrl Shift D in Windows, Shift ⌘ D on the Mac.

2. Choose Format > Time (**Figure 12.29**), which will open the Time Format dialog box (**Figure 12.30**).

3. Make your choices (for specifics on the dialog box, see step 2 of *To set formatting defaults*, on page 178). Click *OK*.

Figure 12.29 To format a time-type field only, choose Format > Time.

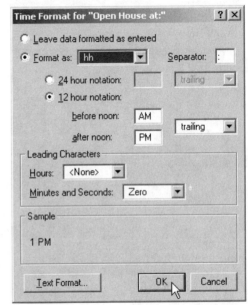

Figure 12.30 The Time Format dialog box's settings are applied to selected time fields or used to set *default* time settings if no field is selected.

Figure 12.31 To format a container-type field only, choose Format > Graphic.

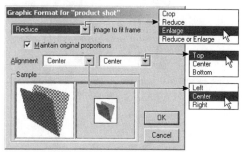

Figure 12.32 The Graphic Format dialog box's settings are applied to selected graphics or used to set *default* graphic settings if no field is selected.

To format a graphic field:

1. Make sure the field you want to format is a container-type field, which is the only kind that can accept a graphic (see page 100). You can do this by checking the Define Fields dialog box: Ctrl Shift D in Windows, Shift ⌘ D on the Mac.

2. Choose Format > Graphic (**Figure 12.31**), which will open the Graphic Format dialog box (**Figure 12.32**).

3. Make your choices, using the three pop-up menus to control the placement of the graphic within its field, then click *OK*.

Working with Graphics

The Layout status area includes a powerful collection of tools for adding graphic interest and emphasis to your layouts (**Figure 12.33**).

Pointer Tool: Use this tool to select or resize fields and objects.

Text Tool: Though it's nestled amid the draw tools, this tool's really for, well, text. See *Working with Text* on page 176 for more information.

Line Tool: Use this tool with the Pen Tools to create lines of varying width, color, and pattern.

Shape Tools (rectangle, rounded rectangle, oval): Use the three tools with the Fill Tools to create shapes of varying colors and patterns. Also see *To change the stack order of objects* on page 167 for information on how to arrange overlapping shapes.

Button, Portal Tools: Buttons are used to trigger scripts and, so, are covered in *Using Templates and Scripts*, on page 199. Portals are views of data from other databases and, so, are covered in *Creating Relational Databases*, on page 221.

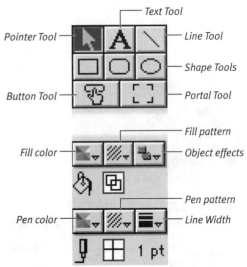

Figure 12.33 The Layout mode's status area contains drawing, fill, and pen tools for adding graphic impact to your layouts.

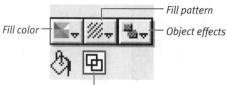

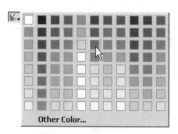

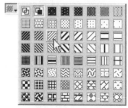

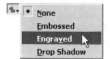

Figure 12.34 The Fill Tools control colors and patterns for shapes.

Figure 12.35 Use the drop-down menus to reach the fill colors, patterns, and effects.

Fill Tools (color, pattern, object effects): Use these three tools (**Figure 12.34**) with the Shape Tools. Each offers a variety of choices via their drop-down menus (**Figure 12.35**). The Objects Effects tool lets you easily add some visual flourishes previously confined to full-fledged graphics programs.

Pen Tools (color, pattern, line width): Use this trio of tools (**Figure 12.36**) with the Line Tool. Like the Fill Tools, these three tools operate via drop-down menus (**Figure 12.37**).

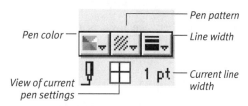

Figure 12.36 The Pen Tools control line colors, patterns, and widths.

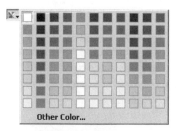

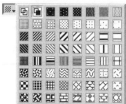

Figure 12.37 Use the drop-down menus to choose line colors, patterns, and widths.

WORKING WITH GRAPHICS

191

To select a drawing tool:

◆ Switch to Layout mode ([Ctrl][L] in Windows, [⌘][L] on the Mac), then click on the tool of your choice. When it's active, it will become gray (left in **Figure 12.38**).

✔ Tips

■ It's easy to accidentally unselect a tool. To keep it selected until you deliberately click on another tool, double-click the tool. It will become black to indicate it's locked on (right in **Figure 12.38**).

■ To toggle between any tool and the Pointer tool, press [Enter] (the one by the numeric keypad).

To draw an object:

1. Switch to Layout mode ([Ctrl][L] in Windows, [⌘][L] on the Mac), then click on the drawing tool of your choice: Line, Rectangle, Rounded Rectangle, or Oval.

2. Click with your cursor where you want the shape to begin and drag the cursor to where you want the shape to end. See **Table 12.1**, *FileMaker's Object Drawing Tools*, for more details.

Figure 12.38 When a tool's selected it becomes gray (left); when it's selected and locked it becomes black (right).

Table 12.1

FileMaker's Object Drawing Tools		
Tool Icon **Shape**	**Action**	
 Line	Select Line Tool, click on start point, and press cursor until end point reached.	
Horizontal, vertical, or 45-degree line	Select Line Tool. Press [Alt] (Windows) or [Option] (Mac) while clicking on start point, and dragging cursor until end point reached.	
▭ Rectangle	Select Rectangle Tool. Click on start point and drag cursor until rectangle is the size you want.	
Square	Select Rectangle Tool. Press [Alt] (Windows) or [Option] (Mac) while clicking on start point, and dragging cursor until square is the size you want.	
▢ Rounded rectangle	Select Rounded Rectangle Tool. Click on start point and drag cursor until rectangle is the size you want.	
⬭ Oval	Select Oval Tool. Click on start point and drag cursor until oval is the size you want.	
Circle	Select Oval Tool. Press [Alt] (Windows) or [Option] (Mac) while clicking on start point, and dragging cursor until circle is the size you want.	

DRAWING OBJECTS

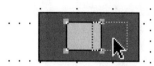

Figure 12.39 To move an object, click on it with the Pointer Tool and drag it. A dotted outline marks your progress.

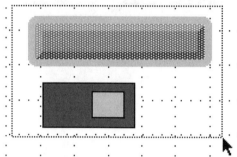

Figure 12.40 Click and drag the Pointer Tool to select multiple objects.

To select and move an object:

1. Make sure you're in Layout mode (Ctrl L in Windows, ⌘L on the Mac), then click on the object. To select multiple objects, hold down Shift before clicking on the objects.

2. Small squares will appear on each corner of the object to let you know it's been selected. Continue holding down your cursor and drag the object where you want it. A dotted outline of the object will mark your movement until you release the cursor (**Figure 12.39**).

✔ Tips

- You also can select multiple objects with the Pointer Tool by pressing and holding down the cursor, then dragging the resulting square to include the objects (**Figure 12.40**).

- To select everything in a layout, use the Select All keyboard command (Ctrl A in Windows, ⌘A on the Mac).

SELECTING AND MOVING OBJECTS

To deselect an object:

◆ Simply click your cursor anywhere within the layout or select a tool other than the Pointer Tool within the tool palette.

To resize an object:

1. Select the Pointer Tool, then click on the object.

2. Handles (small black squares) will appear at the object's corners. Click on any handle and drag it to reshape the object. A dotted outline of the object's new shape will mark your movement until you release the cursor (**Figure 12.41**).

✔ Tip

■ If you want more precision in resizing an object (such as making its size identical to other objects), use the Size palette: Click on the object, then choose View > Object Size, and use the palette to enter measurements for the object. When done, press [Enter] in Windows, [Return] on the Mac. The selected object will assume the sizing you entered.

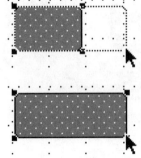

Figure 12.41 To resize an object, grab on the corner handles and drag until it reaches the size you want. A dotted outline marks your progress.

DESELECTING AND RESIZING OBJECTS

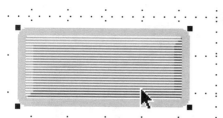

Figure 12.42 To change an object's pattern, first select it with the Pointer Tool.

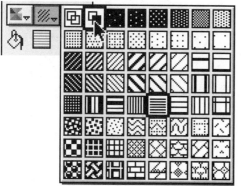

Figure 12.43 Use the Fill Tool's pattern drop-down menu to select a new pattern. The arrow marks the new solid choice; the dark box marks the previous pattern.

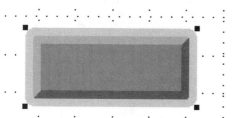

Figure 12.44 The object with its new solid pattern.

Changing fill colors, patterns, and effects

Setting a fill color, pattern, or effect is like setting a default: You start by making sure *nothing* is selected.

To set or change an object's fill color, pattern, or effect:

1. To change an object's *existing* fill color or pattern, select the object using the Pointer Tool (**Figure 12.42**).

2. Now click on one of the Fill tools to select a color, pattern, or effect (**Figure 12.43**).

3. When the tool's drop-down menu appears, drag your cursor to the choice you want and release the cursor. The fill will be applied to the object (**Figure 12.44**).

✔ Tip

- If you want to start all over on the pattern, select the object and then click the transparent pattern, found in the upper-left corner of the pop-down choices.

Changing lines

Setting the pen color, pattern, or width is like setting a default: You start by making sure nothing is selected.

To set or change line color, pattern, or width:

1. To change an existing line, select it using the Pointer Tool (**Figure 12.45**).

2. Now click on any of the Pen tools that control color, pattern, or line width (**Figure 12.46**).

3. When the tool's drop-down menu appears, drag your cursor to the line style choice you want and release the cursor. The selected line will change to reflect your choice (**Figure 12.47**).

✔ Tip

■ Use the pen color to change the border color of objects (fields use a separate process, see *To set or change field borders, fills, and baselines* on the next page). Just select the object and click the pen color drop-down menu to make your choice.

Figure 12.45 To change a line's width, first select it with the Pointer Tool.

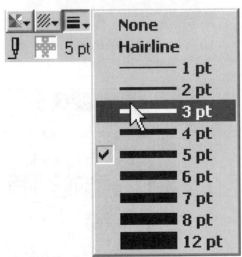

Figure 12.46 Use the Pen Tool's line-width drop-down menu to select a new line width. The check marks the previous line width.

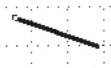

Figure 12.47 After using the drop-down menu, the line assumes its new, sleek look.

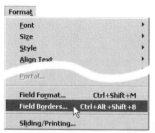

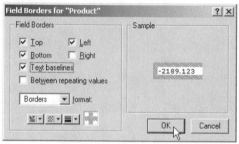

Figure 12.48 The Field Borders command under the Format menu is only available for fields, not objects.

Figure 12.49 When the Field Borders dialog box first opens, the lower-left drop-down menu is already set to *Borders*.

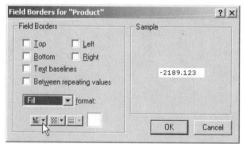

Figure 12.50 Choose *Fill* from the Field Borders dialog box's drop-down menu to control field color and pattern.

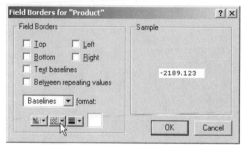

Figure 12.51 Choose *Baselines* from the Field Borders dialog box's drop-down menu to control the baseline pattern and weight.

Changing borders, fills, and baselines

To set the defaults for field borders, fills, or baselines, first make sure nothing is selected.

To set or change field borders, fills, and baselines:

1. To change an existing field's borders, fills, or baselines, first select it using the Pointer Tool. This procedure applies to fields only, not other objects.

2. Choose Format > Field Borders (**Figure 12.48**).

3. When the Field Borders dialog box appears (**Figure 12.49**), use the lower-left drop-down menu to set the borders, fill, or baselines.

   In setting field borders, the four upper-left boxes control the boundary around the field. The results of your choices appear in the upper-right *Sample* area. Checking *Text baselines* will place horizontal lines within fields containing multiple lines of text. Checking *Between repeating values* will separate repeating field entries with lines.

   In setting field fills (**Figure 12.50**), the action is down at the bottom left where two drop-down menus let you set the color and the pattern. In our example, we've selected a dark color, which is shown in the *Sample* area.

   In setting field baselines (**Figure 12.51**), your choices are confined to the three bottom drop-down menus: color, pattern, and line weight.

4. When you've made your choices, click *OK*.

Using Templates and Scripts

Why reinvent the wheel when FileMaker has rounded up a terrific collection of templates and predefined scripts for you? Templates can give you a quick start in creating records, fields, and layouts. Scripts take things another step by helping you automate many parts of the database process, from record entry to finding and sorting records, from dialing a modem to greeting users with personalized messages. Even if you choose to work from scratch, these templates and scripts contain a trove of ideas and inspiration.

Working with Templates

FileMaker comes with 16 templates–each with multiple layouts–that run the gamut: business cards, expense reports, purchase orders, field trip forms, memos, recipes—the list goes on.

If that's not easy enough, FileMaker comes with its own database, "Template Information," which contains brief descriptions of all the templates and suggestions on which templates best suit your purposes.

To review the available templates:

1. Choose File > New Database. When the New Database dialog box appears, click *Template Info* to see information about the available templates (**Figure 13.1**).

2. When the Template Information database's main screen appears, click *Templates* (**Figure 13.2**).

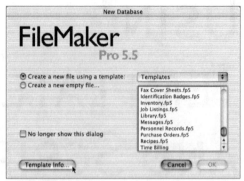

Figure 13.1 To see descriptions of FileMaker's templates, click *Template Info* in the New Database dialog box.

Figure 13.2 Click the *Templates* button when the Template Information database appears.

Figure 13.3 Scroll through the list of FileMaker's templates to find one that suits your needs.

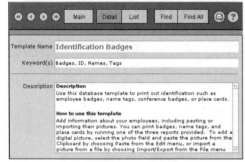

Figure 13.4 If the template isn't quite right for your needs, click the *List* button to resume your search.

3. When the list of FileMaker's templates appears (**Figure 13.3**), scroll through it for an appropriate template. (You can click the *Template Name* and *Keywords* tabs to resort how the list is displayed.)

4. Once you find a likely template in the list, click the arrow left of the template's name and a more detailed description will appear (**Figure 13.4**). If the template isn't quite right for your needs, click the *List* button and resume your search until you find one that works for you.

5. Once you find the appropriate template, click *Main*, which returns you to the Template Information database's main screen (**Figure 13.2**). Click the *New* button and when FileMaker's New Database dialog box appears (**Figure 13.1**), see step 2 of *To create a template-based file* on the next page.

To create a template-based file:

1. Choose File > New Database.

2. When the New Database dialog box appears, select *Create a new file using a template*, select the template you want to use from the right-side list, and click *OK* (**Figure 13.5**).

3. When the dialog box for creating a copy appears (**Figure 13.6**), navigate to the folder where you want to store the file. By default, FileMaker gives the file the same name as the original template but it'll be less confusing if you use a distinctive name. Click *Save*.

Figure 13.5 To create a template-based file, select *Create a new file using a template*, pick a template from the list, and click *OK*.

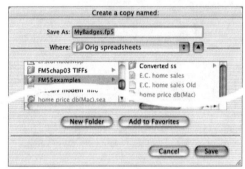

Figure 13.6 Use the create a copy dialog box to navigate to where you want to store the file and give it a distinctive name.

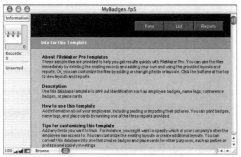

Figure 13.7 Template-based files automatically open to an Information layout that explains how to use the template.

Figure 13.8 Use the layout pop-up menu to choose the layout you want to use for the template-based file.

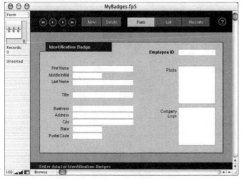

Figure 13.9 Once the template-based file appears, you're ready to start adding records (Ctrl)(N) in Windows, (⌘)(N) on the Mac).

4. A copy of the template appears, which FileMaker automatically opens in an Information layout that explains how to best use the template (**Figure 13.7**).

5. Use the layout pop-up menu to choose the layout you want to use (**Figure 13.8**).

6. When the layout appears (**Figure 13.9**), you're ready to create your first record by choosing Records > New Record ((Ctrl)(N) in Windows, (⌘)(N) on the Mac).

✔ Tip

- Once you create a template-based file, use the book's various chapters—particularly *Creating Layouts* on page 129 and *Formatting and Graphics in Layouts* on page 175—to further customize the template.

WORKING WITH TEMPLATES

Working with Scripts

Creating a script is a lot like designing a database: The more you plan it out in advance, the smoother the actual construction will go.

Running a script simply triggers a series of automatic commands that you've strung together. A script can be a one-step task such as opening a record, or it can involve a cascade of actions that would take a person much longer to do manually. By automating certain tasks, scripts can reduce the chance of data-entry errors and ease the demands on those less comfortable with databases in general. To make scripts even easier to use, you can link them to buttons placed within different layouts (see *Using Buttons with Scripts* on page 216).

In planning a script, break the task you want to perform into the smallest pieces possible. These pieces, what FileMaker calls *steps*, are easier to build than a long, single script. With this modular approach, you can recombine the steps into other scripts later on. FileMaker contains many pre-defined scripts, reducing the need for you to generate a step from scratch. FileMaker 5.5 includes four new script steps: Open Hosts, Allow Toolbars, Set Next Serial Value, and Execute SQL. You'll find the Execute SQL step particularly useful in querying enterprise-level databases. Take a look at the complete list of FileMaker's scripting steps in *Script Commands* on page 315.

Remember as well that a script need not be entirely automatic. For example, inserting pauses into a script can let users enter data at particular points and resume the script when they're ready.

Figure 13.10 Use the Define Scripts dialog box to create, rename, edit, duplicate, delete, import, print out, and perform (test) scripts.

Most of FileMaker's scripting steps are used within just two dialog boxes. The Define Scripts dialog box is where you create (name), rename, edit, duplicate, import, print out, and delete scripts, as well as test them (**Figure 13.10**). All available script steps are listed within the Script Definition dialog box, which is where you build a script once you name it (**Figure 13.11**).

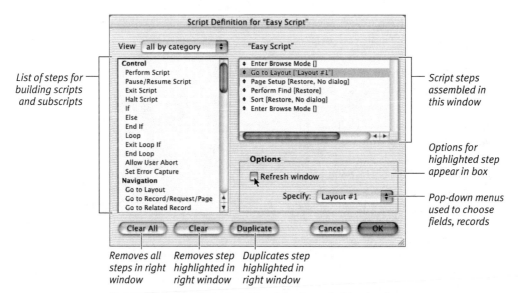

List of steps for building scripts and subscripts

Script steps assembled in this window

Options for highlighted step appear in box

Pop-down menus used to choose fields, records

Removes all steps in right window

Removes step highlighted in right window

Duplicates step highlighted in right window

Figure 13.11 Use the Script Definition dialog box to build scripts by selecting script steps on the left-hand list and building your script in the right-hand window.

Preparing to create a script

When you begin defining a script, you'll find that FileMaker has saved some of the open database's current settings, if they exist, and included them in the Script Definition dialog box. For that reason, it's best to select such things as the file's layout, view, and sort order *before* you define a script for it. FileMaker calls this storing pre-script settings. Mind you, you don't have to do this, but it saves you some scripting work.

To create a file's pre-script settings:

1. Open the file for which you want to create a script.

2. Now, set up your file to reflect how you want the script to handle each of these items:

   Layout: Use the layout pop-up window above the flipbook to choose which layout you'll be using in the script.

   View: Use the View menu to place your database in the mode you'll be using in the script.

   Find Request: If you'll be building a script that needs to use a particular found set of records, go ahead and set up the appropriate Find Request (Ctrl F in Windows, ⌘ F on the Mac). You need not actually run the Find, just specify the Find Request.

   Sort Order: If your script will depend on a particular sort, switch to Browse and set up the sort (Ctrl S in Windows, ⌘ S on the Mac). You don't need to run the sort, just set it up.

Figure 13.12 To create or change any script, choose Scripts > ScriptMaker.

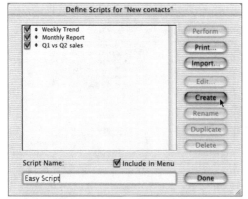

Figure 13.13 When the Define Scripts dialog box appears, give your planned script a distinctive name and click *Create*.

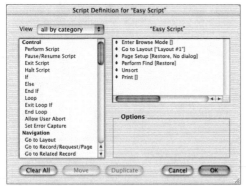

Figure 13.14 The pre-script settings will appear on the right side of the Script Definition dialog box.

Print/Page Setup and **Print Options:** If your script will depend on specific print settings, choose File > Print Setup. You need not actually print the file, just specify the setup. If you want the script to include any specific print options, such as the number of copies, choose File > Print (Ctrl P in Windows, ⌘ P on the Mac) and select those options.

Import/Export Order: If your script involves either importing or exporting data, you'll want to set the order of the fields. Choose File > Import/Export and make your choices in the related Field Mapping and Field Order dialog boxes.

3. When you're done setting up these items for the file, choose Scripts > ScriptMaker (**Figure 13.12**).

4. When the Define Scripts dialog box appears, type in a name for the script you'll be creating, and click *Create* (**Figure 13.13**).

5. The Script Definition dialog box will appear with all of the file's pre-script settings (**Figure 13.14**). You can click *OK* to close the dialog box, then click *Done* when the Define Scripts dialog box reappears, and define the rest of the script later.

Or you can start the real work of creating a script by staying in the Script Definition dialog box and jumping straight to step 3 of *To define a script* on the next page.

PREPARING TO CREATE A SCRIPT

To define a script:

1. Open the file for which you want to define a script and choose Scripts > ScriptMaker (**Figure 13.15**).

2. When the Define Scripts dialog box appears, type in a name for your new script and click *Create* (**Figure 13.13**).

3. When the Script Definition dialog box appears, any pre-script settings will be listed in the right-side window (**Figure 13.14**). (For details see *To create a file's pre-script settings* on page 206.) Delete any settings you don't need for the script by selecting each and then clicking *Clear* (**Figure 13.16**).

Figure 13.15 To define a script, choose Scripts > ScriptMaker.

Figure 13.16 Get rid of settings you don't need for the script by highlighting each and clicking *Clear*.

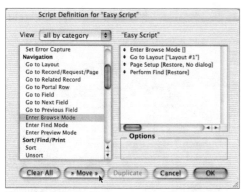

Figure 13.17 Highlight steps you want to add to the script and click *Move*.

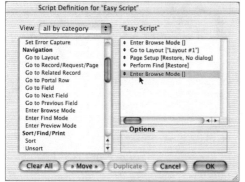

Figure 13.18 After you click *Move*, the steps will be added to those listed in the right-hand window.

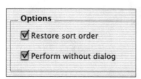

Figure 13.19 If an available step has options, use the *Options* panel's checkboxes to make your choices.

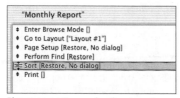

Figure 13.20 To reorder the steps in a script, click the double-arrow next to the script name and drag it up or down.

4. Look in the dialog box's left-hand list of script steps, click to highlight the first step you want to add, and click *Move* (**Figure 13.17**). The step will be added to the script's steps in the right-hand list (**Figure 13.18**).

   If there are any, set the added step's options in the lower-right *Options* panel (**Figure 13.19**). For a complete list of script steps and their uses, see *Script Commands* on page 315.

5. Repeat step 4 until you've added all the scripting steps you need.

6. If you need to reorder the steps in the right-side list, highlight a step and use the double-arrow next to the script name to drag it to another spot in the list (**Figure 13.20**).

(continued)

7. When you're done working in the Script Definition dialog box, click *OK*.

8. If you included any pre-script settings in your script—and have since changed those settings—a dialog box will appear asking whether you want to keep the original settings or replace them with the settings now in use (**Figure 13.21**). Make your choice among the radio buttons and click *OK*.

9. The script is now listed in the Define Scripts dialog box. If you want to test whether your new script runs correctly, click *Perform* to see if the scripting actions play out as you desire (**Figure 13.22**).

10. If you're happy with the script, click *Done*. If your script needs more work, click *Edit* and see *To change a script* on the next page. After you click *Done*, your new script is available under the Scripts menu (**Figure 13.23**). To run the script just select it with your cursor.

✔ Tip

■ To make it easier to find the script step you want to use in the Script Definition dialog box (**Figure 13.14**), use the *View* pop-up menu to show only a specific category of scripts (**Figure 13.24**).

Figure 13.21 If your script changes predefined settings, a dialog box will ask whether to keep or replace them.

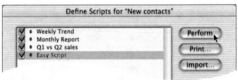

Figure 13.22 To test whether your new script works correctly, click *Perform* in the Define Scripts dialog box.

Figure 13.23 After you've finished building a script, it appears under the Scripts menu.

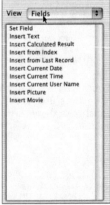

Figure 13.24 To reduce the clutter in the Script Definition dialog box (left), use the *View* pop-up menu to select a specific category of script steps (right).

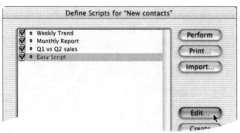

Figure 13.25 Select the script you want to change and click *Edit*.

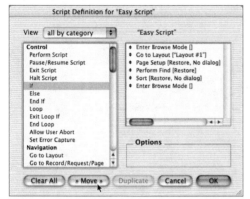

Figure 13.26 Select in the left-hand list any script steps you want to add and click *Move*.

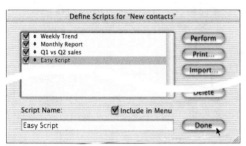

Figure 13.27 Once you've finished changing the script, click *Done*.

To change a script:

1. Choose Scripts > ScriptMaker.

2. When the Define Scripts dialog box appears, select the script you want to change, and click *Edit* (**Figure 13.25**).

3. When the Script Definition dialog box appears, select in the right-hand window any script steps you want to delete and click *Clear* (**Figure 13.16**).

4. Select in the left-hand window any script steps you want to add and click *Move* (**Figure 13.26**). If necessary, rearrange the order of the steps.

5. When you're satisfied with the script, click *OK*. Again, if you included any pre-script settings in your script—and have since changed those settings—a dialog box will appear asking whether you want to keep the original settings or replace them with those now in use (**Figure 13.21**). Make your choice among the radio buttons and click *OK*.

6. When the Define Scripts dialog box reappears, click *Done* (**Figure 13.27**). Your changed script now is available under the Scripts menu.

CHANGING SCRIPTS

To copy a script:

1. Choose Scripts > ScriptMaker.

2. When the Define Scripts dialog box appears, select the script you want to copy, and click *Duplicate* (**Figure 13.28**).

3. If you want to give the copy a distinctive name, type it into the *Script Name* text window, and click *Rename* (**Figure 13.29**). The new name will be applied to the duplicate (**Figure 13.30**). If you're finished, click *Done* or, if you want to change the script, click *Edit*.

✔ Tip

■ If you just want to rename an existing script, skip step 2.

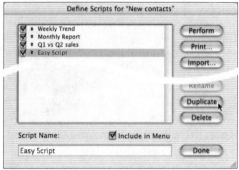

Figure 13.28 Select the script you want to copy and click *Duplicate*.

Figure 13.29 Once you've given the duplicated script a distinctive name, click *Rename*.

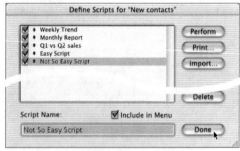

Figure 13.30 The renamed script is added to the Define Scripts dialog box.

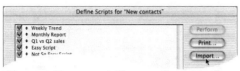

Figure 13.31 To use a script from *another* database, click *Import*.

Figure 13.32 The Import Scripts dialog box lists all the scripts existing in the other database (left). Check one and click *OK* (right).

Figure 13.33 Once the imported script appears in the Define Scripts dialog box, you can click *Edit* to fine-tune it for the new database.

Importing a script

Prior to FileMaker 5, you could only duplicate scripts created within the particular file you were working on. FileMaker now lets you import a script from another file, in effect letting you duplicate scripts created in other databases.

To import a script:

1. Choose Scripts > ScriptMaker.

2. When the Define Scripts dialog box appears, click *Import* (**Figure 13.31**).

3. When the Open File dialog box appears, navigate to the FileMaker database that contains the script you want to use and click *Open*.

   When the Import Scripts dialog box appears, it will list all the scripts in that database (left, **Figure 13.32**).

4. Choose the checkbox next to the script you want to import and click *OK* (right, **Figure 13.32**). The script will appear in the Define Scripts dialog box (**Figure 13.33**), where you can then click *Edit* to tweak it to work in the new database.

✔ Tip

■ Any scripts you import probably include references to fields or layouts in the original file—which won't work in the new file. To avoid any problems, make sure to update any field references in the imported script once you bring it into the new file.

To delete a script:

1. Choose Scripts > ScriptMaker.

2. When the Define Scripts dialog box appears, highlight the existing script you want to delete and click *Delete* (**Figure 13.34**).

3. Since this step cannot be undone, a warning dialog box will appear (**Figure 13.35**). If you're sure you want to delete the script, click *Delete*. The script will be deleted from the list in the Define Scripts dialog box.

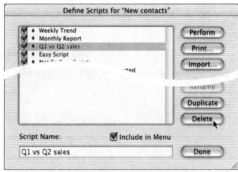

Figure 13.34 To eliminate a script, highlight it in the Define Scripts dialog box and click *Delete*.

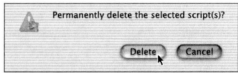

Figure 13.35 Since deleting a script cannot be undone, a warning dialog box appears to let you reconsider.

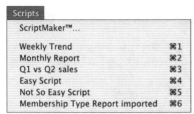

Figure 13.36 Up to 10 scripts listed within the Scripts menu can be assigned keyboard shortcuts.

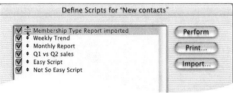

Figure 13.37 To reorder the Scripts menu listings, click and drag in the Define Scripts dialog box.

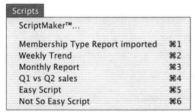

Figure 13.38 After you've rearranged the script order, the Scripts menu will reflect the changes.

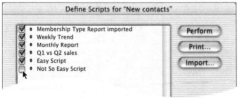

Figure 13.39 Use the checkboxes to control which scripts appear under the Scripts menu.

Reordering script shortcuts

The first 10 scripts listed under the Scripts menu automatically receive keyboard shortcuts ([Ctrl] 1–10 in Windows, [⌘]1–10 on the Mac) (**Figure 13.36**).

To reorder or change the script menu list:

1. To reassign script shortcuts, choose Scripts > ScriptMaker.

2. When the Define Scripts dialog box appears, drag the listed scripts up or down in the order by click-dragging the double-arrows just left of each script (**Figure 13.37**).

3. Once you've fully ordered the list, click *Done* in the Define Scripts dialog box. The Scripts menu will reflect the new order (**Figure 13.38**).

✔ Tip

- You also can shorten the Scripts menu list by toggling off the checkmark next to a script in the Define Scripts dialog box (**Figure 13.39**).

Using Buttons with Scripts

Some folks find the whole notion of scripts intimidating. But put a clearly labeled, script-linked button in a layout and the message is clear: "Click me."

To define a button:

1. Once you've defined a script, switch to Layout mode (Ctrl L in Windows, ⌘ L on the Mac) and select a layout via the pop-up menu just above the flipbook icon.

2. Click the Button Tool within the Layout status area (**Figure 13.40**), then use your cursor to draw a button within the layout. Release the cursor when the button reaches the size you want (**Figure 13.41**).

3. When the Specify Button dialog appears, select a script step from the left-hand list (**Figure 13.42**). Set options for the script step, if any, using the *Specify* pop-up menu in the *Options* panel. Not every step will offer the same options, and steps grayed out in the list don't apply to your particular button.

   or

   If you want to use a script step of your own that you've already defined, select *Perform Script* from the *Control* portion of the left-hand list, then use the *Specify* pop-up menu in the *Options* panel to select your step (**Figure 13.43**).

4. If you do not want the script step applied immediately, use the second pop-up menu in the *Options* panel to select another state: *Halt*, *Exit*, *Resume*, or *Pause* (**Figure 13.44**).

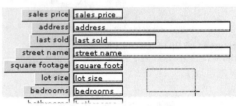

Figure 13.40 Click the Button Tool to add a script-linked button to a layout.

Figure 13.41 Click and drag the cursor in the layout to create a button.

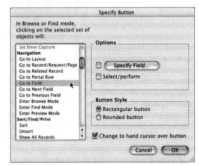

Figure 13.42 Use the Specify Button dialog box to assign a script and shape to the button.

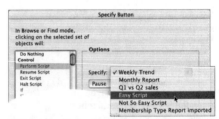

Figure 13.43 To assign one of your own scripts to a button, select *Perform Script* from the left-hand list and use the *Specify* pop-up menu.

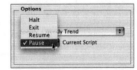

Figure 13.44 If you do not want a script step applied immediately, use the second pop-up menu in the *Options* panel to select one of four other states.

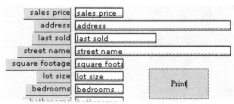

Figure 13.45 When the layout reappears with the new button, type in a label so its function is clear.

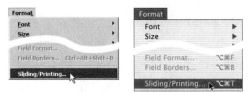

Figure 13.46 To control whether a button appears on printouts, choose Format > Sliding/Printing.

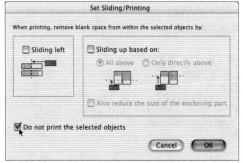

Figure 13.47 Use the lower-left checkbox in the Set Sliding/Printing dialog box to keep buttons from cluttering up printouts.

Figure 13.48 The Specify Button dialog box (top) offers the option of having the cursor switch to a hand when moved over buttons (bottom).

5. Click *OK* to close the Specify Button dialog box.

6. When the layout reappears with the new button, type in a label for it at the I-beam cursor (**Figure 13.45**). When you're done, press [Enter] on the *numeric* keypad. You can now format the button's appearance or switch to Browse mode ([Ctrl][B] in Windows, [⌘][B] on the Mac) and your button's ready for action. See *To set or change a button's appearance* on the next page.

✔ Tips

- The difference between *Halt* and *Pause* (**Figure 13.44**) in controlling a script is small but crucial. *Halt* stops *all* scripts, no matter what level they're running at. *Pause* only pauses the specific script containing that step, which means if it's inside a subscript, the higher-level scripts continue to run.

- Generally, you don't want buttons to appear on printouts, so switch to Layout mode and select the button. Choose Format > Sliding/Printing (**Figure 13.46**). In the Set Sliding/Printing dialog box, check *Do not print the selected objects* and click *OK* (**Figure 13.47**).

- To more closely mimic the standard Web browsing interface, FileMaker now gives you the option of having the cursor switch to a hand when moved over buttons. In step 3, you'll find the checkbox just below the *Button Style* panel in the Specify Button dialog box (**Figure 13.48**).

Setting a button's appearance

Once you've created a button for a script, you still need to format its appearance. Here are a few steps that apply particularly to buttons. For more information, see *Formatting and Graphics in Layouts* on page 175.

To set or change a button's appearance:

1. Switch to Layout mode (Ctrl L in Windows, ⌘ L on the Mac) and click on the button with the Pointer Tool (**Figure 13.49**).

2. To change the button's font, text size, or text color, choose Format and select the appropriate option in the menu's top half (**Figure 13.50**).

3. To change the button's border color, pattern, or width, select one of the Pen Tools (color, pattern, or line width) from the status area and use the related pop-up menu to change the button as desired.

4. To change the button's background color, pattern, or object effects, select one of the Fill Tools from the status area and use the related pop-up menu to change the button as desired. The object effects are particularly handy for giving a 3D look to buttons (**Figure 13.51**).

5. When you're satisfied with the button's appearance, switch to Browse Mode (Ctrl B in Windows, ⌘ B on the Mac) to see the final effect (**Figure 13.52**).

Figure 13.49 To select a button in Layout mode, click on it with the Pointer Tool.

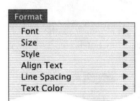

Figure 13.50 To change a button's font, text size, or text color, choose Format and select an option in the menu's top half.

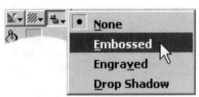

Figure 13.51 Use the Fill Tools' object effects pop-up menu to give a button a 3D look.

Figure 13.52 The same button in Figure 13.49 after changing its font, font size, colors, and effects.

Copying or deleting a button

Copying a button duplicates not just the graphic but the linked script as well.

To copy or delete a button:

1. Switch to Layout mode ([Ctrl][L] in Windows, [⌘][L] on the Mac) and click on the button with the Pointer Tool to select it.

2. To copy the button, use the Copy command ([Ctrl][C] in Windows, [⌘][C] on the Mac), move to the layout where you want the button to appear, and paste it in place ([Ctrl][V] in Windows, [⌘][V] on the Mac).

3. To delete the button, simply press [Delete] or [←Backspace].

✔ Tip

■ You can even copy a button into another database, though you'll probably need to edit the script to reflect the new field names and layouts.

COPYING, DELETING BUTTONS

To resize or move a button:

1. Switch to Layout mode ([Ctrl][L] in Windows, [⌘][L] on the Mac) and click on the button with the Pointer Tool.

2. To resize the button, simply hold down the cursor and drag one of the button's corner handles to the size you want (**Figure 13.53**).

   To move the button, click on its center and drag the button where you want it.

To change a button's definition:

1. Switch to Layout mode ([Ctrl][L] in Windows, [⌘][L] on the Mac) and double-click on the button.

2. When the Specify Button dialog box appears, change the steps or option choices as desired. (To change a step itself, see *To change a script* on page 211.)

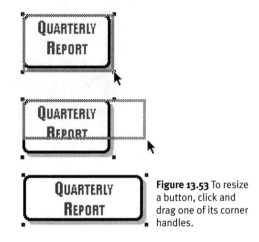

Figure 13.53 To resize a button, click and drag one of its corner handles.

CREATING RELATIONAL DATABASES

As you build databases, sooner or later you want to go relational, that is, to connect one database to another. Relational databases offer a way to make that connection—without slowing performance or requiring gigabytes of extra storage—by sharing data rather than duplicating it.

Instead of creating one big database packed with everything you might ever need to know about a subject, it makes far more sense to create a number of much smaller relational databases. Not only will relational databases help you focus on what's key to each database—contacts in one database, products in another, invoices in still another—they take up far less space. All your product data, for example, stays in the product database. If you need the price of a product while generating an invoice, the relational link lets you see the price data without actually copying it into your invoice database. That way you get speed—without the bulk of FileMaker's original non-relational, flat file design, which required that each database contain *all* the data it needed. One final advantage of relational databases: Different users can update or redesign one of the databases without forcing everyone else to stop using the related databases.

Despite the obvious advantages of relational databases, building them can quickly become a chicken-and-egg problem of which database comes first and which does what. It's easy to become overwhelmed by the possible options. Start small and simple. You can always go back and create more lookups and relationships as you need them. To keep focused, approach the process in six sequential steps:

Step 1—Plan, plan, plan: Take a big-picture look at what you want to accomplish and sketch out the *overall* connections: what kinds of data you want to track and how many databases that might take. Then consider the connections needed between various files and fields. It's common to revise your notions of what information should go where as your plans progress, so don't use the computer just yet. Rely instead on paper, pencil, and eraser—especially the eraser—to draw boxes, arrows, or whatever it takes to identify the best way to organize the data.

Step 2—Define the fields: From the big picture, narrow down to the details of defining exactly what fields need to be in each database. Try to avoid duplicating fields and data from database to database. Instead think about ways the data can be shared.

Step 3—Define the relational links:
Thinking of how to share data leads naturally to defining the relationships between various files. As the *link* between databases, the relationship is simply a formula that names two databases and a field that contains matching data in both databases. The relational link triggers an action, but defining exactly what that action should be comes in the next step.

Step 4—Put the links to use: The actions triggered by a relationship—what FileMaker calls lookups and portals—can be limited to one field or involve the whole database. See *Lookups vs. Portals* on page 226 to better understand the pros and cons of both.

Step 5—Create layouts: Only after the first four steps should you actually begin creating layouts for your lookups and portals. Aim for layouts that present the related information as clearly as possible by using portals, buttons, and scripts to tuck the relational "wiring" out of sight.

Step 6—Enter the data: Now that you've built destinations for your data, you can start importing existing files or entering information record by record as you use your new relational system.

A jargon jump-start

Each relationship in FileMaker includes only one master (destination) file and one related (source) file. But you can create multiple relationships, which means the same file can be the destination (master file) for some data and the source (related file) of other data. Whether you're dealing with a file, a record, or a field, just keep straight where the data's coming *from* (the source) vs. where it's eventually going *to* (the destination). For a bit of lingo help, see **Table 14.1**, *Too Many Terms for Two Simple Ideas*.

The examples in this chapter are based on three database files: "3D," which lists products from 3D software companies; "3D vendor addresses," which lists all the contact information for each company; and "3D Books," which lists information about books that explain how to use the software program (**Figure 14.1**). To put all the information in a single database file would be unwieldy. By dividing it into three files, each database remains focused and simple to use, which is what relational databases are all about. As you read the rest of the chapter, refer back to **Figure 14.1** to see how these three relational files put relationships, match fields, lookups, and portals to use.

Table 14.1

Too Many Terms for Two Simple Ideas	
FILEMAKER TERM	**WHAT IT MEANS**
master file, record, or field *destination* *target* *current*	The file, record, or field you copy data *to*
related *source* *originating*	The file, record, or field you copy data *from*

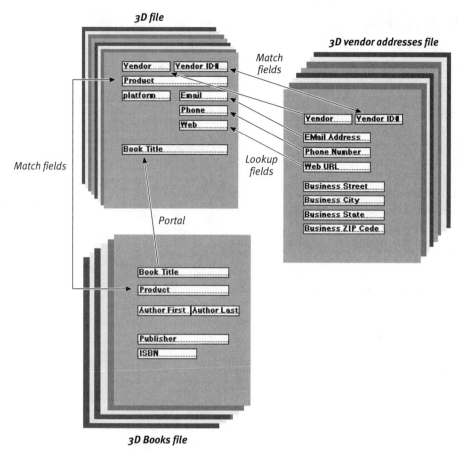

Figure 14.1 How three related files connect: The *Vendor ID#* match fields link the files "3D" to "3D vendor addresses," allowing the separately defined fields to be copied to "3D." The *Product* match fields link "3D" to "3D Books," making the multiple-record portal appear within "3D."

UNDERSTANDING RELATIONAL JARGON

Lookups vs. Portals

Lookup fields *copy* data from one database into another, where it remains unchanged unless you update it manually. A lookup can contain only one record from the related file, whereas a portal can display any number of records from the related file. The portal does not copy the files into the master file, but simply *displays* them via a window (hence the name, portal) back to where the data resides in the related file. For that reason, portals require less storage space since the data remains in just one file. The portal is also "live" in that any change in the linked data is automatically reflected in the portal. There are times, however, when you don't want a live connection. Take, for example, an invoice where you want to preserve the cost of an item at the time of the sale. A portal to item costs would reflect the current price, not the sale price. In that case, a lookup would be better.

Figure 14.2 To create a lookup field, choose File > Define Fields.

Figure 14.3 Pick a *destination* field—the one you want data copied *to*—in the Define Fields dialog box.

Figure 14.4 Checking *Looked-up value* in the Options dialog box will open the Lookup dialog box.

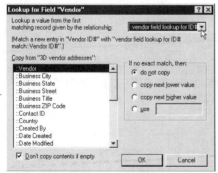

Figure 14.5 Use the Lookup dialog box to pick a field (*Vendor*) from the source file ("3D vendor addresses") that you want to copy into the destination file ("3D").

To define a lookup:

1. Open the database you want to be the master (destination) file. In either Browse or Layout mode, choose File > Define Fields (**Figure 14.2**).

2. When the Define Fields dialog box appears (**Figure 14.3**), double-click on what you want to be the *destination* field—the one data will be copied *to*— and the Options dialog box will open.

3. When the Options dialog box appears, the *Auto-Enter* tab will already be active (**Figure 14.4**). Check *Looked-up value*, which will open the Lookup dialog box.

4. When the Lookup dialog box appears, use the pop-up menu to choose a relationship (**Figure 14.5**). (If no relationships have been defined, choose File > Define Relationships and see step 2 of *To define relationships* on page 230.) In this example, two databases, 3D and 3D vendor addresses, have been linked by matching the *Vendor ID#* field.

   Once you define and choose a relationship from the pop-up menu, pick within the left-side list a *source* field, which is the field you want to copy data *from*.

5. Pick a match option from the *If no exact match, then* panel. Generally you'll use the default *do not copy* but you have the option of using the next lower or higher value, or even using a custom value. Also, leave *Don't copy contents if empty* checked to keep from generating empty lookup fields in your master file. Once you've made your choices, click *OK*.

6. When the Options dialog box reappears, click *OK* again. Finally, when the Define Fields dialog box reappears, click *Done*— and now you really are done.

Creating multiple lookups

Once you've defined a relationship, you can link it to any number of lookup fields.

To create multiple lookups from one relationship:

1. As you did in defining your first lookup, open the database containing the *master* (destination) file and choose File > Define Fields (**Figure 14.2**).

2. When the Define Fields dialog box appears, double-click on a *new* field into which you want data copied.

3. When the Options dialog box appears, check *Looked-up value*.

4. When the Lookup dialog box appears, use the pop-up menu to pick the *same* relationship you previously defined linking this master file with a particular related file (e.g., *vendor field lookup for ID# match*).

5. Unlike the first time you used this box, now pick *another* field from the related file. In our example, since we're defining a lookup for the master 3D file's *Phone* field, the related file's *Phone Number* field has been selected (**Figure 14.6**). Set your options as needed, and click *OK*.

6. Click *OK* again when the Options dialog box reappears, and click *Done* when the Define Fields dialog box reappears. You can continue repeating steps 1–5 to hook even more lookups to the same relationship (**Figure 14.7**). As an example of how this works once you're done, see **Figure 14.8**: When you enter an ID number in the *master* file (the 3D database), FileMaker will see that it matches the ID number in the *related* file (the 3D vendor addresses database), and automatically fill in the *Vendor*, *Phone*, *Email*, and *Web* fields within the 3D database.

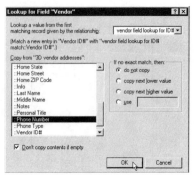

Figure 14.6 Once you've defined a relationship linking a destination and source file, you can use it to lookup data from other fields (e.g., *Phone Number*) in the source file ("3D vendor addresses").

Figure 14.7 It's easy to create multiple lookup fields (e.g., *Book Title*, *Email*, *Web*, and *Phone*) once you've defined a relationship between two files.

Figure 14.8 The lookup in action: Enter a number into the "3D" file's *ID#* field that matches a number in the related database ("3D vendor addresses") and data from that same record will be copied back to the lookup fields (*Vendor*, *Phone*, *Email*, and *Web*).

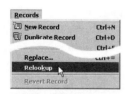 

Figure 14.9 To update a lookup field, open the master file and choose Records > Relookup.

Updating lookups

Lookup fields must be manually updated— unless you create a script to do it. For information on scripting, see *Using Templates and Scripts* on page 199 and *Script Commands* on page 315.

To update a lookup:

1. Open the master (destination) database and use the Find, Sort, and Omit commands to select only the records needing updating.

2. Make sure you're in Browse mode ([Ctrl][B] in Windows, ⌘[B] on the Mac) and select the lookup (destination) field.

3. Choose Records > Relookup (**Figure 14.9**). When the alert dialog box appears asking if you want to update the file's values, click *OK*. The selected records will now contain the latest data from the related file.

To define relationships:

1. Open the database you want to be the master (destination) file. In either Browse or Layout mode, choose File > Define Relationships (**Figure 14.10**).

2. When the Define Relationships dialog box appears, click *New* (**Figure 14.11**).

3. When the Open File dialog box appears, navigate to the *related* (source) file and open it (**Figure 14.12**).

4. When the Edit Relationship dialog box appears, FileMaker will automatically fill in the *Relationship Name* text box with the name of the related file. If you like, rename the relationship to make its function more obvious (**Figure 14.13**).

5. Select a field from the master file's fields (listed on the left side of the Edit Relationship dialog box) and a field from the related file's fields (listed on the right) that *match*—that is, have the *same* name (**Figure 14.13**). For details on the three options at the bottom of the dialog box, see **Table 14.2**, *Edit Relationship Options*. This step can be a conceptual stumbling block: Just remember that you're creating a relationship, which is what *links* the two databases together. Picking fields from one database to show in the other comes later.

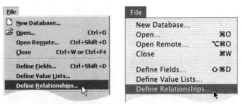

Figure 14.10 Link two databases by choosing File > Define Relationships.

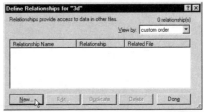

Figure 14.11 To create a relationship between two files, click *New* in the Define Relationships dialog box.

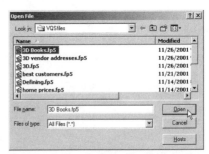

Figure 14.12 Use the Open File dialog box to find the related (source) file you want to link to the master (destination) file.

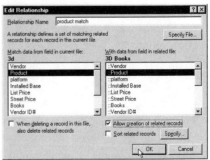

Figure 14.13 It's simple: create a relationship by picking two fields whose contents *match exactly*. Choosing other fields activated by this link comes later.

DEFINING RELATIONSHIPS

Table 14.2

Edit Relationship Options*

CHECK BOX NAMED	TO
When deleting record in this file, also delete related records	Automatically delete records in *related* file when you delete data in *master* file's portal or related field that meets match field criteria. Press Tab to activate.
Allow creation of related records	Automatically create a record in the *related* file if you enter data in *master* file's portal or related field that meets match field criteria. Press Tab to activate.
Sort related records	Sort related records *before* they're displayed in master file. Press Specify to set Sort order.

*Options set in Edit Relationship dialog box. Options activated only if using *master* file in Browse mode.

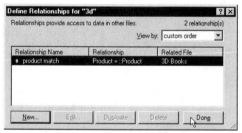

Figure 14.14 Use the Define Relationships dialog box to create new relationships or edit, duplicate, and delete them. When you're finished, click *Done*.

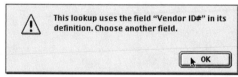

Figure 14.15 FileMaker won't let you define a relationship using a field that you've also included as the match field in the definition.

6. Click *OK*, which will take you back to the Define Relationships dialog box where you can create another relationship. When you've finished defining your relationships, click *Done* (**Figure 14.14**). To now define how these new relationships will be used, see *To define a lookup* on page 227, *To create multiple lookups from one relationship* on page 228, or *To create a portal for multiple related fields* on page 233.

✔ Tips

- You cannot use as a match field the very field for which you're defining a relationship. Otherwise, FileMaker will stop and tell you to pick another field (**Figure 14.15**). Go back and redefine the relationship to use a different field for the lookup (or use a different match field).

- Match fields don't have to be identically *named*, but they must *contain* the very same data.

To change or edit relationships:

1. Choose File > Define Relationships.

2. The Define Relationships dialog box will appear. Select a relationship and then click *Edit*, *Duplicate*, or *Delete*.

3. If you choose *Edit*, the Edit Relationship dialog box will appear where you can rename the relationship, specify another database file to use in the relationship, and pick other source and destination fields. When you're done, click *OK*.

✔ Tip

■ The *Duplicate* and *Delete* choices within the Define Relationships dialog box work similarly to duplicating or deleting layouts or scripts: Duplicate a relationship to save yourself time in creating a variation of an existing relationship; delete relationships you no longer need.

CHANGING OR EDITING RELATIONSHIPS

Figures 14.16–14.17 Click the Portal Tool (left) ...and drag the pointer to set the portal's size in the layout of the "3D" file (right).

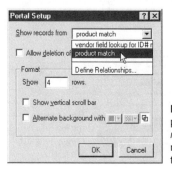

Figure 14.18 By picking *product match* as the relationship for the portal...

Figure 14.19 ...the Product field in the "3D Books" file will be linked to the portal within the "3D" file.

Figure 14.20 Use the *Format* panel to set how many rows are displayed in the portal and if it has a scroll bar or contrasting background.

Creating a portal for multiple fields

Once you've defined a relationship, you can use portals if your layout needs to show *more than one* record from a related file. To show a *single* record, see *To define a lookup* on page 227.

To create a portal for multiple related fields:

1. Open the database you want to be the *master* (destination) file.

2. Make sure you're in Layout mode (Ctrl L in Windows, ⌘L on the Mac) and click the Portal Tool (**Figure 14.16**).

3. Click in the layout and drag the pointer until the portal reaches the shape and size you want (**Figure 14.17**). Release the cursor.

4. When the Portal Setup dialog box appears, use the pop-up menu to choose the relationship you want to use in the portal (**Figure 14.18**). In the example, two databases, 3D and 3D Books, have been linked by matching the *Product* field (**Figure 14.19**). If the relationship hasn't been created yet, choose File > Define Relationships and see step 2 of *To define relationships* on page 230.

5. Use the text window and checkboxes in the *Format* panel of the Portal Setup dialog box to choose how many rows (record listings from the related file) you want to appear in the portal, whether it should have a scroll bar, and whether you want it to have a different color or pattern to stand out from the rest of the layout. You can change these Format options later if need be. When you're done, click *OK* (**Figure 14.20**).

(continued)

CREATING A PORTAL

The portal appears in the layout with a label for which relationship it uses (**Figure 14.21**). However, you still need to place your related fields into the portal.

6. Remain in Layout mode ([Ctrl][L] in Windows, [⌘][L] on the Mac), select the Field Tool, and drag it into the first row of the portal (**Figure 14.22**). When you release the cursor, the Specify Field dialog box will appear (**Figure 14.23**). The top pop-up menu, by default, will be set to the related (source) database you picked in the Portal Setup dialog box in step 4. The list shows all the fields within the source database. Select a field whose data you want to appear in the *destination* database. To reduce any cross-database confusion, leave *Create field label* checked. Click *OK*.

7. The source field will appear *inside* the portal (**Figure 14.24**). You can style and format this field as you would any other. When you switch to Browse mode, related data from multiple records within the 3D Books database appears inside the 3D database's portal (**Figure 14.25**).

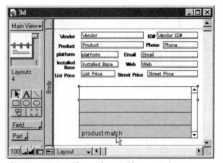

Figure 14.21 Halfway there: The portal appears in the layout with a label for which relationship it uses.

Figure 14.22 Use the Field Tool to drag a field into the portal.

Figure 14.23 Choose which field from the *source* database will appear in the *destination* database's portal.

Figure 14.25 It's magic: The portal within the 3D database displays multiple records (book titles) from the related 3D book database.

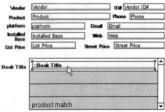

Figure 14.24 Once the field appears within the portal, you can style or format it as you would any other field.

PART IV

PRINTING, NETWORKING, & THE WEB

15

PRINTING

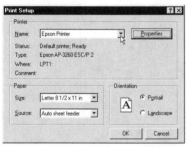

Figure 15.1 To change your printer, choose File > Print Setup.

Figure 15.2 ⓦ The pop-up menu within the Print Setup dialog box lets you select a new printer.

Figure 15.3 ⓜ To change your default printer on a pre-OS X Mac, use the Chooser dialog box.

In general, printing in FileMaker is not too different from printing in your other applications. But there are a few twists worth considering, so read on.

To change the default printer:

◆ Unless you change it, FileMaker will use your regular printer and its default settings. If you want to use a *different* printer for FileMaker files than your regular printer, do this:

ⓦ In Windows, choose File > Print Setup (**Figure 15.1**). When the Print Setup dialog box appears, select a new printer using the pop-up menu (**Figure 15.2**). Make sure your page margins are correct by checking the *Paper* and *Orientation* panels at the bottom of the dialog box. When you're done, click *OK*.

ⓜ On a pre-OS X Mac, select Chooser from the Apple menu. When the Chooser dialog box appears, make your new selection (**Figure 15.3**). Click the close box in the upper-left corner of the title bar.

(continued)

Ⓜ On a Mac running OS X, choose File > Print. When the Print dialog box appears, click the *Printer* drop-down menu and choose *Edit Printer List* (top, **Figure 15.4**). When the Printer List dialog box appears, click *Add Printer* (bottom, **Figure 15.4**). Use the drop-down menu that appears to choose the network connection that leads to the desired printer (e.g., AppleTalk) (top, **Figure 15.5**), navigate to the printer you want and after highlighting it, click *Add* (bottom, **Figure 15.5**). When the Printer List dialog box reappears, the newly selected printer will be highlighted (**Figure 15.6**). Click the dialog box's red close icon in the upper-left corner when you're done.

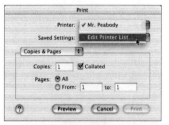

Figure 15.4 Ⓜ To change the default printer on a Mac running OS X, choose *Edit Printer List* from the *Printer* drop-down menu (top), then click *Add Printer* in the Printer List dialog box (bottom).

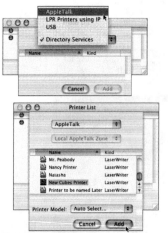

Figure 15.5 Ⓜ Use the drop-down menu that appears to choose the network connection (top), navigate to the desired printer, and click *Add* (bottom).

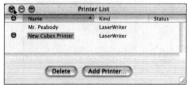

Figure 15.6 Ⓜ When the Printer List dialog box reappears, the newly selected printer will be highlighted.

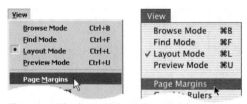

Figure 15.7 Check your margins by switching to Layout mode and choosing View > Page Margins.

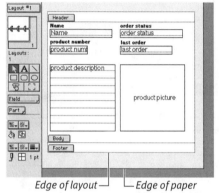

Edge of layout ⎦ ⎣ Edge of paper

Figure 15.8 A gray boundary marks the layout's edge; a darker boundary the paper's edge.

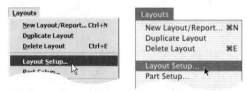

Figure 15.9 Choose Layouts > Layout Setup to change margins.

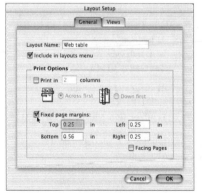

Figure 15.10 Select *Fixed page margins* and enter new numbers to adjust your *Top*, *Bottom*, *Left*, and *Right* margins.

To show page margins:

◆ Switch to Layout mode ([Ctrl][L] in Windows, [⌘][L] on the Mac), and choose View > Page Margins (**Figure 15.7**). The page margin is marked by a gray boundary, while the edge of the paper is marked by a darker boundary (**Figure 15.8**).

To set page margins:

1. First, make sure you have the right paper size selected by choosing File > Print Setup (Windows) or File > Page Setup (Mac) and selecting your paper as necessary using the pop-up menus.

2. Switch to Layout mode ([Ctrl][L] in Windows, [⌘][L] on the Mac), and choose Layouts > Layout Setup (**Figure 15.9**).

3. When the Layout Setup dialog box appears (**Figure 15.10**), select the *Fixed page margins* checkbox and use the four number-entry boxes to adjust your *Top*, *Bottom*, *Left*, and *Right* margins. Check *Facing Pages* to account for a narrower inside margin if you'll be printing on both sides of the paper.

4. Click *OK*.

Removing unwanted space

Data varies: some runs long, some short (**Figure 15.11**). To eliminate wasted field space, create a neater printout—and keep Al and Beauregard happy—you want to use a feature FileMaker calls "sliding." With this feature, FileMaker automatically closes up unused space either to the left or above any fields you select. The great thing about sliding is that FileMaker only applies it when necessary. If you have a field with a long text entry, it gets the room it needs.

To remove unwanted spaces:

1. Switch to Layout mode ([Ctrl][L] in Windows, [⌘][L] on the Mac).

2. Use the Pointer Tool to select all the fields you want to make sure are closed up properly. Choose Format > Sliding/Printing ([Option][⌘][T] on the Mac, no Windows equivalent) (**Figure 15.12**).

3. When the Set Sliding/Printing dialog box appears, check the *Sliding left* box (**Figure 15.13**). (Check *Sliding up based on* to control vertical spacing in a layout, especially within layout *parts*.) Click *OK*.

4. Switch to Preview Mode ([Ctrl][U] in Windows, [⌘][U] on the Mac) to see the change (**Figure 15.14**).

✔ Tips

- Sliding can be applied to objects, along with layout items that aren't in a field, such as lines you've placed in a layout for visual effect. In both cases, just select the item and apply sliding via the Format menu.

- Sliding only works on the body; headers and footers won't slide. Instead, see *To resize a part* on page 153.

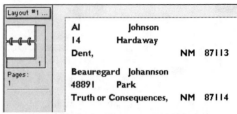

Figure 15.11 The problem with fixed field size printouts: Giving *Beauregard* enough room makes *Al* space out.

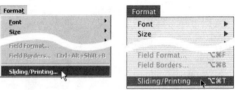

Figure 15.12 To remove unwanted space in fields or parts, choose Format > Sliding/Printing.

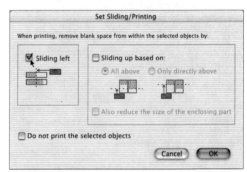

Figure 15.13 Within the Set Sliding/Printing dialog box, check *Sliding left* to close horizontal gaps or *Sliding up based on* to close vertical gaps in fields or parts.

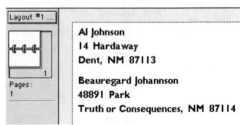

Figure 15.14 With sliding activated, the field size printouts match their entries.

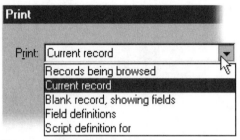

Figure 15.15 Before printing, you can choose View > Preview Mode or use your keyboard: [Ctrl] [U] (Windows) or [⌘] [U] (Mac).

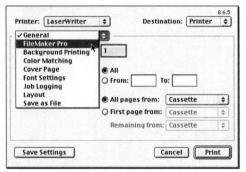

Figure 15.16 ⓦ In Windows, the Print drop-down list lets you choose which FileMaker records you print.

Figure 15.17 ⓜ Use the Print dialog box's pop-up menu to reach the FileMaker settings.

Figure 15.18 ⓜ When the FileMaker settings appear in the lower portion of the Print dialog box, use the radio buttons to control which FileMaker records print.

To preview a printout:

◆ Choose View > Preview Mode ([Ctrl] [U] in Windows, [⌘] [U] on the Mac) to see if your printout will be just as you want it (**Figure 15.15**).

To print:

1. Switch to the layout you want to print from and run any needed Find Requests or Sorts. Choose File > Print ([Ctrl] [P] in Windows, [⌘] [P] on the Mac).

2. When the Print dialog box appears:

   ⓦ Use the Print drop-down list (**Figure 15.16**) to determine whether you print all the records being browsed (the found set), only the current record, a blank record with the fields showing, a list of field definitions, or the script definitions for the current layout.

   ⓜ Use the pop-up menu to choose *FileMaker Pro* (**Figure 15.17**). When the FileMaker settings appear in the lower portion of the Print dialog box (**Figure 15.18**), use the radio buttons to choose whether you print all the records being browsed (the found set), only the current record, a blank record with the fields showing, the script definitions for the current layout, or a list of field definitions. A pop-up menu for the blank record option lets you choose whether you want fields in blank records printed as formatted, with boxes, or with underlines.

3. Once you've set your other choices (print range and number of copies), click *OK* (Windows) or *Print* (Mac).

✔ Tip

■ Printing out a script can be a terrific way to troubleshoot any problems that you can't quite find. Sometimes you see on paper what you can't see on the screen.

NETWORKING

FileMaker's networking abilities make it easy for PCs and Macs to share the same FileMaker database file. Inevitably, layouts will not look exactly the same on each platform. And since the Windows and Mac operating systems use different default fonts—and render them at 96 dpi on Windows and 72 dpi on Macs—text may also appear a bit differently. In some cases, this will force you to add a bit more space to tight Mac-generated layouts used on Windows machines. But, overall, the FileMaker match across platforms is pretty close. Remember: To share version 5 files, everyone on the network must be using FileMaker 5. (Machines running version 5 can open version 5.5 files, though features added in 5.5 will not work.)

To *host* a file simply means being the first user to open a shared FileMaker file. Anyone opening the file after the host is considered a *guest*. The host can set access rights and make file changes that guests cannot. For details, see **Table 16.1**, *Network Rights: Hosts vs. Guests*. FileMaker's network access privileges, by the way, are not the same as the access rights set by your computer's operating system. For information on setting Web access to FileMaker, see *Publishing on the Web* on page 271.

File sharing is set file by file. When a file needs to be shared, it must be set to Multi-User. By default, all FileMaker databases begin as Single User files. When a host needs to make substantial changes to a file, the file must be set back to Single User (see **Table 16.1**, *Network Rights: Hosts vs. Guests*) and guest users temporarily denied access to the file. Once the host finishes the modifications, the file can again be set to Multi-User.

Table 16.1

Network Rights: Hosts vs. Guests	
PARTY	HAS RIGHT TO
Host Only	
(File must be set to Single User. Guests must close file.)	Change file to single-user status or close shared file
	Define, delete, change access rights or groups
	Define fields or change field definitions
	Save file copies (with Save a Copy command)
	Reorder layouts
Any User	
(One at a time)	Edit record or layout
	Define, change value lists
	Define, change own passwords
	Define, change relationships
	Open ScriptMaker dialog box
Any User	
(Any time)	Find, sort, browse records
	Export, import records
	Choose a page setup and print
	Switch layout view or mode
	Check spelling

NETWORKING

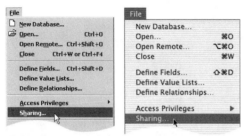

Figure 16.1 To turn FileMaker file sharing on or off, choose File > Sharing.

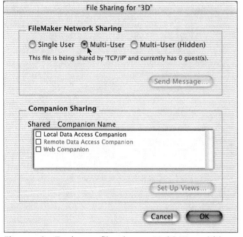

Figure 16.2 To share a file, choose *Multi-User* within the File Sharing dialog box.

Figure 16.3 To stop sharing a file, choose *Single User* within the File Sharing dialog box.

To turn on file sharing:

1. Open the file you want to share: Ctrl O in Windows, ⌘ O on the Mac.

2. Choose File > Sharing (**Figure 16.1**). When the File Sharing dialog box appears (**Figure 16.2**), choose *Multi-User*, then click *OK*.

To turn off file sharing:

1. If you're hosting the file, close it: Ctrl W in Windows, ⌘ W on the Mac.

2. A dialog box will appear listing other users of the file. Click *Ask* and they will be alerted to close the file as well. If they don't respond, FileMaker automatically closes the file in 30 seconds.

3. Choose File > Sharing (**Figure 16.1**). When the File Sharing dialog box appears, choose *Single User*, then click *OK* (**Figure 16.3**). The file will remain set to *Single User* until you turn file sharing back on, so it's best to make any changes promptly and return the file to its original *Multi-User* setting.

To open a database as the host:

1. After making sure no one else has the file open, choose File > Open or use your keyboard: Ctrl O in Windows, ⌘ O on the Mac.

2. When the Open dialog box appears, choose a file and click *Open*.

3. Choose File > Sharing (**Figure 16.1**). Within the File Sharing dialog box, make sure *Multi-User* is selected (**Figure 16.2**). If the button is dimmed, a message will appear in the middle of your screen explaining why. Or choose *Multi-User (Hidden)* to host a file that's somehow linked to a file guests will need to see. For more information, see the *Tip* below.

4. Click *OK*.

✔ Tip

■ The *Multi-User (Hidden)* choice in the File Sharing dialog box (**Figure 16.2**) is designed to grant guests access to a file they need to see while hiding related files that you don't necessarily want them to see. For example, a file may include value list- or relational-links to another file. By opening the related file and choosing *Multi-User (Hidden)*, the host can enable the first file to fetch all the data it needs without giving guests direct access to the related files.

Figure 16.4 To open a database not on your own computer, choose File > Open Remote.

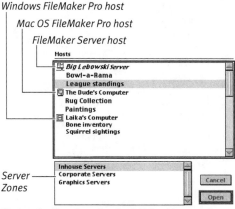

Windows FileMaker Pro host
Mac OS FileMaker Pro host
FileMaker Server host

Server Zones

Figure 16.5 If you're using AppleTalk with several server zones, pick a zone from the lower list and a file on that server in the upper list, and then click *Open*.

Figure 16.6 To find a FileMaker host outside your local area network, click *Specify Host*.

Figure 16.7 Enter the host's name or IP address in the Specify Host dialog box.

To open a database as a guest:

1. Choose File > Open Remote or use your keyboard: Ctrl Shift O in Windows, Shift ⌘ O on the Mac (**Figure 16.4**).

2. When the Hosts dialog box appears (**Figure 16.5**), its appearance and your choices will vary depending on your network setup:

   ◆ If you're using IPX/SPX (Windows) or AppleTalk with no server zones (Mac), select a file in the top list and click *Open*.

   ◆ If you're using AppleTalk with several server zones, pick a zone in the box's lower-left list, then select a file from those that appear in the top list and click *Open* (**Figure 16.5**).

   ◆ If you're using TCP/IP and want to pick a host *outside* your local area network, click *Specify Host* in the lower-left list (**Figure 16.6**). When the Specify Host dialog box appears, enter a host name or IP address (**Figure 16.7**). Click OK and when the Host dialog box reappears, choose a database in the top list. When you're done, click *OK* to close the Hosts dialog box.

   ◆ If you're using TCP/IP on a local area network, click *Local Hosts* in the box's lower-left list (**Figure 16.6**), then select a file from those that appear in the top list and click *Open*.

   (continued)

◆ If you're using a TCP/IP connection
with a Windows machine or a Mac
running OS X and need a host *outside*
your local area network, you also can
click *Directory Service* in the lower-left
list (**Figure 16.6**). When the
Directory Service dialog box appears
(**Figure 16.8**), enter the necessary
configuration information (your network administrator can help with the
specifics). Click *OK* and when the
Hosts dialog box reappears, choose a
database in the top list. When you're
done, click *OK* to close the Hosts dialog box.

✔ Tip

■ If you frequently use a host outside your
local area network, click *Permanently add
entry to Hosts list* within the Specify Host
dialog box.

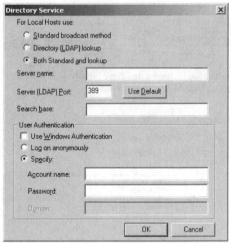

Figure 16.8 Use the Directory Service dialog box to
configure your TCP/IP connection to a host *outside*
your local area network.

Controlling File Access

By giving you the options to set a mix of passwords and group definitions, FileMaker lets you precisely control who can access files on your network. Be careful to not overdo security, however. The first time users can't get to something they need because of a password restriction, you'll hear about it and they won't be happy. Obviously you may need to control access to sensitive records, such as personnel and cost data. But in general, it's better to add passwords as you need them than to set up a security maze from the start. If you're the only one using a database or you're working in a very small group, you may not even need to set passwords.

Passwords should be relatively easy to remember but not so obvious that people outside the group can easily figure them out. The most secure passwords are a random mix of letters and numbers, but these passwords can be very hard to remember. Ultimately, security vs. ease of use requires a balancing act determined by your group's particular needs.

Group and password definitions are so interrelated it can get confusing as to which controls what. Remember: Groups control *access* or what users can *see*; passwords control *actions* or what users can *do*. In practical terms that means only the members of a group can see a particular layout or field, while passwords determine what they can do with the data once they reach it.

The first step in creating passwords is defining what FileMaker calls a master password, which grants access to everything in the database. Only then can you begin creating passwords for individual users. Aside from the master password, passwords are set based on the level of access needed. Password access privileges can run the gamut. For details, see **Table 16.2**, *Password Access Privileges*.

The first step in creating groups is defining them. Only then do you set a group's access privileges. Once passwords have been set and groups linked to them, FileMaker controls all users' access and their layout and field views of the database.

Table 16.2

Password Access Privileges	
CHECK	TO LET USERS
Access the entire file	Do any task via a master password. Only choice that grants right to define, change, or delete passwords. Also grants right to change field or group definitions, and document preferences.
Browse records	View record data
Print records	Print any records
Export records	Export any records, copy a found set, enable Web Companion sharing
Override data entry warnings	Enter data even if it doesn't match preset entry options
Design layouts	Create and change layouts
Edit scripts	Create and change scripts
Define value lists	Create and change value lists
Create records	Create new records and enter data
Edit records	Change data in records
Delete records	Delete any records

Figure 16.9 To work with FileMaker passwords, choose File > Access Privileges > Passwords.

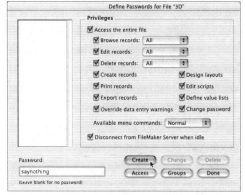

Figure 16.10 Within the Define Passwords dialog box, type a password into the *Password* text box. Create a master password by checking *Access the entire file*.

Figure 16.11 Any time you define other users' passwords, you'll need to confirm that you know the master password.

To set a master password:

1. Open the file for which you want to set a password (Ctrl O in Windows, ⌘ O on the Mac).

2. Turn off File Sharing (see page 245).

3. Choose File > Access Privileges > Passwords (**Figure 16.9**).

4. When the Define Passwords dialog box appears, type a password into the *Password* text box (**Figure 16.10**). It can include up to 31 characters and can include spaces. Capitalization within passwords is ignored.

5. Check *Access the entire file* at the top of the *Privileges* panel.

6. Click *Create*, then click *Done*.

7. When the Confirm dialog box appears, type in the *master* password and click *OK* (**Figure 16.11**). Remember to turn File Sharing back on.

Defining passwords

Only users who know the master password can define a password other than their own. FileMaker 5.5 adds the ability to define password access on a record-by-record basis.

To define user passwords:

1. Open the file for which you want to set a password ([Ctrl][O] in Windows, ⌘[O] on the Mac).

2. Turn off File Sharing (see page 245).

3. Choose File > Access Privileges > Passwords (**Figure 16.9**).

4. When the Define Passwords dialog box appears (**Figure 16.10**), type a password into the *Password* text box.

5. Check the appropriate access boxes within the *Privileges* panel. (See **Table 16.2**, *Password Access Privileges*.)

6. If you want to further limit the password user's ability to browse, edit, or delete only certain records within the file, click any of the three drop-down menus and choose *Limited* (**Figure 16.12**). When the Specify Calculation dialog box appears, use the list of field names, operators, and functions to fine-tune which records can be accessed (**Figure 16.13**). (For more information on using formulas, see *Understanding Formulas* on page 118.) When you're done, click *OK* to close the dialog box.

Figure 16.12 To limit a password's access to only certain records within the file, choose *Limited* in any of the three drop-down menus.

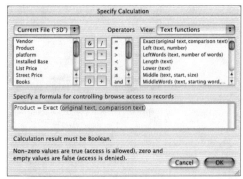

Figure 16.13 Use the Specify Calculation dialog box to fine-tune which records can be accessed within a file.

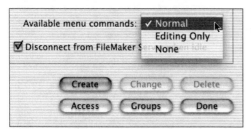

Figure 16.14 Control which FileMaker menu commands are linked to a password with the *Available menu commands* pop-up menu within the Define Passwords dialog box.

7. To grant access to all the FileMaker *menu commands* associated with the privilege boxes you've checked in steps 5–6, leave the *Available menu commands* pop-up menu set to *Normal* (**Figure 16.14**). If you want to enable only commands associated with simple data entry, choose *Editing Only*. To block use of any menu commands, choose *None*.

8. Click *Create*.

9. Repeat the process for as many passwords as you need to define. To associate passwords with existing groups, see *To define groups* on page 256.

10. Click *Done*.

11. When the Confirm dialog box appears, type in the *master* password and click *OK* (**Figure 16.11**).

✔ **Tip**

■ A file can have more than one password with each offering a different degree of access.

To create a blank password:

1. For users who only need limited access and can't be bothered with remembering a password, follow steps 1–3 of *To define user passwords.*

2. When the Define Passwords dialog box appears, leave the *Password* text box entirely blank, but go ahead and define a limited set of access options within the *Privileges* panel (top, **Figure 16.15**). Click *Create.*

3. A *[no password]* password now appears within the left-side list (bottom, **Figure 16.15**). Click *Done.*

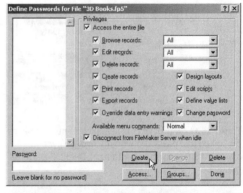

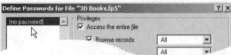

Figure 16.15 Top: Create a blank password by leaving the *Password* text box empty and giving it limited access privileges. Bottom: Once created, a blank password appears in the list as *[no password].*

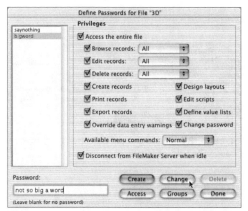

Figure 16.16 To change your own password, select the old password, type in a new password, and click *Change*.

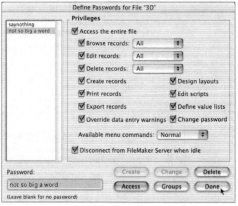

Figure 16.17 Once your password is updated in the left-side list, click *Done*.

Changing or deleting passwords

Only users who know the master password can change or delete passwords other than their own.

To change or delete passwords:

1. Choose File > Access Privileges > Passwords (**Figure 16.9**).

2. When the Define Passwords dialog box appears (**Figure 16.10**), select the password within the left-side list.

3. Type a new password in the *Password* text box and make any changes in *Privileges*. Click *Change*. The new password is now active.

   To delete the password, click *Delete*.

4. Click *Done*.

5. When the Confirm dialog box appears, type in the *master* password and click *OK*. Be sure to alert other users affected by the password changes.

Changing your own password

Even if you don't know the master password, you can change your individual password (if you have one).

To change your own password:

1. Choose File > Access Privileges > Passwords (**Figure 16.9**).

2. When the Define Passwords dialog box appears, select your old password in the left-side list, type your new password into the *Password* text box, and click *Change* (**Figure 16.16**).

3. Once your password is updated in the left-side list, click *Done* (**Figure 16.17**).

To define groups:

1. Open the file for which you want to set group access (Ctrl O in Windows, ⌘ O on the Mac). If you've already created passwords for the file, FileMaker will ask you to enter the master password.

2. Turn off File Sharing (see page 245).

3. Choose File > Access Privileges > Groups (**Figure 16.18**).

4. When the Define Groups dialog box appears, type in the new group name and click *Create* (**Figure 16.19**).

5. Make sure the new group name remains highlighted in the left-side list, then click *Access* (**Figure 16.20**). The Access Privileges dialog box appears, showing the groups, passwords, layouts, and fields for the file you're working in.

Figure 16.18 To create groups with varying rights, choose File > Access Privileges > Groups.

Figure 16.19 Type in a new group's name and click *Create*.

Figure 16.20 Once a group has been created, click *Access* to set its rights to the file.

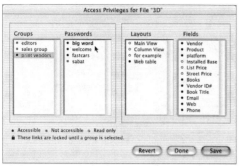

Figure 16.21 Select a group in the left column of the Access Privileges dialog box to see the passwords, layouts, and fields associated with the group.

Table 16.3

Access Symbols

THIS BULLET	MEANS THE LAYOUT OR FIELD
● Solid bullet	Can be read and edited by selected group
○ Hollow bullet	Can only be read by selected group
◉ Dimmed bullet	Cannot be seen by selected group

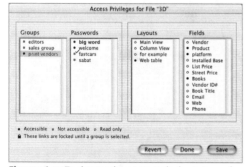

Figure 16.22 To change the passwords, layouts, and fields associated with a group, select the group's name in the left column and then click the bullets next to items in the other columns.

6. Select the group in the far-left column by clicking on it. In **Figure 16.21**, *print vendors* is associated with three passwords, all marked by solid bullets: *welcome, fastcars,* and *bigword.* (As the master password, the bold-face *bigword* is linked to *every* group; the bullet for the password *sabot* is dimmed because it is *not* linked to the *print vendors* group.) For the access level signified by different bullets, see **Table 16.3**, *Access Symbols.*

7. To change passwords linked to a group, keep the group selected in the far-left column and click the bullet next to a password you no longer want linked to the group (**Figure 16.22**). In the example, the bullet next to *fastcars* has changed to gray. To relink a password, click the bullet again.

8. The *print vendors* group in **Figure 16.22** can see *the Web table layout* and 12 fields within it. Of those fields, group members can edit just three: *Product, platform,* and *Books.* To change the group's layout and field access, just click on the adjacent bullets.

9. Click *Save.* If you want to make other changes, repeat the process, clicking *Save* after each round. If you change your mind mid-way through a round of changes, click *Revert* to go back to the version last saved. When you're satisfied, click *Done* twice.

DEFINING GROUPS

Changing group definitions

To change group definitions, you must host the file, know the master password, and first turn off file sharing.

To change a group definition:

1. Choose File > Access Privileges > Overview (**Figure 16.23**).

2. Within the Access Privileges dialog box, select a group in the left column and click the bullets in the other three columns (*Passwords*, *Layouts*, and *Fields*) to change the group's definition (**Figure 16.24**).

3. Click *Save*, and then click *Done*.

Deleting group definitions

To delete any group definitions, you must host the file, know the master password, and first turn off file sharing.

To delete a group definition:

1. Choose File > Access Privileges > Groups.

2. When the Define Groups dialog box appears, select a group name in the left-side list and click *Delete* (**Figure 16.25**).

3. When the warning dialog appears, click *Delete* again (**Figure 16.26**). Click *Done*.

Figure 16.23 The host can control group and password settings by choosing File > Access Privileges > Overview.

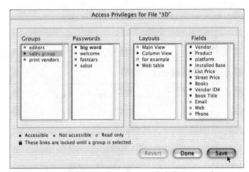

Figure 16.24 Once you've changed definitions for various groups, click *Save*.

Figure 16.25 Select a group name in the left-side list and click *Delete*.

Figure 16.26 When the warning dialog appears, click *Delete* again.

EXCHANGING DATA VIA ODBC

Open Database Connectivity (ODBC) allows FileMaker to easily exchange data with giant enterprise-level databases such as those created by Oracle and Microsoft SQL Server. This lets you sidestep an all-too-common dilemma: either stick with FileMaker and forego connecting with corporate-level databases or give up FileMaker's simpler interface for the complications of using ODBC-based programs. Now you and your co-workers can have the best of both worlds. Those who prefer the scale and power of enterprise-level database programs can still tap your FileMaker data and you can use FileMaker to query the big databases. In either case, of course, you'll need to work with your network administrator to make sure you follow your network's procedures and guidelines. As a FileMaker user *always* stay on your network administrator's good side.

Unfortunately, FileMaker does not yet fully support ODBC on Macs running OS X. But as Apple smoothes out the rough spots in OS X, expect FileMaker to remedy the problem as soon as possible, so make a point of regularly checking www.filemaker.com/support/ for updates. On Macs running OS 8.1–9.1 and Windows machines, the ODBC process is roughly the same: You turn on FileMaker's Data Access Companions, configure the ODBC Control Panel for the particular data source, connect to the data file, and then construct a query (search) of that data. There are a lot of steps involved, but you'll find the process pretty straight-forward once you walk through it. If you're not familiar with Structured Query Language (SQL)—the programming language that controls corporate-level database management systems—find someone within your organization to lend you a hand building those initial queries.

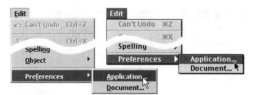

Figure 17.1 To turn on the Data Access Companions, choose Edit > Preferences > Application.

Figure 17.2 Click the *Plug-Ins* tab and check *Local...* or *Remote...* depending on where the ODBC-enabled database resides.

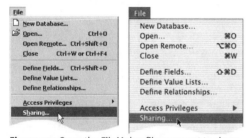

Figure 17.3 Open the FileMaker file you want to share, then choose File > Sharing.

Figure 17.4 Choose *Multi-User* to share a file, then check *Local...* or *Remote...* in the bottom panel to match your choice in Figure 17.2.

To turn on the Data Access Companions:

1. Choose Edit > Preferences > Application (**Figure 17.1**).

2. When the Application Preferences dialog box appears, click the *Plug-Ins* tab (**Figure 17.2**).

3. Check *Local Data Access Companion* if you want to share FileMaker data with an ODBC-enabled database *on the same computer*. If you want to share FileMaker data *across a TCP/IP network*, check the third choice, *Remote Data Access Companion*.

4. Click *OK* and the Application Preferences dialog box will close.

5. Now open the FileMaker file you want to share and choose File > Sharing (**Figure 17.3**).

6. When the File Sharing dialog box appears (**Figure 17.4**), first choose *Multi-User* in the *FileMaker Network Sharing* panel. Within the *Companion Sharing* panel, make the same choice you made in step 3: *Local Data Access Companion* to share the file with an ODBC-enabled database on the same computer; *Remote Data Access Companion* to share the file across a TCP/IP network.

7. Click *OK* and the File Sharing dialog box will close. The FileMaker file can now be reached by an ODBC-enabled database. For more information, see *To use FileMaker data from an ODBC application* on the next page.

✔ Tip

■ To control access to the FileMaker data across the network, it's best to assign a password to the shared file. For more information, see *Defining Passwords* on page 252.

Using FileMaker Data within an ODBC Application

Once you've turned on the Data Access Companions (explained on the previous page), your FileMaker data can be used by any ODBC-compliant application. The exact steps for tapping the FileMaker file will vary depending on which ODBC application you're using. The FileMaker ODBC driver must be installed on the computer that contains the ODBC *client* application. (See your network administrator for help on this.) Once the ODBC control panel has been installed, you'll need to configure the control panel by naming and locating the FileMaker file you'll be using from within the ODBC application. From there, it's just a matter of building queries for the FileMaker data using Structured Query Language (SQL) within your ODBC application.

To use FileMaker data from an ODBC application:

1. You'll need to configure the ODBC by:

   - **W** Choosing Start > Settings > Control Panel. In pre-Windows 2000 machines, double-click *ODBC Data Sources (32bit) w*hen the Control Panel window opens. On machines running Windows 2000 and Windows XP, you'll need to go one level deeper by also opening the *Administrative Tools* folder and choosing *Data Sources (ODBC)*.

   - **M** Choosing System Folder > Control Panels > ODBC Setup PPC if you're using a pre-OS X Mac. (OS X does not yet support ODBC import).

2. When the ODBC Data Source Administrator dialog box appears, make sure the *User DSN* tab is active, and click *Add* (**Figure 17.5**).

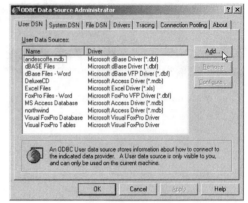

Figure 17.5 To create a new ODBC data source, make sure the *User DSN* tab is active, and click *Add*.

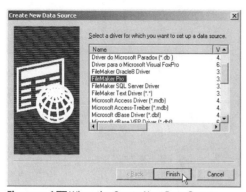

Figure 17.6 Ⓦ When the Create New Data Source dialog box appears, select the *FileMaker Pro* driver, and click *Finish*.

Figure 17.7 Ⓜ When the Create New Data Source dialog box appears, select the *ODBC 3.11 FileMaker Pro PPC* driver, and click *Finish*.

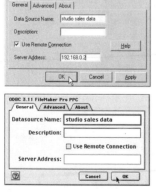

Figure 17.8
Make sure the *General* tab is activated when the driver setup dialog box appears. If the database is not on your local network, check *Use Remote Connection* and enter an IP number in *Server Address* (top).

3. When the Create New Data Source dialog box appears, select the *FileMaker Pro* driver (Windows) (**Figure 17.6**) or the *ODBC 3.11 FileMaker Pro PPC* driver (Mac) (**Figure 17.7**), and click *Finish*.

4. Make sure the *General* tab is activated when the driver setup dialog box appears (**Figure 17.8**), type a distinctive name into the *Data Source Name* text box and a *Description* if it will help users recognize the file.

5. If you'll be using a local file, click *OK* and you're done. If you'll be using a remote file not on the local server, check *Use Remote Connection*, enter the IP number in the *Server Address* text box, and then click *OK*.

(continued)

6. When the ODBC Data Source Administrator dialog box reappears, the newly named FileMaker data source will appear in the *User Data Sources* list (**Figure 17.9**). Click *OK* to close the dialog box. You're now ready to build your SQL query within your ODBC application and execute the query of the FileMaker file.

✔ Tips

- If your ODBC application requires it, you can set such items as a column's maximum text length, the number of rows requested, and multi-threading by clicking the *Advanced* tab in step 4 (**Figure 17.8**).

- To see which drivers you already have installed, in step 2 click the *Drivers* (Windows) or *ODBC Drivers* (Mac) tab in the ODBC Data Source Administrator dialog box (**Figure 17.10**).

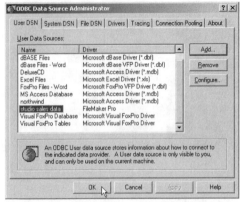

Figure 17.9 Once added, the newly named FileMaker data source appears in the *User Data Sources* list.

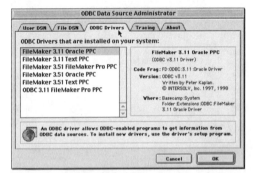

Figure 17.10 To see which drivers you already have installed, just click the *Drivers* (Windows) or *ODBC Drivers* (Mac) tab in the ODBC Data Source Administrator dialog box.

Importing ODBC Data into FileMaker

FileMaker's ODBC capabilities create a two-way street: ODBC-based applications can read FileMaker data, but you also can use FileMaker's simpler interface to tap corporate databases created by such programs as Oracle.

Importing the data involves three distinct procedures: (1) using the ODBC control panel to specify the name and location of the ODBC source data, (2) connecting to the source data from within FileMaker, and (3) building a database query within FileMaker.

To import ODBC data into FileMaker:

1. Open the ODBC control panel by:

- **W** Choosing Start > Settings > Control Panel. In pre-Windows 2000 machines, double-click *ODBC Data Sources (32bit) w*hen the Control Panel window opens. On machines running Windows 2000 and Windows XP, you'll need to go one level deeper by also opening the Administrative Tools folder and choosing Data Sources (ODBC).

- **M** Choosing System Folder > Control Panels > ODBC Setup PPC if you're using a pre-OS X Mac. (OS X does not yet support ODBC import).

2. When the ODBC Data Source Administrator dialog box appears (**Figure 17.5**), make sure the *User DSN* tab is active, and click *Add* if you're setting up a *new* data source.

If you're going to use an existing data source and need to change its settings, select it in the list, click *Configure*, and make the changes in the dialog box that appears.

(continued)

3. When the Create New Data Source dialog box appears, select the appropriate ODBC driver for the data source you'll be importing, and click *Finish* (**Figure 17.11**).

4. The setup dialog box that appears (**Figure 17.12**) will vary, depending on your choice in step 3. Type in a *Data Source Name*, a *Description* if you want, and the *Server Name* where the data source resides. When you're done, click *OK*.

- Click *Select Directory* to navigate your way to the *Database Directory* you want to use (**Figure 17.13**).

Figure 17.11 Select the appropriate ODBC driver for your data source in the Create New Data Source dialog box, and click *Finish*.

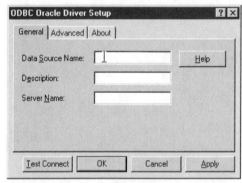

Figure 17.12 Type in a *Data Source Name*, a *Description*, and the *Server Name* where the data source resides. The dialog box will vary depending on your data source.

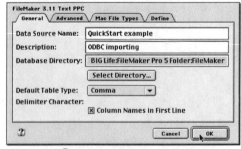

Figure 17.13 Click *Select Directory* to navigate your way to the desired *Database Directory*.

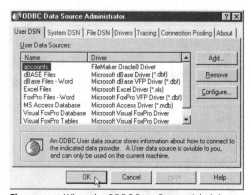

Figure 17.14 When the ODBC Data Source Administrator dialog box reappears, the newly named data source is listed under *User Data Sources*.

5. When the ODBC Data Source Administrator dialog box reappears, the newly named data source will appear in the *User Data Sources* list (**Figure 17.14**). Click *OK* to close the dialog box. You're now ready to import the data source into FileMaker. For more information, see *To connect to and query an ODBC source data* on the next page.

✔ Tip

- If your ODBC application requires it, you can set such items as a column's maximum text length, the number of rows requested, and multi-threading by clicking the *Advanced* tab in step 4 (**Figure 17.12**).

To connect to and query an ODBC data source:

1. Open the FileMaker file into which you'll be importing the source data and define fields for the data you expect to import. For more information on defining fields, see page 98.

2. Make sure you're in Browse mode ([Ctrl] [B] in Windows, [⌘][B] on the Mac), then choose File > Import Records (**Figure 17.15**).

3. When the Open File dialog box appears, use the *Files of type* (Windows) or *Show* (Mac) drop-down menu to select *ODBC Data Sources* (Windows) or *ODBC* (Mac) (**Figures 17.16** and **17.17**).

Figure 17.15 To tap an ODBC data source, begin by choosing File > Import Records.

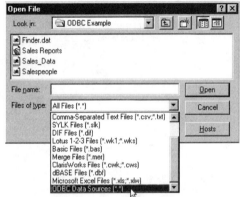

Figure 17.16 ⬛ When the Open File dialog box appears, use the *Files of type* drop-down menu to select *ODBC Data Sources*.

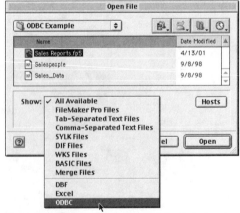

Figure 17.17 ⓜ When the Open File dialog box appears, use the *Show* drop-down menu to select *ODBC*.

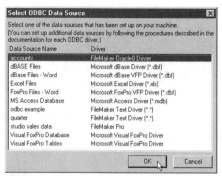

Figure 17.18 🖳 When the Select ODBC Data Source dialog box appears, select a data source and click *OK*.

Figure 17.19 Ⓜ When the Select ODBC Data Source dialog box appears, select a data source and click *OK*.

Figure 17.20 Enter a name and password for the ODBC database or, if none exists, just click *OK*.

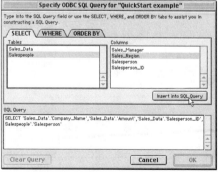

Figure 17.21 Use the *SELECT* tab to begin building your query (search) of the ODBC database.

4. When the Select ODBC Data Source dialog box appears (**Figures 17.18** and **17.19**), select a data source (such as the one you first configured in step 4 of *To import ODBC data into FileMaker* on page 265), and click *OK*.

5. When the password dialog box appears, enter the required password or, if none was created, press *OK* (**Figure 17.20**).

6. When the Specify ODBC SQL Query dialog box appears, the *SELECT* tab already will be activated (**Figure 17.21**). Within the *Tables* list, click the table you want to import, then click a choice in the *Columns* list. Click *Insert into SQL Query* and the request will appear in the *SQL Query* list.

(continued)

7. If you want to fine-tune which data will be imported, click the *WHERE* tab (**Figure 17.22**). Use the drop-down menus (similar to creating a Find request) to narrow which records and values you want to import. Again, click *Insert into SQL Query* to add the criteria to your query.

8. If you want to sort the records before you import them, click the *ORDER BY* tab (**Figure 17.23**). As you select items in the *Columns* list, click *Move* to add them to the *Order By* list. Choose *Ascending* or *Descending* as needed for each item added to the *Order By* list. Click *Insert into SQL Query* to add the ordering criteria to your query.

9. Click *Execute* (Windows) or *OK* (Mac) to start the query.

10. When the Import Field Mapping dialog box appears (**Figure 17.24**), use the *Scan Data* arrows to make sure the data and fields match up properly. If necessary, reorder the fields in your FileMaker database. For more information on import mapping, see page 84.

11. Click *Import* and the ODBC data source will be imported into the FileMaker database.

✔ Tip

- If you are familiar with building SQL queries, you can type SQL statements directly into the dialog box's *SQL Query* window (**Figure 17.21**).

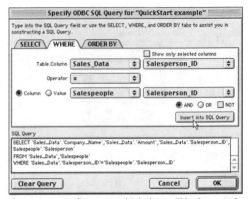

Figure 17.22 To fine-tune which data will be imported, use the *WHERE* tab much as you would create a Find request.

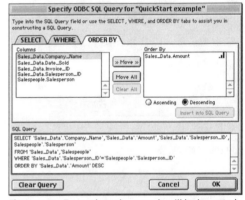

Figure 17.23 To sort how the records will be imported, use the *ORDER BY* tab.

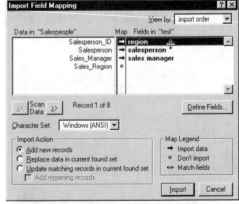

Figure 17.24 Once you begin the query, the Import Field Mapping dialog box will appear. Make sure the data and fields match up before you click *Import*.

PUBLISHING ON THE WEB

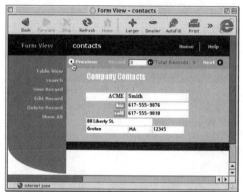

Figure 18.1 The Instant Web Publishing feature makes it easy to generate Web pages that let Web users take advantage of virtually all FileMaker's database powers.

FileMaker's Instant Web Publishing component has become even easier to set up and more Web-like in version 5.5. Here's what makes Instant Web Publishing so appealing: Any computer with a Web browser can view and (if you allow it) even edit FileMaker data (**Figure 18.1**).

Thanks to buttons in the Instant Web Publishing layouts, which run behind-the-scenes scripts, Web users can perform many of the same actions once limited to machines running FileMaker itself. They can search records, update information, sort tables—the list goes on. A company's sales force, for example, can place orders from the road, outside vendors can check delivery dates, and you can check the latest product deadlines from home. Don't worry—Web Companion includes security options to let you precisely control who sees your data and what they can do with it. Timeliness is one of the best things about Web database publishing. Too much of the Web still uses static pages, which look the same every time you visit them. With the Web Companion feature, if a shared FileMaker database changes, Instant Web Publishing makes those changes immediately visible over the Web.

How It Works and What You'll Need

FileMaker's Web Companion acts like a Web server by handling the file requests placed by Web browsers visiting your database. It does this by interpreting the HTTP (HyperText Transfer Protocol) commands from the browser, along with operating as a de facto CGI (Common Gateway Interface) application between FileMaker and visiting Web browsers. Web Companion handles all this in the background so you don't have to deal with it. Instead, FileMaker's Web Companion uses its Instant Web Portal and a built-in home page to automatically generate and display links to your Web databases (**Figure 18.2**). The Web Companion also offers you a variety of page styles for presenting your databases (**Figure 18.3**).

If you elected not to include the Web Companion in your initial FileMaker installation, go back and add it by running the Custom installation. (See page 292 for Windows, page 297 for the Mac.) Besides FileMaker and Web Companion, if you're running the Web Companion on a company intranet, that is all you need. If you're going to publish to the Web, however, you'll also need a *full-time* Internet connection (DSL, ISDN, T1, T2, or T3). In theory, you could publish a Web database via a part-time dial-up connection, but no one could use the database unless you were online at the very same time. The IP address for most part-time connections also changes from session to session, which would make it all but impossible for users to keep track of your database's latest location.

Figure 18.2 The Web Companion's Instant Web Portal automatically generates and displays links to your Web databases.

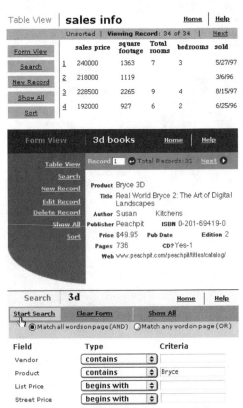

Figure 18.3 The Web Companion now includes a variety of styles and colors, including (top to bottom): a table view in fern green, a form view in lavender, and a search-only view.

What if you're just running a small business and don't have the dough to install a Web server, a T1 line, and a closet of cables? Not to worry—many of the same Internet Service Providers who offer dial-up connections can host your FileMaker database on one of their Internet-linked computers for a small monthly fee. FileMaker offers a partial list of such ISPs at: www.filemaker.com/products/isp.html

Aside from setting up and configuring the Web Companion, which controls FileMaker's *general* Web publishing features, you'll need to decide which *individual* files to share over the Web. As part of preparing those individual files for the Web, you'll probably want to create layouts tailored for your Web users. Not only will that make it easier for your Web viewers, it also prevents the Web Companion from displaying database fields you may not want the world to see. For details, see *Sharing and Viewing Web Files* on page 279.

HOW IT WORKS; WHAT YOU'LL NEED

Setting Up and Configuring the Web Companion

Generally, you'll only need to set up Web Companion once. Selecting which FileMaker files will be published on the Web, however, must be done file by file using the File Sharing dialog box.

To set up the Web Companion:

1. If you are using a Windows machine or a pre-OS X Mac, choose Edit > Preferences > Application (**Figure 18.4**). If you are running OS X, choose FileMaker Pro > Preferences > Application (**Figure 18.5**).

2. When the Application Preferences dialog box appears, click the *Plug-Ins* tab and check *Web Companion* (**Figure 18.6**). Most of the Web Companion's default settings are fine for most users, so click *OK* to close the Application Preferences dialog box. If you want to customize the settings, see *To configure the Web Companion* on the next page.

✔ Tips

- The Web Companion works independently of the two Data Access Companions, so whether they're checked or not doesn't affect the Web Companion.

- In step 2, if you are running OS X on a Mac, an alert dialog box will appear the first time you check *Web Companion* (top, **Figure 18.7**). Click *Continue* and, when the Authenticate dialog box appears, enter your user name and password, click *OK*, and you'll be returned to the Application Preferences dialog box. Unless you want to reconfigure the Web Companion's default settings, click *OK* and you're done.

Figure 18.4 To set up the Web Companion on a Windows or pre-OS X machine, choose Edit > Preferences > Application.

Figure 18.5 To set up the Web Companion on a Mac running OS X, choose FileMaker Pro > Preferences > Application.

Figure 18.6 Click the *Plug-Ins* tab and check *Web Companion* in the Application Preferences dialog box.

Figure 18.7 In step 2, if you are running OS X on a Mac, an alert dialog box will appear when you first check *Web Companion* (top). Click *Continue* and enter your user name and password in the Authenticate dialog box (bottom).

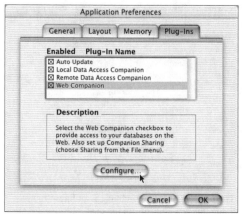

Figure 18.8 To set its preferences, select *Web Companion* and click *Configure*.

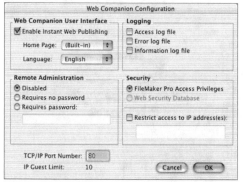

Figure 18.9 The Web Companion Configuration dialog box controls the user interface, logging activities, remote administration, and security.

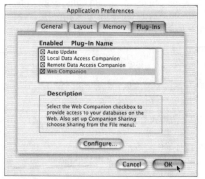

Figure 18.10 After you've configured the Web Companion's preferences, click *OK* when the Application Preferences dialog box reappears.

To configure the Web Companion:

1. To customize the Web Companion's settings on a Windows machine or a pre-OS X Mac, choose Edit > Preferences > Application (**Figure 18.4**). If you are running OS X, choose FileMaker Pro > Preferences > Application (**Figure 18.5**).

2. When the Application Preferences dialog box appears, click the *Plug-Ins* tab. Then select *Web Companion* in the *Enabled Plug-In Name* panel and—assuming the Web Companion is already activated—click *Configure* (**Figure 18.8**). (If you haven't turned on the Web Companion, see *To set up the Web Companion* on the previous page.)

3. When the Web Companion Configuration dialog box appears (**Figure 18.9**), make your configuration choices. For details on each choice, see *Web Companion options* on page 276.

4. When you're done, click *OK* to close the Web Companion Configuration dialog box. When the Application Preferences dialog box reappears, click *OK* again (**Figure 18.10**) and you're done.

SETTING UP AND CONFIGURING WEB COMPANION

275

Web Companion options

The Web Companion Configuration dialog box (**Figure 18.11**) controls the user interface, remote administration, the TCP/IP port number, logging activities, and security. Here's a quick rundown of each:

Enable Instant Web Publishing: By default, this is checked. Even if you plan on using the FileMaker Developer edition to create custom pages, you'll find the Instant Web Publishing option will be fine for certain pages.

Home Page: By default, the Web Companion uses its own *Built-in* home page. You can, however, use your own custom page (**Figure 18.12**) as a home page—if you first place it in FileMaker's Web folder (FileMaker Pro 5.5\Web in Windows; FileMaker Pro 5.5 Folder\Web on the Mac). Once you put your custom HTML file in the Web folder, it will be visible in the *Home Page* pop-up menu (**Figure 18.13**).

Language: This only affects the Instant Web Publishing interface and its built-in Help feature—not your data or layouts. Use the pop-up menu to select one of seven languages.

Remote Administration: The three radio buttons in this panel allow you to upload and download Web Companion files if they reside on an offsite server, a handy feature if you depend on an Internet Service Provider for hosting your FileMaker database. You can leave this option off or enable it. If you choose to use remote administration, always select *Requires password* and enter a password in the text box. For more details, see *Security* on page 278.

For more details, see *Security* on page 278.

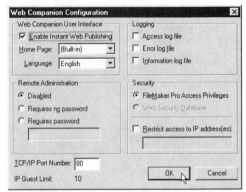

Figure 18.11 The Web Companion Configuration dialog box lets you control the user interface, logging activities, remote administration, and security.

Figure 18.12 You can use a custom home page with links to your data if you place the page inside FileMaker's Web folder.

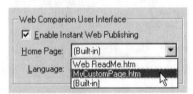

Figure 18.13 Use the *Home Page* pop-up menu to choose FileMaker's Built-In page or your own custom page.

TCP/IP Port Number: Unless you've already got a Web server connected to your computer, the default setting of 80 is fine. Otherwise, you'll have to set it to 591 and users visiting your Web site will have to add ":591" to the end of your normal IP address (e.g., 146.98.21:591).

IP Guest Limit: Unless you're using the $999 FileMaker Unlimited edition, this number will be set at 10. That means only the first 10 users in a rolling 12-hour period will be able to use the Web database. More precisely, the limit is 10 *computers* since FileMaker tracks the use by the IP address. Any Web browser logging into the database after the first 10 users will get an error message. If one of your first 10 computers has not used the Web database in 12 hours, then FileMaker will let a new computer log into the database. If three of your first 10 computers don't use it in 12 hours, three additional computers will be able to log in, and so on.

The problem with this approach, obviously, is FileMaker makes no distinction between 10 computers regularly logging into the Web database and a situation where several computers only tap into the database for one request or just spend five minutes using it. You're limited to 10 IP addresses per 12 hours, no exceptions. If you're a small firm, the workaround is musical chairs: designate 10 machines for tapping the Web database and have people sit at those machines to make their requests. If you're trying to use FileMaker's Web publishing features to serve a Web database to the wider world, you should get FileMaker Unlimited.

(continued)

Logging: By default, Web Companion does not store a log of Web activity. Check *Access log file* if you want to record which IP addresses log into the site and which pages are viewed. Check *Error log file* if you want a record kept of errors generated by the Web Companion. Check *Information log file* only if you're creating custom Web publishing files using the FileMaker Developer edition. The log files are stored in the FileMaker Pro 5.5 folder.

Security: The Web Companion's security default is *FileMaker Pro Access Privileges*, which are set file by file using passwords and groups as explained in *Networking* on page 243. With this option activated, Web browsers enter the same passwords, and have the same privileges, as they would if they opened those files directly within FileMaker. You should choose *Web Security Database* only if you'll be creating custom Web pages with FileMaker's Developer Edition. You can, however, add another level of security by checking *Restrict access to IP address(es)* and then entering specific IP numbers into the text window. Separate multiple IP addresses with a comma. You also can use wildcard character (e.g. 192.168.0.*) to specify a range of addresses, a common setup for inhouse intranets.

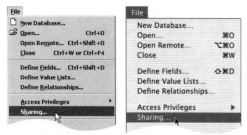

Figure 18.14 To share a file over the Web, open it and choose File > Sharing.

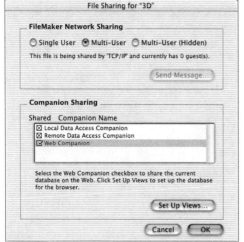

Figure 18.15 When the File Sharing dialog box appears, check *Web Companion* in the lower *Companion Sharing* panel.

Sharing and Viewing Web Files

Once you've configured the Web Companion, you need to designate which files will be shared over the Web. This must be done separately for every file you want to share. FileMaker also requires that you specify how you want each shared file to be viewed. Before you start using the Web Companion to configure each file's Web views, however, be sure to create a Web-only layout for those same files. That will speed up the display of your files over the Web—and ensure that visitors don't have to wade through irrelevant fields.

To share a file over the Web:

1. Open the FileMaker file you want to share: Ctrl O in Windows, ⌘ O on the Mac.

2. Choose File > Sharing (**Figure 18.14**).

3. When the File Sharing dialog box appears, ignore the *FileMaker Networking Sharing* panel. Instead, look within the lower *Companion Sharing* panel and check *Web Companion* (**Figure 18.15**).

4. If you want to go ahead and set how the file will look over the Web, see step 2 in *To set up the browser views* on page 280. Otherwise, click *OK*. Once you also configure Web Companion, the file will be shared over the Web. Repeat the steps for every file you want to share.

✔ Tips

■ If you ever want to stop sharing a file, open the File Sharing dialog box, uncheck *Web Companion*, and click *OK*.

■ You won't be able to activate file sharing unless your password allows you to export records, which is effectively what you're doing by sharing files over the Web. If your password doesn't include that privilege, see the person who assigns FileMaker passwords to get export rights.

Setting up the browser views

The Web Companion View Setup dialog box lets you control what visitors see when they call up your Web database. Depending on your needs, you may not need to set all the views.

To set up the browser views:

1. Open the FileMaker file whose views you want to set, then choose File > Sharing (**Figure 18.14**).

2. Make sure that *Web Companion* is not only checked but selected (highlighted), then click *Set Up Views* (**Figure 18.16**).

3. When the Web Companion View Setup dialog box appears, the *Web Style* tab will be selected (**Figure 18.17**). Use the *Styles* pop-up menu to select a look for your Web pages (**Figure 18.18**). Not every style will work with every Web browser, so see **Table 18.1** for help in making your choice. If you don't need to set any of the other tabs, skip to step 8.

Figure 18.16
To set how the database will appear within a Web browser, highlight the *Web Companion* and click *Set Up Views*.

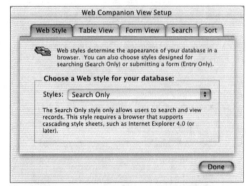

Figure 18.17 To set a style for your Web database, click the *Web Style* tab in the Web Companion View Setup dialog box.

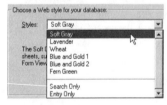

Figure 18.18
Use the pop-up menu to select a style. See Table 18.1 for help on making a choice.

Table 18.1

Choosing a Web Style

WEB STYLE	WORKS WITH BROWSERS	DETAILS
Soft Gray	version 4 or later; must support Cascading Style Sheets (CSS)	Opens in Form View
Lavender	version 4 or later; must support CSS	Opens in Form View
Wheat	version 4 or later; must support CSS	Opens in Form View
Blue and Gold 1	version 3 or later; must support CSS	Opens in Form View
Blue and Gold 2	version 3 or later	Opens in Table View
Fern Green	version 3 or later	Opens in Table View
Search Only	version 4 or later; must support CSS	Uses can only find and view records
Entry Only	version 4 or later; must support CSS	Users can only add records (works like a guestbook)

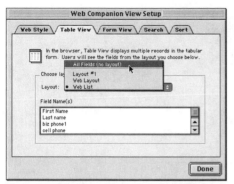

Figure 18.19 To set how the Web Companion displays *multiple* records, click the *Table View* tab and use the *Layout* pop-up menu to choose which layout Web visitors will see.

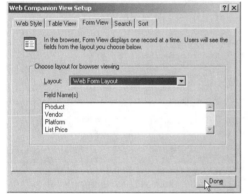

Figure 18.20 To set how the Web Companion displays *single* records, click the *Form View* tab and use the *Layout* pop-up menu.

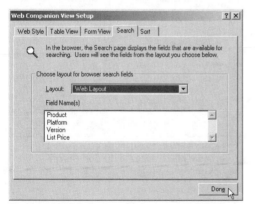

Figure 18.21 Click the *Search* tab to see which fields your Web visitors will see, based on the *Layout* chosen. (You may need to create a more restrictive layout.)

4. After you make your style choice, click the *Table View* tab (**Figure 18.19**) to set how the Web Companion will display *multiple* records. Use the *Layout* pop-up menu to choose which layout you want Web visitors to see. The *Field Name(s)* window will list *all* the fields in the chosen layout. This is where the advantage of creating special Web layouts for the file with a limited number of fields becomes obvious. If, however, you want to include every single field, select the *Layout* pop-up menu's first choice: *All Fields (no layout)*. If you don't need to set any of the other tabs, skip to step 8.

5. Click the *Form View* tab (**Figure 18.20**) to set how the Web Companion will display *single* records. Again, use the *Layout* pop-up menu to choose which layout you want Web visitors to see. If you don't need to set any of the other tabs, skip to step 8.

6. Click the *Search* tab (**Figure 18.21**) to see which fields will be visible to your Web visitors based on the *Layout* chosen. If you need to narrow which fields can be searched, you'll need to exit the Web Companion View Setup dialog box and create a new layout for the file. If you don't need to set any of the other tabs, skip to step 8.

(continued)

SHARING AND VIEWING WEB FILES

7. Click the *Sort* tab (**Figure 18.22**) to set how the Web Companion will handle sorting. By default, the *Do not sort records* radio button will be selected. If you don't want users to be able to sort the records, skip to step 8.

To let users sort the file, select the second radio button (*User defines sorting...*) and click *Specify* (**Figure 18.23**). When the Specify Sort dialog box appears (**Figure 18.24**), *all* the file's fields—even those not visible in the chosen layout—will be listed on the left. Select any field in the left-hand list that you want to sort by, click *Move*, and it will be added to the *Sort Order* list. Continue adding fields, reordering them if needed by dragging the double arrows, and click *OK* when you're done.

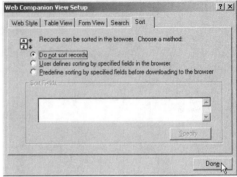

Figure 18.22 By default, sorting is turned off in the Web Companion. Select the second or third radio button to enable sorting.

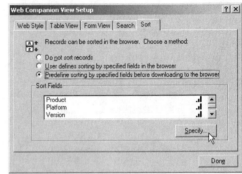

Figure 18.23 To let *users* sort the file, select the second radio button and click *Specify*.

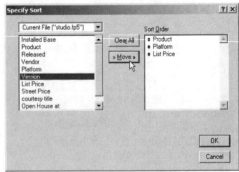

Figure 18.24 Select a field in the left-hand list, click *Move*, and it will be added to the *Sort Order* list. See the *Tips* on the next page for a workaround.

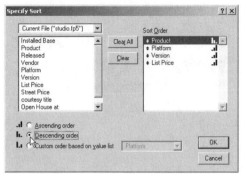

Figure 18.25 To control the sort yourself, choose the third radio button in Figure 18.22 and use the buttons in the Specify Sort dialog box.

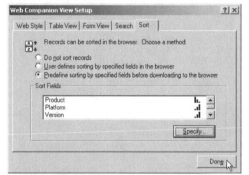

Figure 18.26 After you've set the sort, click *Done* to close the setup dialog box.

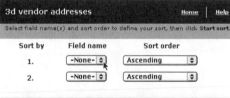

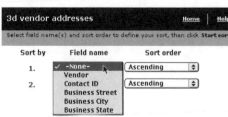

Figure 18.27 Top: If you forget to enable sorting, Web users will see a pop-up menu only listing *None*. Bottom: With sorting enabled, users can select a field to sort.

If you want to control the sort, choose the third radio button (*Predefine sorting...*) and click *Specify*. When the Specify Sort dialog box appears (**Figure 18.25**), select fields on the left and click *Move* to add them to the *Sort Order* list. To set how each field is sorted, select it in the *Sort Order* list, then choose *Ascending order...*, *Descending order...*, or *Custom order....* Click *OK* when you're done and your sort orders will appear in the *Sort* tab (**Figure 18.26**).

8. When you are finished with the Web Companion View Setup dialog box, click *Done* and the current Web database will be configured based on your choices.

✔ Tips

■ If you forget to set up sorting in step 7, the Web user won't be able to set any fields for sorting (top, **Figure 18.27**). If you select the *User defines sorting...* radio button in step 7, users will be able to choose fields for sorting (bottom, **Figure 18.27**).

■ As noted in step 7, all of a file's fields will be visible in the Specify Sort dialog box (**Figure 18.24**). If you don't want Web visitors to see those fields, duplicate your original file, delete all the extraneous fields, and publish that file on the Web instead.

Testing your Web Database Locally

You can see how your Web databases look and test how they operate *before* publishing them to the Web or your inhouse intranet by setting up a local connection on your own computer. In Windows, it couldn't be easier. On the Mac, it's a wee bit more involved.

ⓦ To test the Web Companion on your Windows computer:

1. Make sure you've opened the FileMaker databases you want to share and that you've activated Web sharing for each.

2. Launch your Web browser and in the *Address* or *Location* text window type http://localhost/ and press ⟨Enter⟩. FileMaker's Instant Web Portal will appear within the browser, displaying all the open databases for which you have activated Web sharing (**Figure 18.28**). Click any of the listed databases to test their various views.

✔ Tip

■ During testing you may decide to choose another Web style, view, or sort. Those changes won't appear in the Instant Web Portal unless you first quit and restart FileMaker.

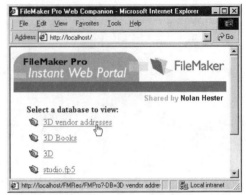

Figure 18.28 ⓦ By testing the Instant Web Portal locally, you can double-check your databases before publishing them on an intranet or the Web.

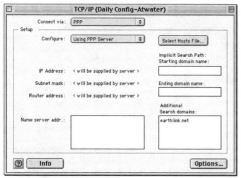

Figure 18.29 ⓜ To test your database locally, you'll have to change the settings in your TCP/IP control panel.

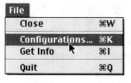

Figure 18.30 ⓜ After you've opened the TCP/IP control panel, choose File > Configurations.

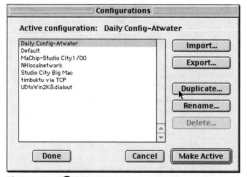

Figure 18.31 ⓜ Select your current configuration and choose *Duplicate*.

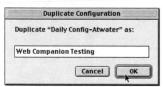

Figure 18.32 ⓜ Name the duplicate setting Web Companion Testing and click *OK*.

ⓜ To test the Web Companion on your Mac:

1. Open your TCP/IP control panel (**Figure 18.29**), then choose File > Configurations (**Figure 18.30**).

2. When the Configurations dialog box appears, select your current configuration and choose *Duplicate* (**Figure 18.31**).

3. When the Duplicate Configuration dialog box appears, type in Web Companion Testing and click *OK* (**Figure 18.32**).

(continued)

TESTING YOUR WEB DATABASE LOCALLY

4. When the Configurations dialog box reappears, select the *Web Companion Testing* configuration and click *Make Active* (**Figure 18.33**).

5. When the TCP/IP control panel for Web Companion testing appears, use the *Connect via* pop-up menu to select *AppleTalk (MacIP)* and choose *Using MacIP Manually* in the *Configure* pop-up menu. Type 10.10.10.10 into the *IP Address* text window and 10.10.10.1 into the *Router address* text window. When you're done (**Figure 18.34**), close the window.

6. Click *Save* when asked if you want to save the new configuration (**Figure 18.35**).

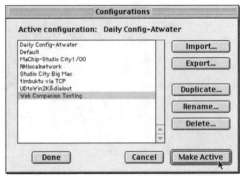

Figure 18.33 Ⓜ When the Configurations dialog box reappears, select *Web Companion Testing* and click *Make Active*.

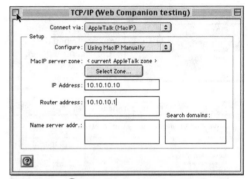

Figure 18.34 Ⓜ Enter the settings shown in the TCP/IP control panel above to test the Web Companion locally.

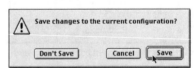

Figure 18.35 Ⓜ When asked, click *Save* to preserve the new settings.

TESTING YOUR WEB DATABASE LOCALLY

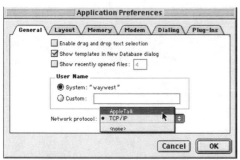

Figure 18.36 ⓜ Back in FileMaker, use the Application Preferences dialog box to switch your *Network protocol* to *AppleTalk*. Restart FileMaker after you click *OK*.

Figure 18.37 ⓜ Launch your Web browser and enter 10.10.10.10/ in the *Address* or *Location* text box.

Figure 18.38 ⓜ Finally: The Instant Web Portal appears with all your shared FileMaker databases.

7. Switch to FileMaker and choose Edit > Preferences > Application. When the Application Preferences dialog box appears, switch the *Network protocol* to *AppleTalk* using the pop-up menu (**Figure 18.36**). Click *OK* to close the dialog box.

8. Restart FileMaker to switch the networking protocol, then open the FileMaker databases you want shared.

9. Now, launch your Web browser and type into the *Address* or *Location* text box: 10.10.10.10/ and press ⟨Return⟩ (**Figure 18.37**). (The http:// part of the address will be added automatically.)

10. The Instant Web Portal will appear in the browser window and display the names of any FileMaker databases with Web sharing activated (**Figure 18.38**). Click any of the listed databases to test their various views.

11. Once you're done testing, be sure to switch your TCP/IP control panel back to its original setting and switch FileMaker back to its original network protocol.

✔ Tip

■ During testing you may decide to choose another Web style, view, or sort. Those changes won't appear in the Instant Web Portal until you restart FileMaker.

Once You Publish the Database

Once you publish your database to the Web or company intranet, you'll need to let users know how to reach it so they can put it to work. Typically these first users will be customers or co-workers. There are a couple of ways to point them your way.

You can simply tell them the IP address for the computer hosting the Web database, which they can type directly into their Web browser's location window. Tell visitors to bookmark your database's page in their browsers once they reach the page, and they'll never have to key in that pesky number again.

If you already have a Web site, you can avoid the whole "What's an IP address?" issue by putting a Web link on the site that points to the Instant Web Publishing home page.

PART V

APPENDICES

INSTALLING & CONFIGURING FILEMAKER

Unlike most of the book, this appendix has separate sections for Windows and Macintosh machines.

 For installing FileMaker on computers running Windows, turn to the next page.

 For installing FileMaker on computers running the Macintosh operating system, turn to page 297.

Once you've installed FileMaker, go ahead and configure its major preferences before you start using the program. See *Setting FileMaker's Preferences* on page 301.

Installing FileMaker on Windows

FileMaker runs on a variety of Windows operating systems:Windows 95, Windows 98, Windows Me, and Windows NT 4.0 (Service Pack 3), Windows 2000, and Windows XP. (Officially, FileMaker is "Windows XP ready" but at press time had not yet been certified to include the XP logo in FileMaker's packaging. The upshot: FileMaker will work fine on Windows XP machines.) To use the Web Companion and ODBC features, however, you need to be using Windows 98 or later.

What you'll need before starting:

◆ A PC with an Intel-compatible chip equivalent to at least the 486/33 with at least 32 MB of RAM (memory).

◆ A CD-ROM drive for using FileMaker's installation CD.

◆ A hard drive with at least 20 MB of free space for the *Typical* installation.

◆ The installation code for FileMaker. Look for the peel-off label on the sleeve containing the FileMaker CD.

✔ Tip

■ If you've been using an earlier version of FileMaker, it's easy to import the old files into FileMaker 5.5. See *To convert files from earlier FileMaker versions* on page 80.

Figure A.1 W When the CD's initial screen appears, choose *Install FileMaker Pro 5.5* to get started.

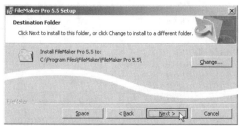

Figure A.2 W When the Destination Folder dialog box appears, click *Next* to install FileMaker in a new folder of its own or click *Change* to navigate to an existing folder.

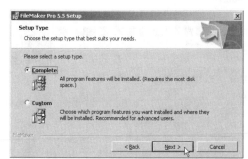

Figure A.3 W Unless you're hard pressed for space, click *Complete* for the full FileMaker installation, and then click *Next*.

To install FileMaker on a Windows computer:

1. Exit any other programs you may be running.

2. Put the FileMaker disc into your CD-ROM drive. Once the CD launches, you'll be presented with several choices (**Figure A.1**). Choose *Browse CD Contents* if you want to look around. The *View the ReadMe* choice includes information on potential conflicts with other programs. To get started, click *Install FileMaker Pro 5.5*.

3. When the InstallShield Wizard appears, click *Next* and a series of setup dialog boxes will appear. In the first, the Licensing Agreement dialog box, select the *I accept* option button and click *Next*. In the Customer Information dialog box enter your name, organization, and choose whether FileMaker will be used for all users of the computer or just yourself. Click *Next* and when the Destination Folder dialog box appears, click *Next* to have FileMaker installed in its own folder (**Figure A.2**). If you want to install FileMaker elsewhere, click *Change* to navigate to that folder and click *Next*.

4. The Setup Type dialog box offers two configuration choices: *Complete* and *Custom* (**Figure A.3**).

   If the *Complete* choice suits your purposes—and in most cases it will—simply click the *Next* button and skip ahead to step 6. You should choose *Complete* unless you're short on hard drive space, in which case choose *Custom*.

(continued)

5. To install only certain FileMaker files, click *Custom* and the Custom Setup dialog box will appear (**Figure A.4**). Click any item listed in the dialog box's main window and a brief description of its purpose and the size of the file will appear in the right-side panel. Click the drop-down menu of any item to select your installation option for that item (**Figure A.5**). Once you've made your choices, click *Next*.

6. Once you select your installation type, FileMaker will ask you what networking protocol you prefer (**Figure A.6**). The default setting is *TCP/IP*, which will cover most situations, so click *Next* and move on. For more information on networking, see page 243.

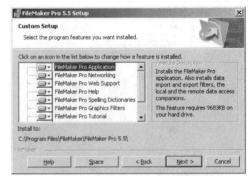

Figure A.4 The Custom installation lets you use only the files you want. The right column shows each file's size; the *Feature Description* area explains each highlighted file's purpose. Once you have made your choices, click *Next*.

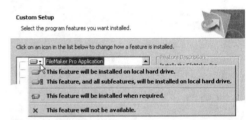

Figure A.5 Click the drop-down menu of any item in the Custom Setup dialog box to select an installation option.

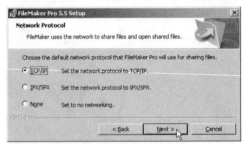

Figure A.6 The *TCP/IP* default will work for most network installations, so click Next. For more on networking, see page 243.

Figure A.7 🖳 You can make launching FileMaker easier by leaving the Application Shortcuts dialog box set to Yes.

Figure A.8 🖳 You'll find the 17-digit Installation Code on the sleeve of your FileMaker CD. When you're ready, click Next.

Figure A.9 🖳 A bar graph marks the progress of the installation.

Figure A.10 🖳 Once the installation is completed, click Finish.

7. When the Application Shortcuts dialog box appears, *Yes* will be selected by default (**Figure A.7**). Click *Next* to enable installation of a FileMaker icon on your desktop and in the Windows Quick Launch toolbar.

8. When the Installation Code dialog box appears, enter your 17-digit *code* (**Figure A.8**), (You'll find the code on the sleeve of your FileMaker CD.) Click *Next* and a dialog box will ask you to confirm your registration information. Click *Yes*. The installation will begin, with a bar graph marking its progress (**Figure A.9**).

9. Once the installation is completed, another dialog box will appear (**Figure A.10**). Click *Finish* and one final dialog box will appear. Choose *Yes, I want to restart my computer now* and click *Finish*.

(continued)

INSTALLING FILEMAKER ON WINDOWS

10. Once your machine restarts, launch FileMaker by double-clicking the FileMaker icon on your desktop (**Figure A.11**). Or choose Start > Programs > FileMaker Pro.

11. FileMaker's registration process will start (top, **Figure A.12**). Enter the necessary information in the series of dialog boxes that appear until you're done and click *Finish* (bottom, **Figure A.12**). FileMaker will start up. You're *almost* ready to get to work, but first see page 301 to set your FileMaker preferences.

✔ Tip

■ You can use the *Custom* installation if your hard drive is short on space. But anything less than the *Complete* installation will restrict what you can do with FileMaker. Consider tidying up your hard drive to make room for the *Complete* installation.

Figure A.11 W Navigate via your Start menu to launch FileMaker and you're off.

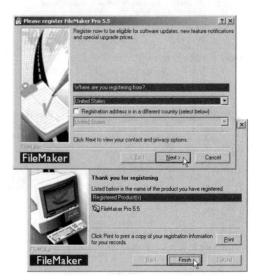

Figure A.12 W The first time you launch FileMaker, the program's registration process will guide you through a series of data-entry dialog boxes (top). Once you're done and click Finish (bottom), FileMaker will start up.

Installing FileMaker on the Mac

Unlike so many software programs, FileMaker doesn't demand the very latest operating system software to work. While it works well with OS X, it also will work with OS 7.6.1–9.1. To use the Web Companion and ODBC features, however, you need to be using at least OS 8.6.

What you'll need before starting:

◆ A Macintosh or Mac OS-compatible computer running System 7.6.1–9.1 with at least 32 MB of RAM. If you're running OS X, you'll need at least 128 MB of RAM.

◆ A hard drive with at least 30 MB of free space. If you simply can't free up the space for the regular installation, see the *Tips* on page 300 for help on creating a minimum installation.

◆ A CD-ROM drive for using the FileMaker installation CD.

◆ The installation code for FileMaker. Look for the peel-off label on the sleeve containing the FileMaker CD.

To install FileMaker on a Macintosh:

1. Turn off any anti-virus program you may have running in the background. Such programs sometimes cause problems for FileMaker's installer program.

2. If it's running, turn off File Sharing by clicking on the Apple at the upper-left corner of your screen and navigating to the Control Panels folder. Continue holding the mouse button down until you locate the File Sharing control panel, then release the mouse button. When the File Sharing control panel opens, click the *Cancel* button, then close the control panel. (Remember to turn File Sharing back on once you're done with the installation.)

3. Put the FileMaker disc into your CD-ROM drive.

4. Once the CD launches, depending on which system you're running double-click either the *Start Here Mac OS X* or the *Start Here Mac OS Classic* icon (**Figure A.13**), which will present the software license agreement. Click *Accept* to move to the next step.

5. FileMaker's Start Here dialog box will appear with *Easy Install* as the default setting, which will install all the FileMaker files (**Figure A.14**).

   Use the *Installation Location* pop-up menu to select a hard drive on which you want to install FileMaker. By default, your startup hard drive is chosen. Note that the approximate disk space needed to install FileMaker appears on the right just above the *Quit* button. If you don't have enough disk space for the full installation, switch to another hard drive or see the first *Tip* on page 300 on making a custom installation. Once you've chosen a hard drive, click *Install*.

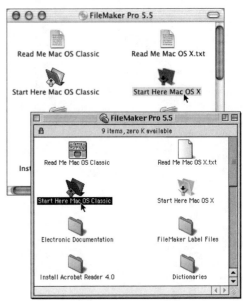

Figure A.13 🅜 Double-click the Start Here icon to begin installation on the Macintosh.

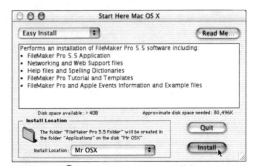

Figure A.14 🅜 If you choose Easy Install, be sure to note the default destination drive in the lower left and change it if necessary. The disk space needed appears above the Quit button.

INSTALLING FILEMAKER ON THE MAC

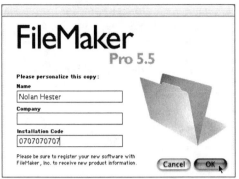

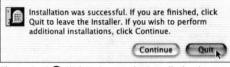

Figure A.15 ⓜ You'll find the Installation Code on the sleeve of your FileMaker CD. When you're done, click OK.

Figure A.16 ⓜ Click Quit once the installation is complete.

6. Fill out the registration dialog box when it appears (**Figure A.15**). You'll find the 17-digit *Installation Code* on the sleeve of your FileMaker CD. Click *OK* and the installation will begin, with a bar graph marking its progress.

7. One final dialog box will appear, announcing that the installation is finished (**Figure A.16**). Click *Quit* and you're done installing the program.

(continued)

INSTALLING FILEMAKER ON THE MAC

8. The new FileMaker Pro 5.5 folder will automatically open on your desktop (**Figure A.17**). Launch the program by double-clicking the *FileMaker Pro* icon and FileMaker's registration process will start (**Figure A.18**). Choose how you want to register and enter the necessary information in the series of dialog boxes that appear. You're *almost* ready to get to work, but first see the next page to set your FileMaker preferences.

✔ Tips

■ If you do not have enough hard drive space to install all the FileMaker files in step 5, click the *Easy Install* button in the upper left of the installation window and choose *Custom Install* (**Figure A.19**). You can then select only the files you need. The *Approximate disk space needed* figure in the lower right will change as you check or uncheck items, helping you decide how many FileMaker items to install.

The *Custom Install* requires much less space than the *Easy Install* but also restricts what you can do with FileMaker. Consider tidying up your hard drive to make room for the *Easy Install*.

■ In making a *Custom Install*, if you're not sure which items you truly need, click on the I to the right of any item for more information on its purpose (**Figure A.20**).

Figure A.17 ⓜ The new FileMaker Pro 5.5 folder opens automatically. Launch the program by double-clicking the *FileMaker Pro* icon.

Figure A.18 ⓜ The first time you launch FileMaker, the program's registration process will guide you through a series of data-entry dialog boxes.

Figure A.19 ⓜ To perform a custom installation of FileMaker, use your cursor to toggle the install button in the upper left of Figure A.14.

Figure A.20 ⓜ Within the *Custom Install* window, click the I if you want a description of a file's purpose.

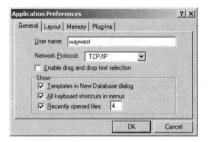

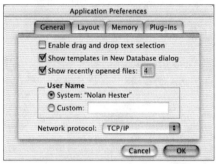

Figure A.21 The settings in the Application Preferences dialog box affect every FileMaker database. From top, the dialog box's appearance in Windows, Mac OS X, and pre-OS X Macs.

Figure A.22 The *Layout* preferences tab.

Setting FileMaker's Preferences

FileMaker gives you control over three kinds of preferences: application, document, and Web. Application-level preferences affect *every* document used by FileMaker. Document-level preferences apply only to the *open* database, which if you like, lets you create a different set of preferences for a particular database. The Web preferences are covered separately in *Setting Up and Configuring the Web Companion* on page 274.

Application preferences

Before you start setting your preferences, here's a quick rundown of the choices for each tab of the Application Preferences dialog box:

General: Most items in this tab are fairly self explanatory (**Figure A.21**). While you chose a *Network Protocol* when installing FileMaker, you can use this drop-down menu if you ever need to change the protocol. The *Templates in New Database dialog* option is great if you'll regularly use templates as layout starting points; otherwise it adds an extra step to the file-opening process.

Layout: Most items in this tab are fairly self explanatory (**Figure A.22**). The *Always lock layout tools* option helps keep you from accidentally deselecting a tool, though you can also lock any tool by double-clicking it as you work within a particular file. The *Web palette* choice ensures that the colors used in layouts published on the Web will appear consistently across platforms and browsers. Unless you absolutely need to use a color outside the 216-color Web palette, go ahead and turn on this choice.

(continued)

Memory: Unlike many programs, FileMaker has no Save command and instead saves automatically. Here's where you control how often it saves—an interval based on your own comfort zone—or whether it saves only when the computer's idle, which is the default (**Figure A.23**).

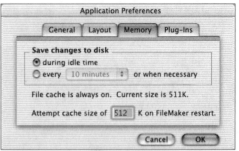

Figure A.23 Use the *Memory* preferences tab to set how often FileMaker automatically saves your database.

 Modem: Most of the items in this tab, which appears only in pre-OS X Macs, are fairly self explanatory (**Figure A.24**). Unless you know your AT modem control commands cold or have specific settings recommended by your modem manufacturer, leave the *Modem Commands* settings alone. As for the lower *Connection* panel's settings, check the *Speed*—it's easy to forget to bump it up as you upgrade modems or switch to a full-time connection.

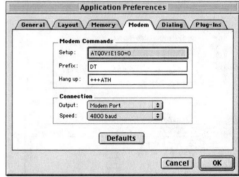

Figure A.24 This tab appears only in pre-OS X Macs.

 Dialing: FileMaker uses this tab, which appears only in pre-OS X Macs, to set part of the Dial Phone script to call numbers in a database. The entry boxes let you account for the varying dialing needs of phone systems in handling outside, long-distance, and local extension calls (**Figure A.25**).

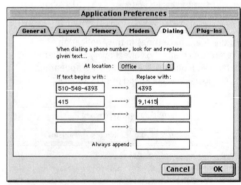

Figure A.25 This tab, which appears only in pre-OS X Macs, lets you control outside, long-distance, and extension settings.

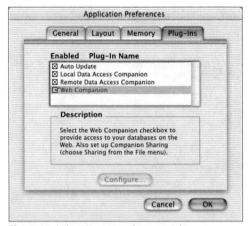

Figure A.26 The *Plug-Ins* preferences tab.

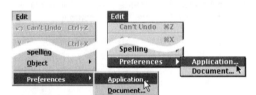

Figure A.27 To set preferences for the entire program on a Windows or pre-OS X machine, choose Edit > Preferences > Application.

Figure A.28 To set program preferences on a Mac running OS X, choose FileMaker Pro > Preferences > Application.

Plug-Ins: This tab is used to enable your Data Access and Web connection plug-ins (**Figure A.26**). It also includes Auto Update, which works with FileMaker Server to automatically update the FileMaker plug-ins. For details, see *To turn on the Data Access Companions* on page 261 and *Setting Up and Configuring the Web Companion* on page 275.

To set application preferences:

1. If you are using a Windows machine or a pre-OS X Mac, open a FileMaker database (Ctrl O in Windows, ⌘ O on the Mac), then choose Edit > Preferences > Application (**Figure A.27**). If you are running OS X, choose FileMaker Pro > Preferences > Application (**Figure A.28**).

2. When the Application Preferences dialog box appears, choose a category with the tabs.

3. Make your choices based on the information described in the preceding section. Click *OK*.

Document preferences

If a document is shared, only users who know the master password can change its preferences. (For more on passwords, see *Controlling File Access* on page 249.) Before you start setting a document's preferences, here's a quick rundown of the choices:

General: The options in this tab give you a fair amount of control over individual databases (**Figure A.29**).

◆ Check *Use smart quotes* to automatically substitute the more typographically polished curly quotes for straight quotes.

◆ Check *Store compatible graphics* to automatically store database objects in cross-platform formats such as JPEG, GIF, or PICT. This will take a little more space on your hard drive but makes cross-platform work more consistent.

◆ Check *Try default password* and type in a password if you want FileMaker to automatically enter that password when you open the database. Obviously, this option only makes sense for password-protected databases.

◆ Check *Switch to layout* and enter a specific layout name if you want FileMaker to automatically change to that layout whenever this document is open. This can be particularly handy if you're spending multiple sessions designing a complicated database.

◆ Check either of the two *Perform script* boxes and enter a script's name if you want a particular set of actions performed at that time (one to run upon opening a file, the other upon closing it). This is very useful if, as host of a database, you regularly work on a database but want guests to see it presorted or set up in a particular view.

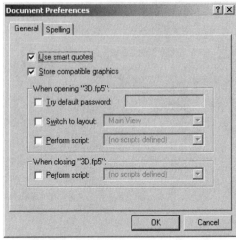

Figure A.29 The document-level *General* preferences tab affects only the currently open database.

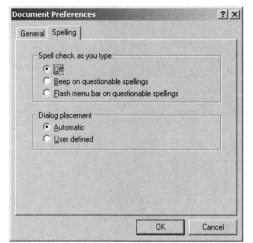

Figure A.30 The *Spelling* preferences apply only to the currently open database.

Figure A.31 To set preferences for the current file on a Windows or pre-OS X machine, choose Edit > Preferences > Document.

Figure A.32 To set preferences for the current file on a Mac running OS X, choose FileMaker Pro > Preferences > Document.

Spelling: Most items in this tab are fairly self explanatory (**Figure A.30**). Some users love *Spell check as you type*; others can't stand it. Selecting *User defined* under *Dialog placement*, lets you move the Spelling dialog box when it appears the first time to a set spot on your screen. Unless you move it again for this database, it will appear in that same spot every time, making it quick to find.

To set document preferences:

1. If you are using a Windows machine or a pre-OS X Mac, open a FileMaker database ([Ctrl]O in Windows, [⌘]O on the Mac), then choose Edit > Preferences > Document (**Figure A.31**). If you are running OS X, choose FileMaker Pro > Preferences > Document (**Figure A.32**).

2. When the Document Preferences dialog box appears, choose a tab (*General* or *Spelling*).

3. Make your choices based on the information in the preceding section and click *OK*.

FUNCTIONS

Here's an all-in-one-place listing of FileMaker's various functions, organized by type. FileMaker 5.5 has 17 new functions, including 10 status functions. Before digging into these tables, be sure you understand formulas and how to use expressions, constants, and operators. If you don't, these tables won't make much sense. For more information, see *Defining Fields* on page 99.

Text Functions

SYNTAX	DEFINITION
Exact *(original text, comparison text)*	Returns a comparison of *original text* and *comparison text* in two text strings
Exact *(original container, comparison container)*	Returns a comparison of *original container* and *comparison container* in two container fields
Left *(text, number)*	Returns the specified *number* of characters in the supplied *text*, counting from the left
LeftWords *(text, number of words)*	Returns a text result containing the specified *number of words* in the supplied *text*, counting from the left
Length *(text)*	Returns the number or characters of *text*, including all spaces, numbers, and special characters
Lower *(text)*	Converts all letters in the given *text* to lowercase
Middle *(text, start, size)*	Returns characters from the supplied *text*, counting from *start* through number of characters in *size*
MiddleWords *(text, starting word, number of words)*	Returns the middle words from the supplied *text*, from *starting word* through the *number of words*
PatternCount *(text, search string)*	Returns the number of occurrences of the *search string* in *text*
Position *(text, search string, start, occurrence)*	Scans the supplied *text* from *start* for the nth *occurrence* of a *search string*
Proper *(text)*	Converts first letter in each word of *text* to uppercase and rest to lowercase
Replace *(text, start, size, replacement text)*	Substitutes a series of characters for others in a string
Right *(text, number)*	Returns the specified *number* of characters in the supplied *text*, counting from the right
RightWords *(text, number of words)*	Returns a text result containing the specified *number of words* in the supplied *text*, counting from the right
Substitute *(text, search string, replace string)*	Substitutes every occurrence of a specified set of characters in a text string with another set of characters you specify, and returns the revised text string
TextToDate *(text)*	Returns the date equivalent of the supplied *text*, for use with formulas involving dates or date-oriented functions
TextToNum *(text)*	Returns the numeric equivalent of the supplied *text*, for use with formulas involving numbers or numeric functions
TextToTime *(text)*	Returns the time equivalent of the supplied *text*, for use with formulas involving time or time-oriented functions
Trim *(text)*	Returns the supplied *text*, stripped of all leading and trailing spaces
Upper *(text)*	Converts all letters in the given *text* to uppercase
WordCount *(text)*	Returns a count of the total number of words in the given *text*

Number Functions

SYNTAX	DEFINITION
Abs (*number*)	The absolute value (a positive value) of the *number* supplied
Exp (*number*)	The value of the constant "e", raised to the power specified by the supplied *number*
Int (*number*)	The integer part of the supplied *number*, dropping any digits to the right of the decimal point
Mod (*number, divisor*)	The remainder after the specified *number* is divided by a *divisor*
NumToText (*number*)	The text equivalent of the specified *number*
Random	A random number between 0 and 1
Round (*number, precision*)	The supplied *number*, rounded off to the number of decimal places supplied in *precision*
Sign (*number*)	One of three possible values, representing whether the supplied *number* is negative, zero, or positive
Sqrt (*number*)	The square root of the supplied *number*
Truncate (*number, precision*)	The supplied *number*, truncated to the specified number of decimal places supplied in *precision*

Date Functions

SYNTAX	DEFINITION
Date (*month, day, year*)	The calendar date (*year* must be four digits)
DateToText (*date*)	The text equivalent of the supplied *date*
Day (*date*)	A number representing the day of the month for the given *date*
DayName (*date*)	Text containing the name of the weekday for the given *date*
DayofWeek (*date*)	A number representing the day of the week for the given *date*
DayofYear (*date*)	A number representing the number of days since January 1 for the given *date*
Month (*date*)	A number representing the month of the year for the given *date*
MonthName (*date*)	Text containing the name of the month for the given *date*
Today	The current date
WeekofYear (*date*)	The number of weeks since January 1 for the given *date*
WeekofYearFiscal (*date, starting day*)	A number between 1 and 53 representing the week containing the given *date*, figured according to the *starting day* used as the first day of the week
Year (*date*)	A number representing the year for the given *date*

Time Functions

SYNTAX	DEFINITION
Hour (*time*)	A number representing the number of hours embedded in a *time* value
Minute (*time*)	A number representing the number of minutes embedded in a *time* value
Seconds (*time*)	A number representing the number of seconds embedded in a *time* value
Time (*hours, minutes, seconds*)	A time result with the given number of *hours*, *minutes*, and *seconds*, counting from zero and adding the supplied duration of time to each unit
TimeToText (*time*)	The text equivalent of the supplied *time*, for use with formulas involving text or text-oriented functions

FUNCTIONS

FUNCTIONS

Aggregate Functions

SYNTAX	DEFINITION
Average (*field*) Average (*relationship::field*)	Returns the average for all non-blank values in a single repeating field (*field*) or (*relationship::field*)
Average (*field1, field2,...*) Average (*relationship::field1, relationship::field2...*)	Returns the average for all non-blank values in each corresponding repetition of one or more repeating fields or non-repeating fields (*field1, field2,...*) or (*relationship::field1, relationship::field2...*)
Count (*field*) Count (*relationship::field*)	Returns the number of valid, non-blank entries in a repeating field (*field*) or (*relationship::field*)
Count (*field1, field2,...*) Count (*relationship::field1, relationship::field2...*)	Returns the number of valid, non-blank values in each corresponding repetition of one or more repeating fields or non-repeating fields (*field1, field2,...*) or (*relationship::field1, relationship::field2...*)
Max (*field*) Max (*relationship::field*)	Returns the highest non-blank value in a repeating field (*field*) or (*relationship::field*)
Max (*field1, field2,...*) Max (*relationship::field1, relationship::field2...*)	Returns the highest non-blank values in each corresponding repetition of one or more repeating fields or non-repeating fields (*field1, field2,...*) or (*relationship::field1, relationship::field2...*)
Min (*field*) Min (*relationship::field*)	Returns the lowest non-blank value in a repeating field (*field*) or (*relationship::field*)
Min (*field1, field2,...*) Min (*relationship::field1, relationship::field2...*)	Returns the lowest non-blank values in each corresponding repetition of one or more repeating fields or non-repeating fields (*field1, field2,...*) or (*relationship::field1, relationship::field2...*)
StDev (*field*) StDev (*relationship::field*)	Returns the standard deviation of the sample represented by a series of non-blank values in a repeating field (*field*) or (*relationship::field*)
StDev (*field1, field2,...*) StDev (*relationship::field1, relationship::field2...*)	Returns the standard deviation of the sample represented by a series of non-blank values in each corresponding repetition of one or more repeating fields or non-repeating fields (*field1, field2,...*) or (*relationship::field1, relationship::field2...*)
StDevP (*field*) StDevP (*relationship::field*)	Returns the standard deviation of a population represented by a series of non-blank values in a repeating field (*field*) or (*relationship::field*)
StDevP (*field1, field2,...*) StDevP (*relationship::field1, relationship::field2...*)	Returns the standard deviation of a population represented by a series of non-blank values in each corresponding repetition of one or more repeating fields or non-repeating fields (*field1, field2,...*) or (*relationship::field1, relationship::field2...*)
Sum (*field*) Sum (*relationship::field*)	Returns the sum of non-blank values in a repeating field (*field*) or (*relationship::field*)
Sum (*field1, field2,...*) Sum (*relationship::field1, relationship::field2...*)	Returns the sum of non-blank values in each corresponding repetition of one or more repeating fields or non-repeating fields (*field1, field2,...*) or (*relationship::field1, relationship::field2...*)

Summary Functions

SYNTAX	DEFINITION
GetSummary (*summary field, break field*)	Returns the value of the specified *summary field* for the current range of records when the database is sorted by *break field*; otherwise returns an empty result. (Equivalent to calculating a sub summary.)
GetSummary (*summary field, summary field*)	Returns the value of the *summary field* for the current found set of records. (Equivalent to calculating a grand summary.)

Repeating Functions

SYNTAX	DEFINITION
Extend (*non-repeating field*)	Allows the value of a *non-repeating field* (a field defined to contain only one value) to be used in calculations involving repeating fields
GetRepetition (*repeating field, repetition number*)	Returns the contents of the *repetition number* specified in a *repeating field*
Last (*repeating field*)	Returns the last valid, non-blank value in a *repeating field*. The Last function can also return the contents of the last related record.

Financial Functions

SYNTAX	DEFINITION
FV (*payment, interest rate, periods*)	The future value of an investment, based on a constant *interest rate* and *payment* amount for the *periods*
NPV (*payment, interest rate*)	The net present value of a series of unequal *payments* made at regular intervals, assuming a fixed *interest rate* per interval
PMT (*principal, interest rate, term*)	The payment required to meet the requirements of the *term*, *interest rate*, and *principal* supplied
PV (*payment, interest rate, periods*)	The present value of a series of equal *payments* made at regular intervals (*periods*), assuming a fixed *interest rate* per interval

Trigonometric Functions

SYNTAX	DEFINITION
Atan (*number*)	The trigonometric arc tangent (inverse tangent) of the *number* supplied
Cos (*number*)	The cosine of the angle (in radians) of the *number* supplied
Degrees (*number*)	The supplied *number* (in radians) converted to degrees
Ln (*number*)	The base-e (natural) logarithm of the *number* supplied
Log (*number*)	The common logarithm (base 10) of any positive *number*
Pi	The value of the constant *pi* (approximately 3.14159)
Radians (*number*)	The supplied *number* (in degrees) converted to radians
Sin (*number*)	The sine of an angle expressed in *number* of radians
Tan (*number*)	The tangent of an angle in *number* of radians

Logical Functions

SYNTAX	DEFINITION
Case (*test1, result1 [, test2, result2, default result]...*)	Evaluates each in a series of expressions, in order, and when a True expression is found, returns the result supplied for that expression. Returns one of any number of results from a supplied list.
Choose (*expression, result0 [, result1, result2]...*)	Searches a list of arguments and returns a result. Returns one of any number of results from a supplied list. Use Choose to look up one value in a list of possibilities.
GetField (*fieldname*)	The name of the field whose contents should be retrieved
If (*test, resultIfTrue, resultIfFalse*)	Tests the number or expression for a True or False condition
IsEmpty (*value*)	Determines whether a *value* is an empty (null) value
IsValid (*field*)	Determines if a given *field* is missing or contains an invalid entry

Status Functions

SYNTAX	DEFINITION
Status (CurrentAppVersion)	The FileMaker Pro version number that is currently in use
Status (CurrentDate)	The current calendar date
Status (CurrentError)	A number representing the current error value
Status (CurrentFieldContents)	The contents of the active field or the current repetition in a repeating field
Status (CurrentFieldName)	The name of the field currently containing the insertion point
Status (CurrentFileName)	The name of the file currently in use
Status (CurrentFilePath)	The file path for a local or remote file
Status (CurrentFileSize)	The size (in bytes) of the current file
Status (CurrentFoundCount)	The number of records in the current found set
Status (CurrentGroups)	The group (or groups) that the current user is a member of, based on the current password
Status (CurrentHighContrast)	The availability of Windows high contrast accessibility option
Status (CurrentHighColor)	The name of current high contrast default color scheme if Windows high contrast option available
Status (CurrentHostName)	The host name FileMaker Pro registers on the network
Status (CurrentLanguage)	The current language set on the current system
Status (CurrentLayoutAccess)	A number representing a layout's access privileges
Status (CurrentLayoutCount)	The total number of layouts defined in the database file
Status (CurrentLayoutName)	The name of the layout currently displayed in the file
Status (CurrentLayoutNumber)	The number of the current layout in the file
Status (CurrentMessageChoice)	A number indicating user input from an alert message displayed using the Show Message step in a script
Status (CurrentMode)	The FileMaker Pro mode at the time of the calculation
Status (CurrentModifierKeys)	A number representing which keyboard modifier keys (for example, Shift) are being pressed by the user
Status (CurrentMultiUserStatus)	A value representing single user file, multiuser file on the host computer, or multi-user file on a guest computer
Status (CurrentNetworkChoice)	The name of the network protocol that is currently loaded
Status (CurrentODBCError)	A string representing an ODBC error
Status (CurrentPageNumber)	The current page being printed or previewed
Status (CurrentPlatform)	A value representing the current platform (Windows or Mac OS)
Status (CurrentPortalRow)	The number of the current row in a selected portal (when no portal is selected, returns 0)
Status (CurrentPrinterName)	A text string identifying the current printer type
Status (CurrentRecordAccess)	A number representing a record's access privileges
Status (CurrentRecordCount)	A number that represents the total number of records in the current file
Status (CurrentRecordID)	The unique ID of the current record
Status (CurrentRecordModificationCount)	The number of times changes are saved for the current record since it was created
Status (CurrentRecordNumber)	The number of the current record in the found set
Status (CurrentRepetitionNumber)	A number representing the current (active) iteration of a repeating field
Status (CurrentRequestCount)	The total number of find requests currently defined in the database file
Status (CurrentScreenDepth)	The number of bits needed to represent the color of a pixel on the main screen
Status (CurrentScreenHeight)	The number of pixels displayed vertically on the screen in which the window of the current file is open

Status Functions (continued)

SYNTAX	DEFINITION
Status (CurrentScreenWidth)	The number of pixels displayed horizontally on the screen in which the window of the current file is open
Status (CurrentScriptName)	The name of the script currently running (or paused)
Status (CurrentSortStatus)	A value representing whether the records in the current file are unsorted, sorted, or partially sorted
Status (CurrentStatusArea)	A number representing whether the status area is hidden, visible, and locked, or hidden and locked
Status (CurrentSystemVersion)	A text string containing the current system version
Status (CurrentTime)	The current time
Status (CurrentUserCount)	The number of users currently accessing the file
Status (CurrentUserName)	The name of the FileMaker Pro user, as specified in the General area of the Application Preferences dialog box
Status (CurrentView)	A number representing whether current view of database is a form, list, or table
Status (CurrentWebSharing)	A number representing whether the Web Companion is enabled and active, and whether the current file has been opened with a password that allows records to be exported

Design Functions

SYNTAX	DEFINITION
DatabaseNames	The names of the currently opened databases
FieldBounds (*database name, layout name, field name*)	The location and size of a specified field
FieldIDs (*database name, [layout name]*)	The field IDs in a specified database file
FieldNames (*database name, [layout name]*)	The names of fields in a specified database file
FieldRepetitions (*database name, layout name, field name*)	The number of repetitions of a specified repeating field
FieldStyle (*database name, layout name, field name*)	How a specified field is formatted on a layout (for example, a radio button), and whether a value list is associated with the field
FieldType (*database name, field name*)	The field definition for a specified field
GetNextSerialValue (*database name, field name*)	The next serial number for a specified field
LayoutIDs (*database name*)	The layout IDs in a specified database file
LayoutNames (*database name*)	The names of layouts in a specified database file
RelationIDs (*database name*)	The relation IDs in a specified database file
RelationInfo (*database name, relationship name*)	The name of the related file for a specified relationship
RelationNames (*database name*)	The relationships defined in a specified database file
ScriptIDs (*database name*)	The script IDs in a specified database file
ScriptNames (*database name*)	The scripts defined in a specified database file
ValueListIDs (*database name*)	The value list IDs in a specified database file
ValueListItems (*database name, value list name*)	The values defined for a specified value list
ValueListNames (*database name*)	The value lists defined in a specified database file

FileMaker Pro Web Companion External Functions

SYNTAX	DEFINITION
External ("Web-Version", 0)	The version of FileMaker Pro Web Companion that loads when you open FileMaker Pro
External ("Web-ClientAddress", 0)	The domain name (for example, www.filemaker.com) of a Web user whose HTTP request is being processed by FileMaker Pro Web Companion
External ("Web-ClientIP", 0)	The IP address (for example, 12.34.56.78) of the Web user whose HTTP request is being processed by FileMaker Pro Web Companion
External ("Web-ClientName", 0)	The value that the Web user types for user name in the Web browser password dialog box
External ("Web-ClientType", 0)	The name and version of the Web browser being used by the Web user
External ("Web-ToHTML", field name or text value)	The contents of the specified field or text value encoded in HTML
External ("Web-ToHTTP", field name or text value)	The contents of the specified field or text value encoded in HTTP

FUNCTIONS

SCRIPT COMMANDS

Virtually any script step you can think of has been predefined within FileMaker. You build scripts within ScriptMaker's Script Definition dialog box where all the available script steps are listed in the left-hand column (**Figure C.1**). Use this appendix as you work within the dialog box to quickly look up what actions each script step will trigger. The appendix is arranged in the same order and groups as the steps displayed in the left-hand column. For more on using FileMaker's ScriptMaker, see *Using Templates and Scripts* on page 199.

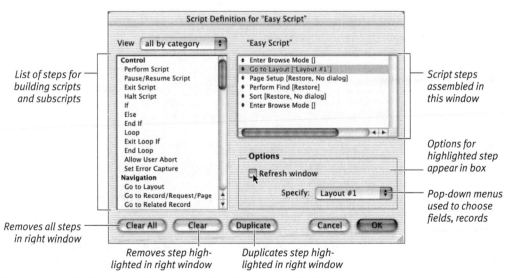

List of steps for building scripts and subscripts

Script steps assembled in this window

Options for highlighted step appear in box

Pop-down menus used to choose fields, records

Removes all steps in right window

Removes step highlighted in right window

Duplicates step highlighted in right window

Figure 13.11 Use the Script Definition dialog box to build scripts by selecting script steps on the left-hand list and building your script in the right-hand window.

Control Script Steps

Use	To
Perform Script	Run another script, specified by options, within a script
Pause/Resume Script	Pause (or resume) script, based on option chosen
Exit Script	Exit the current script
Halt Script	Stop current script (allowing for user inputs)
If	Perform script if calculation is True
Else	Perform another step if calculation is False
End If	Mark end of script started by If script
Loop	Repeat a set of steps
Exit Loop If	Exit a loop if a calculation is True
End Loop	Mark end of Loop script
Allow User Abort	Let user stop (or not stop) script, based on option chosen
Set Error Capture	Move (or not move) error messages to Status function, based on option chosen

Navigation Script Steps

Use	To
Go to Layout	Move to layout specified by option
Go to Record, Request, Page	Move to record, request, or page specified by option
Go to Related Record	Move to record in related database specified by option
Go to Portal Row	Move to portal row or field in portal row specified by option
Go to Field	Move to field specified by option
Go to Next Field	Move to next field in current layout
Go to Previous Field	Move to previous field in current layout
Enter Browse Mode	Switch to Browse mode with option to pause
Enter Find Mode	Switch to Find mode
Enter Preview Mode	Switch to Preview mode

Sort, Find, Print Script Steps

Use	To
Sort	Sort records in found set based on current sort settings
Unsort	Restore records to unsorted state
Show All Records	Find all records in database
Show Omitted	Find records not in found set
Omit Record	Omit current record from found set
Omit Multiple	Omit number of records from found set, starting with current record
Perform Find	Find records matching current find request
Modify Last Find	Change find request
Page Setup/Print Setup	Open Page Setup dialog box (Mac); Open Print Setup dialog box (Windows)
Print	Print current record

Editing Script Steps

Use	To
Undo	Undo last action
Cut	Delete contents of field specified by option and place in Clipboard
Copy	Copy contents of field specified by option and place in Clipboard
Paste	Paste Clipboard contents into field specified by option
Clear	Delete contents of field specified by option
Select All	Select all items in layout

Field Script Steps

Use	To
Set Field	Replace contents of field specified by option with results of calculation, also specified by option
Insert Text	Paste text specified by option into field specified by option
Insert Calculated Result	Paste result of calculation specified by option into field specified by option
Insert from Index	Paste contents of field specified by option
Insert from Last Record	Paste contents of field, specified by option, from last active record
Insert Current Date	Paste current system date into field specified by option
Insert Current Time	Paste current system time into field specified by option
Insert Current User Name	Paste current user name into field specified by option
Insert Picture	Paste graphic into active container field
Insert QuickTime/Insert Movie	Paste movie into active container field
Insert Object	Insert embedded or linked object into container field (Windows only)
Update Link	Update an OLE link in container field (Windows only)

Record Script Steps

Use	To
New Record/Request	Add a new record or find request
Duplicate Record/Request	Duplicate a record or find request
Delete Record/Request	Delete current record or find request
Delete Portal Row	Delete current portal row
Revert Record/Request	Revert current record or find request to state before most recent action
Exit Record/Request	Leave current record or find request, with no field selected
Copy Record	Copy contents of current record to Clipboard
Copy All Records	Copy contents of records in found set to Clipboard
Delete All Records	Delete all records in found set
Replace	Replace contents of field, specified by options, within current record
Relookup	Update current record from lookup value
Import Records	Import records, specified by options, to current field
Export Records	Export records, specified by options, to another database format

Window Script Steps

Use	To
Freeze Window	Hide action from user
Refresh Window	Update screen
Scroll Window	Scroll window to position specified by options
Toggle Window	Toggle window size to choice specified by options
Toggle Status Area	Toggle status area to choice specified by options
Toggle Text Ruler	Show or hide text ruler based on options
Set Zoom Level	Change window's zoom based on options
View As	Show single record or list of records, based on options

File Script Steps

Use	To
New	Create new database
Open	Open a database specified by options
Close	Close a database specified by options
Change Password	Change existing password
Set Multi-User	Allow or block network access to current file
Set Use System Formats	Use date, time, number formats of current file or use system formats
Save Copy As	Save a database specified by options
Recover	Recover a damaged database specified by options

Spelling Script Steps

Use	To
Check Selection	Check spelling in field specified by options
Check Record	Check spelling in record specified by options
Check Found Set	Check spelling in all records within found set
Correct Word	Display Spelling dialog box so user can correct misspelled word
Spelling Options	Display Spelling Options dialog box
Set Dictionaries	Display Select Dictionaries dialog box
Edit User Dictionary	Display Edit User Dictionary dialog box

Open Menu Item Script Steps

Use	To
Open Application Preferences	Display Application Preferences dialog box
Open Document Preferences	Display Document Preferences dialog box
Open Define Fields	Display Define Fields dialog box
Open Define Relationships	Display Define Relationships dialog box
Open Define Value Lists	Display Define Value Lists dialog box
Open Help	Display FileMaker's Help contents window
Open Hosts	Open the Hosts dialog box to select and open shared database over network
Open ScriptMaker	Display Define Scripts dialog box and halt current script
Open Sharing	Display File Sharing dialog box

Miscellaneous Script Steps

Use	To
Show Message	Display specified text message for user
Allow Toolbars	Hide or show FileMaker's toolbars and related menu items
Beep	Play system alert sound
Speak	Generate speech from text specified by options (Mac only)
Dial Phone	Dial phone number specified by options
Open URL	Open a Web URL specified by options
Send Mail	Send email with To, Cc, Subject, and Message fields specified by options (available in Mac OS X in FileMaker 5.5v2 or later)
Set Next Serial Value	Update next value in an auto-enter serial number value field
Send Apple Event	Start Apple Event specified by options (Mac only)
Perform AppleScript	Run AppleScript specified by options (Mac only)
Send DDE Execute	Send a Dynamic Data Exchange command to application specified by options (Windows only)
Execute SQL	Execute any SQL statement to control interaction with ODBC data source
Send Message	Start or print using another application specified by options (Windows only)
Comment	Add explanatory note to a script
Flush Cache to Disk	Save FileMaker internal cache to disk
Exit Application	Close all files and exit FileMaker (Windows only)
Quit Application	Close all files and quit FileMaker (Mac only)

SCRIPT COMMANDS

KEYBOARD SHORTCUTS

This appendix aims to help you quickly find the FileMaker keyboard command shortcuts you need. For that reason, they are organized by menu and by function—reflecting the two most common ways people remember commands and do their work.

Shortcuts by Menu: Sometimes you really have to dig around in a menu to find all the available commands. The Shortcuts by menu tables list every keyboard shortcut hiding beneath FileMaker's 12 menus. Many keyboard shortcuts, however, do not appear under any menu. That's where the Shortcuts by function tables come to the rescue.

Shortcuts by Function: FileMaker's menus arrangement sometimes does not really mirror the way you use the program. If you're deep into creating a new layout, for example, it's easier to see all the layout-related functions at a glance rather than listed under a bunch of menus. The same goes for text selection and formatting.

Shortcuts by Menu

The File Menu

To	WINDOWS	MACINTOSH	WORKS IN MODE
Create new file	none	none	All
Open file	Ctrl O	⌘ O	All
Open Remote	Ctrl Shift O	Shift ⌘ O	All
Close file	Ctrl W	⌘ W	All
Open Define fields dialog box	Ctrl Shift D	Shift ⌘ D	All
Redefine field	Double-click field	Double-click field	Layout
Print	Ctrl P	⌘ P	All
Print without dialog box	Ctrl Alt P	Option ⌘ P	All
Exit/Quit	Ctrl Q	⌘ Q	All

The Edit Menu

To	WINDOWS	MACINTOSH	WORKS IN MODE
Undo an action	Ctrl Z	⌘ Z	All
Cut a selection	Ctrl X	⌘ X	All
Copy a selection	Ctrl C	⌘ C	All
Paste a selection	Ctrl V	⌘ V	All
Delete a selection	Del	Del	All
Duplicate object	Ctrl D	⌘ D	Layout
Select All	Ctrl A	⌘ A	All
Spelling—Correct Word	Ctrl Shift Y	Shift ⌘ Y	Browse, Find, Layout

The View Menu

To SWITCH To	WINDOWS	MACINTOSH	WORKS IN MODE
Browse mode	Ctrl B	⌘ B	All
Find mode	Ctrl F	⌘ F	All
Layout mode	Ctrl L	⌘ L	All
Preview mode	Ctrl U	⌘ U	All
Turn on/off T-squares	Ctrl T	⌘ T	Layout

The Insert Menu

To INSERT	WINDOWS	MACINTOSH	WORKS IN MODE
Current Date	Ctrl − (hyphen)	⌘ − (hyphen)	Browse, Find
Current Time	Ctrl ;	⌘ ;	Browse, Find
Current User Name	Ctrl Shift N	Shift ⌘ N	Browse, Find
Merge Field	Ctrl M	⌘ M	Layout
From Index	Ctrl I	⌘ I	Browse, Find
From Last Record	Ctrl ' (apostrophe)	⌘ ' (apostrophe)	Browse, Find

The Format Menu

To Format	Windows	Macintosh	Works in Mode
Selected text via Text Format dialog box	`Alt`+Double-click	`Option`+Double-click	Browse, Layout
Size—Increase by one point size	`Ctrl` `Shift` `>`	`Shift` `⌘` `>`	Browse, Layout
Size—Decrease by one point size	`Ctrl` `Shift` `<`	`Shift` `⌘` `<`	Browse, Layout
Size—Select menu's next larger size	`Ctrl` `.`	`Shift` `Option` `⌘` `>`	Browse, Layout
Size—Select menu's next smaller size	`Ctrl` `,`	`Shift` `Option` `⌘` `<`	Browse, Layout
Style—Plain text	`Ctrl` `Shift` `P`	`Shift` `⌘` `P`	Browse, Layout
Style—Bold	`Ctrl` `Shift` `B`	`Shift` `⌘` `B`	Browse, Layout
Style—Italic	`Ctrl` `Shift` `I`	`Shift` `⌘` `I`	Browse, Layout
Style—Outline	none	`Shift` `⌘` `O`	Browse, Layout
Style—Shadow	none	`Shift` `⌘` `S`	Browse, Layout
Style—Underline	`Ctrl` `Shift` `U`	`Shift` `⌘` `U`	Browse, Layout
Style—Superscript	none	`Shift` `⌘` `+`	Browse, Layout
Style—Subscript	none	`Shift` `⌘` `-`	Browse, Layout
Align Text—Left	`Ctrl` `[`	`⌘` `[`	Browse, Layout
Align Text—Center	`Ctrl` `\`	`⌘` `\`	Browse, Layout
Align Text—Right	`Ctrl` `]`	`⌘` `]`	Browse, Layout
Align Text—Full (Justify)	`Ctrl` `Shift` `\`	`Shift` `⌘` `\`	Browse, Layout
Field Format	`Ctrl` `Shift` `M`	`Option` `⌘` `F`	Browse, Layout
Field Borders	`Ctrl` `Alt` `Shift` `B`	`Option` `⌘` `B`	Browse, Layout

The Records Menu (appears in Find & Preview only)

To Switch To	Windows	Macintosh	Works in Mode
Create new record	`Ctrl` `N`	`⌘` `N`	Browse
Duplicate record	`Ctrl` `D`	`⌘` `D`	Browse
Delete record	`Ctrl` `E`	`⌘` `E`	Browse
Delete record w/o dialog confirmation	`Ctrl` `Shift` `E`	`Option` `⌘` `E`	Browse
Modify Last Find	`Ctrl` `R`	`⌘` `R`	Browse
Show all records	`Ctrl` `J`	`⌘` `J`	Browse, Find
Omit record	`Ctrl` `M`	`⌘` `T`	Browse
Omit multiple records	`Ctrl` `Shift` `M`	`Shift` `⌘` `T`	Browse
Sort records	`Ctrl` `S`	`⌘` `S`	Browse, Preview
Replace	`Ctrl` `=`	`⌘` `=`	Browse

The Requests Menu (appears in Find only)

To Switch To	Windows	Macintosh	Works in Mode
Add new request	`Ctrl` `N`	`⌘` `N`	Find
Duplicate request	`Ctrl` `D`	`⌘` `D`	Find
Delete request	`Ctrl` `E`	`⌘` `E`	Find
Delete find request w/o dialog confirmation	`Ctrl` `Shift` `E`	`Option` `⌘` `E`	Find
Show all records	`Ctrl` `J`	`⌘` `J`	Browse, Find

The Layouts Menu (appears in Layout only)

To	WINDOWS	MACINTOSH	WORKS IN MODE
Create new layout	Ctrl N	⌘ N	Layout
Duplicate layout	none	none	Layout
Delete layout	Ctrl E	⌘ E	Layout

The Arrange Menu (appears in Layout only)

To	WINDOWS	MACINTOSH	WORKS IN MODE
Group selected objects or fields	Ctrl G	⌘ G	Layout
Ungroup selected object(s) or field(s)	Ctrl Shift G	Shift ⌘ G	Layout
Lock selected object(s) or field(s)	Ctrl H	⌘ H	Layout
Unlock selected object(s) or field(s)	Ctrl Shift H	Shift ⌘ H	Layout
Bring selected object(s) to front	Ctrl Alt Shift F	Shift Option ⌘ F	Layout
Bring selected object(s) forward	Ctrl Shift F	Shift ⌘ F	Layout
Send selected object(s) to back	Ctrl Alt Shift J	Shift Option ⌘ J	Layout
Bring selected object(s) backward	Ctrl Shift J	Shift ⌘ J	Layout
Rotate selected object(s) or part(s)	Ctrl Shift R	Option ⌘ R	Layout
Align selected object(s)	Ctrl K	⌘ K	Layout
Open alignment dialog box	Ctrl Shift K	Shift ⌘ K	Layout
Turn on/off autogrid	Ctrl Y	⌘ Y	Layout

The Scripts Menu

(no keyboard shortcuts)

The Window Menu

To	WINDOWS	MACINTOSH	WORKS IN MODE
Tile horizontally	Shift F4	none	All
Cascade	Shift F5	none	All

The Help Menu

To	WINDOWS	MACINTOSH	WORKS IN MODE
Launch Help	F1	⌘ ?	All

Shortcuts by Function

Navigating

To Move To	Windows	Macintosh	Works in Mode
Beginning of line	`Home`	`⌘` `←`	Browse, Find, Layout
End of line	`End`	`⌘` `→`	Browse, Find, Layout
Previous word	`Ctrl` `←`	`Option` `←`	Browse, Find, Layout
Next word	`Ctrl` `→`	`Option` `→`	Browse, Find, Layout
Beginning of text	`Ctrl` `Home`	`⌘` `↑`	Browse, Find, Layout
End of text	`Ctrl` `End`	`⌘` `↓`	Browse, Find, Layout
Next character	`→`	`→`	Browse, Find, Layout
Previous character	`←`	`←`	Browse, Find, Layout
Next line	`↓`	`↓`	Browse, Find, Layout
Previous line	`↑`	`↑`	Browse, Find, Layout
Next field	`Tab`	`Tab`	Browse, Find
Previous field	`Shift` `Tab`	`Shift` `Tab`	Browse, Find
Next record, layout, request	`Ctrl` `↓`	`⌘` `Tab`	Browse, Find
Previous record, layout, request	`Ctrl` `↑`	`Ctrl` `↑` or `Shift` `⌘` `Tab`	Browse, Find
Flipbook icon if nothing selected	none	`Esc`	All

Formatting

To Format	Windows	Macintosh	Works in Mode
Size—Increase by one point size	`Ctrl` `Shift` `>`	`Shift` `⌘` `>`	Browse, Layout
Size—Decrease by one point size	`Ctrl` `Shift` `<`	`Shift` `⌘` `<`	Browse, Layout
Size—Select menu's next larger size	`Ctrl` `.`	`Shift` `Option` `⌘` `>`	Browse, Layout
Size—Select menu's next smaller size	`Ctrl` `,`	`Shift` `Option` `⌘` `<`	Browse, Layout
Style—Plain text	`Ctrl` `Shift` `P`	`Shift` `⌘` `P`	Browse, Layout
Style—Bold	`Ctrl` `Shift` `B`	`Shift` `⌘` `B`	Browse, Layout
Style—Italic	`Ctrl` `Shift` `I`	`Shift` `⌘` `I`	Browse, Layout
Style—Outline	none	`Shift` `⌘` `O`	Browse, Layout
Style—Shadow	none	`Shift` `⌘` `S`	Browse, Layout
Style—Underline	`Ctrl` `Shift` `U`	`Shift` `⌘` `U`	Browse, Layout
Style—Superscript	none	`Shift` `⌘` `+`	Browse, Layout
Style—Subscript	none	`Shift` `⌘` `−`	Browse, Layout
Align Text—Left	`Ctrl` `[`	`⌘` `[`	Browse, Layout
Align Text—Center	`Ctrl` `\`	`⌘` `\`	Browse, Layout
Align Text—Right	`Ctrl` `]`	`⌘` `]`	Browse, Layout
Align Text—Full (Justify)	`Ctrl` `Shift` `\`	`Shift` `⌘` `\`	Browse, Layout
Insert tab into text	`Ctrl` `Tab`	`Option` `Tab`	Browse, Layout
Insert nonbreaking space	`Ctrl` `Spacebar`	`Option` `Spacebar`	Browse, Layout

Editing

To	WINDOWS	MACINTOSH	WORKS IN MODE
Select a word	Double-click	Double-click	All
Select a line	Triple-click	Triple-click	All
Select a paragraph	Four clicks	Four clicks	All
Select All	Ctrl A	⌘ A	All
Select back to beginning of line	Shift Home	Option ⌘ ←	Browse, Find, Layout
Select back to beginning of previous word	Shift Ctrl ←	Shift Option ←	Browse, Find, Layout
Select back to beginning of text block	Ctrl Shift Home	Shift Option ⌘ ↑	Browse, Find, Layout
Select to end of line	Shift End	Shift Option ⌘ →	Browse, Find, Layout
Select to end of next word	Shift Ctrl →	Shift Option →	Browse, Find, Layout
Select to end of text block	Ctrl Shift End	Shift Alt ⌘ ↓	Browse, Find, Layout
Select next character	Shift →	Shift →	Browse, Find, Layout
Select next line	Ctrl Shift ↓	Ctrl Shift ↓	Browse, Find, Layout
Select previous character	Shift ←	Shift ←	Browse, Find, Layout
Select previous line	Ctrl Shift ↑	Ctrl Shift ↑	Browse, Find, Layout
Delete a selection	Del	Del	Browse, Find, Layout
Delete next character	Del	⌦ (below Help key)	Browse, Find, Layout
Delete next word	Ctrl Del	Option ⌦	Browse, Find, Layout
Delete previous character	← Backspace	Delete	Browse, Find, Layout
Delete previous word	none	Option Delete	Browse, Find, Layout
Undo	Ctrl Z	⌘ Z	Browse, Find, Layout
Copy selection	Ctrl C	⌘ C	Browse, Find, Layout
Copy all text in record (nothing selected)	Ctrl C	⌘ C	Browse, Find, Layout
Cut selection	Ctrl X	⌘ X	Browse, Find, Layout
Paste a selection	Ctrl V	⌘ V	Browse, Find, Layout
Paste from index	Ctrl I	⌘ I	Browse, Find
Paste from last record	Ctrl ' (apostrophe)	⌘ ' (apostrophe)	Browse, Find
Paste from last record & move to next field	Ctrl Shift '	Shift ⌘ '	Browse, Find
Paste current date	Ctrl – (hyphen)	⌘ – (hyphen)	Browse, Find
Paste current time	Ctrl ;	⌘ ;	Browse, Find
Paste current user name	Ctrl Shift N	Shift ⌘ N	Browse, Find
Paste merge field	Ctrl M	⌘ M	Layout
Paste without styling	Ctrl Shift V	Option ⌘ V	Browse, Find
Replace current field contents in found set	Ctrl =	⌘ =	Browse
Spelling—Correct Word	Ctrl Shift Y	Shift ⌘ Y	Browse, Find, Layout

Switching Modes

To switch to	Windows	Macintosh	Works in Mode
Browse mode	Ctrl B	⌘ B	All
Find mode	Ctrl F	⌘ F	All
Layout mode	Ctrl L	⌘ L	All
Preview mode	Ctrl U	⌘ U	All

Working with Records

Creating, duplicating records, layouts, requests

To	Windows	Macintosh	Works in Mode
Switch to Browse mode	Ctrl B	⌘ B	All
Create new record, layout, request	Ctrl N	⌘ N	Browse
Duplicate record, layout object, request	Ctrl D	⌘ D	Browse
Copy the found set (no fields selected)	Ctrl Shift C	Option ⌘ C	Browse

Finding records

To	Windows	Macintosh	Works in Mode
Switch to Find mode	Ctrl F	⌘ F	All
Find all records	Ctrl J	⌘ J	Browse, Find
Modify Last Find	Ctrl R	⌘ R	Browse
New find request	Ctrl N	⌘ N	Find
Duplicate request	Ctrl D	⌘ D	Find
Delete find request	Ctrl E	⌘ E	Find
Delete find request w/o dialog confirmation	Ctrl Shift E	Option ⌘ E	Find
Perform Find	Enter	Return	Find

Omitting records

To	Windows	Macintosh	Works in Mode
Omit record	Ctrl M	⌘ T	Browse
Omit multiple records	Ctrl Shift M	Shift ⌘ T	Browse

Deleting records, requests

To	Windows	Macintosh	Works in Mode
Delete record, request	Ctrl E	⌘ E	Browse
Delete record, request w/o dialog confirmation	Ctrl Shift E	Option ⌘ E	Browse

Sorting records

To	Windows	Macintosh	Works in Mode
Sort records	Ctrl S	⌘ S	Browse, Preview

Working with Layouts

Layout tools, formats

To	WINDOWS	MACINTOSH	WORKS IN MODE
Switch current tool to pointer tool (and back)	Enter	Return	Layout
Constrain line tool to 45 degree increments	Ctrl +drag	Option +drag	Layout
Constrain movement horizontally/vertically	Shift +drag	Shift +drag	Layout
Constrain oval tool to a circle	Ctrl +drag	Option +drag	Layout
Constrain rectangle tool to a square	Ctrl +drag	Option +drag	Layout
Constrain resize to horizontal/vertical	Shift +drag handle	Shift +drag handle	Layout
Square object being resized	Ctrl +resize	Option +resize	Layout
Turn on/off T-squares	Ctrl T	⌘ T	Layout
Turn on/off autogrid	Ctrl Y	⌘ Y	Layout
Open alignment dialog box	Ctrl Shift K	Shift ⌘ K	Layout
Display selected object's format	Alt Double-click	Option Double-click	Layout
Reset default field format	Ctrl Click field	⌘ Click field	Layout
Open define fields dialog box	Ctrl Shift D	Shift ⌘ D	All
Redefine a field	Double-click field	Double-click field	Layout
Field Format	Ctrl Shift M	Option ⌘ F	Browse, Layout
Field Borders	Ctrl Alt Shift B	Option ⌘ B	Browse, Layout

Moving, selecting layout objects

To	WINDOWS	MACINTOSH	WORKS IN MODE
Move object	Click+drag	Click+drag	Layout
Move selected object pixel by pixel	Arrow keys	Arrow keys	Layout
Drag layout *part* past object	Alt +drag part	Option +drag part	Layout
Duplicate *object* by dragging	Ctrl +drag part	Option +drag part	Layout
Turn off autogrid while dragging	Alt +drag	⌘ +drag	Layout
Resize object	Drag handle	Drag handle	Layout
Turn off autogrid while resizing	Alt +drag handle	⌘ +drag handle	Layout
Bring selected object(s) to front	Ctrl Alt Shift F	Shift Option ⌘ F	Layout
Bring selected object(s) forward	Ctrl Shift F	Shift ⌘ F	Layout
Send selected object(s) to back	Ctrl Alt Shift J	Shift Option ⌘ J	Layout
Bring selected object(s) backward	Ctrl Shift J	Shift ⌘ J	Layout
Rotate selected object(s) or part(s)	none	Option ⌘ R	Layout
Reorder selected part	Shift +drag part	Shift +drag part	Layout
Reorient part labels (horizontal/vertical)	Ctrl Click	⌘ Click	Layout
Align selected object(s)	Ctrl K	⌘ K	Layout
Select objects by type	Ctrl Shift A	Option ⌘ A	Layout
Select objects via marquee	Ctrl +drag	⌘ +drag	Layout
Group selected objects or fields	Ctrl G	⌘ G	Layout
Ungroup selected object(s) or field(s)	Ctrl Shift G	Shift ⌘ G	Layout
Lock selected object(s) or field(s)	Ctrl H	⌘ H	Layout
Unlock selected object(s) or field(s)	Ctrl Shift H	Shift ⌘ H	Layout

Working with Windows

To	Windows	Macintosh	Works in Mode
Scroll document window down	Page Down	Page Down	All
Scroll document window up	Page Up	Page Up	All
Scroll left in document window	Ctrl Page Up	none	All
Scroll right in document window	Ctrl Page Down	none	All
Show/Hide mode status area	Ctrl Shift S	Option ⌘ S	All
Maximize/Restore (Toggle full size/previous)	Ctrl Shift Z	Shift ⌘ Z	All
Cascade windows	Shift F5	none	All
Tile windows	Shift F4	none	All
Zoom in	F3	none	All
Zoom out	Shift F3	none	All

Working with Files, Dialog Boxes

To	Windows	Macintosh	Works in Mode
Quit FileMaker	Ctrl Q , Alt F4	⌘ Q	All
Close database	Ctrl W , Ctrl F4	⌘ W	All
Save	Automatic	Automatic	All
Print	Ctrl P	⌘ P	All
Print without dialog box	Ctrl Shift T	Option ⌘ P	All
Open a dialog box	Ctrl O	⌘ O	All
Cancel a dialog box	Esc	Esc	All
Open Hosts/Network dialog box	Ctrl Shift O	Option ⌘ O	All
Open Remote Host	Ctrl Shift O	Shift ⌘ O	All
Cancel an operation	none	⌘ . (period)	All
Cancel a paused script	Alt N	none	All
Move object up in dialog box list	Ctrl ↑	⌘ ↑	All
Move object down in dialog box list	Ctrl ↓	⌘ ↓	All
Select layout in Layout pop-up menu	F2 ↑ or ↓ Enter	none	Layout
Select symbol in Symbols pop-up menu	Alt B ↑ or ↓	none	Find
Check/Uncheck Omit box in status area	Alt O	⌘ M	Find

INDEX

INDEX

PEACHPIT PRESS

Quality How-to Computer Books

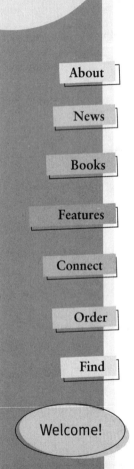

About

News

Books

Features

Connect

Order

Find

Welcome!

Visit Peachpit Press on the Web at www.peachpit.com

- Check out new feature articles each Monday: excerpts, interviews, tips, and plenty of how-tos

- Find any Peachpit book by title, series, author, or topic in Books

- See what our authors are up to on the News page: signings, chats, appearances, and more

- Meet the Peachpit staff and authors in the About section: bios, profiles, and candid shots

- Use Connect to reach our academic, sales, customer service, and tech support areas

Peachpit.com is also the place to:

- Chat with our authors online
- Take advantage of special Web-only offers
- Get the latest info on new books